COLLECTED WORKS OF CHARLES BAUDOUIN

Volume 4

PSYCHOANALYSIS AND AESTHETICS

PSYCHOANALYSIS AND AESTHETICS

CHARLES BAUDOUIN

Translated from the French by
EDEN AND CEDAR PAUL

LONDON AND NEW YORK

First published in 1924

This edition first published in 2015 by
Routledge
4 Park Square, Milton Park, Abingdon, Oxon OX14 4RN
605 Third Avenue, New York, NY 10017

Routledge is an imprint of the Taylor & Francis Group, an informa business

© 1924 Charles Baudouin

All rights reserved. No part of this book may be reprinted or reproduced or utilised in any form or by any electronic, mechanical, or other means, now known or hereafter invented, including photocopying and recording, or in any information storage or retrieval system, without permission in writing from the publishers.

Trademark notice: Product or corporate names may be trademarks or registered trademarks, and are used only for identification and explanation without intent to infringe.

British Library Cataloguing in Publication Data
A catalogue record for this book is available from the British Library

ISBN: 978-1-138-82541-3 (Set)
ISBN: 978-1-315-73901-4 (ebk)(Set)
ISBN: 978-1-138-82652-6 (Volume 4)
ISBN: 978-1-315-73904-5 (ebk)(Volume 4)
ISBN: 978-1-138-82905-3 (pbk)

Publisher's Note
The publisher has gone to great lengths to ensure the quality of this reprint but points out that some imperfections in the original copies may be apparent.

Disclaimer
The publisher has made every effort to trace copyright holders and would welcome correspondence from those they have been unable to trace.

EMILE VERHAEREN
From a photograph by G. Kéfer

PSYCHOANALYSIS AND AESTHETICS

BY
CHARLES BAUDOUIN

TRANSLATED FROM THE FRENCH BY
EDEN AND CEDAR PAUL

LONDON: GEORGE ALLEN & UNWIN LTD.
RUSKIN HOUSE, 40 MUSEUM STREET, W.C.1

First published in 1924

(All rights reserved)

Printed in Great Britain by
UNWIN BROTHERS, LIMITED, THE GRESHAM PRESS, LONDON AND WOKING

FACSIMILE OF VERHAEREN'S MS.

TRANSLATORS' PREFACE

Two thoughtful book-notices, published in the "Westminster Gazette" last year, give the clue to much of the interest and value of Charles Baudouin's *Psychoanalysis and Aesthetics*. The first of these notices, a review of a translation of Benedetto Croce's *The Poetry of Dante*, appeared in the "Weekly Westminster Gazette" for August 12, 1922. The writer says of Dante: "To understand him, . . . we require first some clue to his symbolism and the world-view which inspires it. . . . Next, we require, at least in some degree, poetry of soul; conferring on us the power of sympathetic communion with the spirit of the poet. These are the essentials of the 'historico-aesthetic' understanding of the Divine Comedy; or, indeed, of any supreme work of art." The other notice, signed "E. U.," was a review of F. C. Prescott's *The Poetic Mind*, and was published in the "Weekly Westminster Gazette" for September 2, 1922. "To be complete," writes the reviewer, "such a book should be written, as it were, by spiritual Siamese twins, one a poet and the other a psychologist, in vital union and complete sympathy of soul. Where Professor Prescott fails he does so because of an almost inevitable limitation in such imaginative sympathy; because he doesn't really know what it feels like to be a poet. . . . He throws a new and interesting light on many phases and peculiarities of poetic creation; yet its concrete reality escapes him still."

Now, Charles Baudouin has, not merely "in some

degree," but in a high degree, that poetry of soul which confers on us the power of sympathetic communion with the spirit of the poet. There is no need, as far as he is concerned, to search for "spiritual Siamese twins," since he is himself, in one and the same person, both poet and psychologist. As the latter, the author of *Suggestion and Autosuggestion, Studies in Psychoanalysis*, and *The Power Within Us*, is sufficiently well known to English and American readers. But his reputation as a poet can hardly be supposed to have crossed the Channel and the Atlantic, for neither *Ecce Homo*, nor *L'arche flottante*, nor any other of his poems and lyrical dramas, has yet appeared in English translation. Indeed, for reasons presently to be considered, their full poetic beauty is only accessible to those who can read them in the original.

It is, then, both as poet and as psychologist that Baudouin has written *Psychoanalysis and Aesthetics*, has made this study of poetic symbolism in the works of Emile Verhaeren. The book is not by any means the first venture into the province of psychoanalytical aesthetics and psychoanalytical literary criticism, but it is perhaps the most notable hitherto published—notable no less for the mode of treatment than for the fact that it deals with so outstanding a figure as Emile Verhaeren. In the introductory chapter on "The Laws of the Imagination and Poetic Symbols" the author expounds the principles that guide him throughout the subsequent analysis of Verhaeren's life and works, illustrating the way in which the newer psychological outlooks are gradually modifying the canons of "literary" criticism. This modification has hitherto been in large measure unconscious; but in *Psychoanalysis and Aesthetics* at one stride it becomes aware of itself. Take, for instance, the passage at the close of Chapter One which shows how phrases which critics of the old school would have pilloried as examples of literary inelegance, acquire a profound poetical significance from their bearing on Verhaeren's most intimate personal experiences. The literary "inelegances" are psychologically vital.

Thus quite apart from its value and interest, thanks to the understanding it brings to the study of one of the supreme figures in contemporary imaginative literature, *Psychoanalysis and Aesthetics* solves, as only the new psychology is able to solve, the riddle of artistic appreciation. Hard upon forty years ago, Edmund Gurney, in two essays respectively entitled *Poets, Critics, and Class-lists*, and *The Appreciation of Poetry*, laid stress upon what he termed " the non-reasonable element in poetry " as a factor in appreciation, and showed that this element was not identical with the purely musical or sensory element in verse. But Gurney, well equipped though he was with the psychological knowledge of his day, could not run this " non-reasonable " factor to earth. For the psychology of the eighteen-eighties was still intellectualist. It was concerned with the " reason," the " judgment," the shallows of the mind. Having thus limited the scope of its enquiries, it naturally could not perceive how, in artistic appreciation, deep calls to deep. The delight in poetry is largely an affair of the subconscious. The symbols in which the mind of the imaginative writer or the painter seeks self-expression, are tinged with an affect that wells up from the depths ; and in the hidden recesses of the mind of the observer or the reader there is an affect that rings responsive. This is Gurney's " non-reasonable factor " of appreciation. In both the artist and the appreciator there is (to use Baudouin's own term in *Suggestion and Autosuggestion*) an "outcropping of the subconscious," and they are outcroppings from kindred strata. When the symbol makes a very wide appeal, it is an outcropping from a stratum that exists universally in the minds of all the individuals that comprise the human race—an outcropping from what Jung terms the " collective unconscious."

Being a surge from the unconscious, it is " non-reasonable."
For, as Ralph Hodgson writes :

> Reason has moons, but moons not hers
> Lie mirrored on her sea,
> Confounding her astronomers,
> But Oh ! delighting me.

Baudouin phrases the same thought in the language of the new analytical psychology : " In the course of our analysis we have seen that these poems are the outcome of a very strong and very precise condensation of images. That is why they have guided us into the most intimate recesses of Verhaeren's soul. Such condensations would seem to favour the genesis of great works. This is natural, for condensation is the sign of an emotion or of a conflict in the soul of the poet ; such poems give expression to the profoundest feelings, and for this reason they profoundly react on the reader's emotions. A noteworthy fact is that the real object of the emotion or of the conflict may be subconscious, may be quite unknown both to the author and to the reader, and yet an intimate vibration is awakened which may not be understood but will certainly be felt. We are led to the view that it is wise and proper to analyse the symbols employed by a poet, and especially those which he introduces into his masterpieces ; seeing that the most moving of works are at the same time, and in general, the most explicative of works."

To sum up, the present book must not be looked upon simply as a treatise upon psychoanalysis and aesthetics, nor simply as an attempt at the appreciation of the writings of a particular poet. It is an application of psychoanalysis to the theory of aesthetics, as illustrated by a detailed study of Verhaeren's works. The " interpretation " Freud has supplied for dreams, Baudouin achieves for the imagery of the artistic creator.

A few words may be permitted upon the task of the

translators. The introduction, the conclusion, and the comments interspersed throughout the chapters, were a straightforward piece of work, offering no exceptional difficulties. It was otherwise with the illustrative passages from Verhaeren, which bulk so largely in the book. After much consideration we decided that the best plan would be to reserve the use of footnotes for the references to the titles of the poems from which extracts are made, and to print the translations of these extracts in the text (enclosed in brackets) immediately following the French citation in each case. Thus those who read French will be enabled to enjoy Verhaeren's actual phrasing with the least effort, whilst those who need to have recourse to the translation will find it close at hand, and will not have the trouble of turning to an appendix.

No attempt has been made to give a metrical translation. The rendering is as literal as possible. In view of the need for accuracy—this work being a study of Verhaeren's symbolism—we have not always succeeded in avoiding roughness. Though we have, in general, translated verse by verse, we have not translated word for word. The latter would have produced a mere semblance of accuracy at the expense of real meaning. Those curious in such matters will note that we have not followed what some authorities regard as a canon of " good translation "; we have not invariably translated the same foreign word by the same English word—not even within the limits of a single citation. Human beings think in sentences, rather than in words. The connotations of the same word will vary in different sentences, and one of the things which makes " good " translation so difficult an art is that (except in the case of terms for which there is a precise scientific definition) words can never be translated in a way that is universally applicable. That is why even the best of dictionaries is often nothing better than a lame guide. That is why, in the last resort, the translator has always to depend upon what the Germans call *Sprachgefühl*—linguistic tact. And one of the first requisites for the competent translator is the possession of this linguistic tact in both the languages in question.

For the most part, in the rendering of Baudouin's extracts from Verhaeren, we have had to rely entirely on ourselves, for not many of the poems have been translated into English. (See bibliography.) Wherever possible, however, the prose versions in the present work have been checked by the renderings—mostly metrical—made by other translators. Readers of Baudouin's psychoanalytical study of a great poet will not be slow to realise that it is impossible to reproduce the meaning of poetry in another language while preserving the original rhythms, and rhyming wherever the original was rhymed. The result of any such attempt is to reproduce the jingle, at the sacrifice of the message despatched from the poet's subconscious in the forms of thought and imagery.

EDEN AND CEDAR PAUL.

LONDON, *October*, 1923.

CONTENTS

	PAGE
TRANSLATORS' PREFACE	7
INTRODUCTION: THE LAWS OF THE IMAGINATION. POETIC SYMBOLS	15

CHAPTER
I.	LES TENDRESSES PREMIÈRES	35
II.	LES FLAMANDES AND LES MOINES	70
III.	THE CRISIS	106
IV.	CONVERSION AND DELIVERANCE	155
V.	AN OEDIPUS TRILOGY	202
VI.	LIFE IN ALL ITS ARDOUR	242
	CONCLUSION	293
	CE SOIR (*poem by Verhaeren, here first published*)	310
	BIBLIOGRAPHY	315
	INDEX	321

INTRODUCTION

IF there be one thing in the world which seems to have no other law than caprice, it is the imagination. We need not, therefore, be surprised that in this domain psychology is still in its infancy. For a long time science was content with the rudimentary laws of the association of ideas—or, to speak more precisely, the laws of the association of images. It was said that one mental image called up another because the objects had been perceived side by side, as when the image of an individual made us think of the street in which he lived. This was termed association by contiguity. Or else one image called up another because the two images were alike, as when a carrot makes us think of a peaked hat. This was termed association by similarity. It must be admitted that these explanations, these laws beloved of the pundits, do not take us far. We are not informed why, from among an infinite number of like things, one thing in particular is selected. Is the choice the outcome of pure caprice, or rather of physiological chance? Does the brain process resemble the shaking of dice in a box, when a number turns up without there being any intelligent motive to account for the result? In view of the incoherence of day-dreams and of dreams, there seemed good reason for the contention. But it is no longer possible to hold such a view. We are beginning to understand that what appears to be the outcome of chance, depends upon a strict psychological determinism. The lovers of fantasy may take heart none the less. This determinism, far from robbing the imagination of its charm, lends a new grace to the faculty. Whereas we had been inclined to regard the imagination as blooming capriciously on the very surface of the mind, and as having no more significance than wreaths of cigarette smoke, we now perceive that it springs from the very depths of our being.

How has this knowledge been secured ? As long as we tried to explain the imagination in terms of the imagination alone, we could get no further. At length, however, we have become aware that *the imagination is wholly guided by the affective life* ; by the sentiments, the emotions, the instincts, that accompany the images. These are the poles round which the images crystallise. Thus the images disclose the affective kernel around which they have been aggregated ; and the affective kernel, in its turn, accounts for the formation of the images. We instantly perceive that this reciprocal illumination of inner sensibility by the imagination, on the one hand, and of the laws of the imagination by sensibility, on the other, must be peculiarly typical in the poet, who is at one and the same time a great affective and a great imaginative. The new psychology would almost seem to have been specially designed to explain the poet.

No doubt the existence of such a relationship between the life of feeling and the life of imagination has always been suspected. It is almost self-evident in the case of poets and in that of other persons of artistic temperament. Moreover, instances in which the relationship is conspicuous are familiar to us all. Fear creates phantoms, and from the character of the phantoms may be inferred the nature of the fear that induced them. Reveries and fantasies are ripe at puberty, and the images with which the mind is then filled leave us in no doubt as to the nature of the emotions which have called them into being. We see once again that our novelty is not new. But the psychology of our own days, cautious and modest in the hands of Ribot, ambitious in the

INTRODUCTION

hands of Freud, has for the first time been able to discover the laws of a relationship which has long been suspected. Ribot set out from the idea of association, but was struck by the inadequacy of this theory, and grasped the importance of the "affective factor" in the genesis and interconnexion of images. A fundamental matter, and one whose importance was fully realised by this author, is what we may term *condensation*.[1] He describes it as follows: "Representations which have been accompanied by the same affective state, tend henceforward to be associated; their affective similarity forms a link between the separate representations. This is not the same as association by contiguity, which is a repetition of the experience; nor is it the same as association by similarity in the intellectual sense. The states of consciousness are linked, not because they have previously occurred together, nor because we perceive similarities between them, but because they have a common affective tone. Joy, sadness, love, hatred, surprise, boredom, pride, fatigue, etc., can each become a centre of attraction, grouping representations or events which are devoid of any intellectual interconnexion, but which have the same emotional tinge—joyful, melancholy, erotic, etc. This form of association is common in dreams and in day-dreams, that is to say, in states of mind when imagination works in perfect freedom."[2]

In another work, Ribot writes: "Substantially, this form corresponds to what official psychology denotes by the vague term 'the influence of the feeling on the intelligence.'"[3]

The influence of which Ribot speaks is not accidental but constant. The intellectual life as a whole does not become truly intelligible unless we take into consideration

---
[1] See Baudouin, Studies in Psychoanalysis, 1922, pp. 43 et seq.
[2] Essai sur l'imagination créatrice, 1900, p. 31.
[3] Logique des sentiments, 1905, p. 22.

the underlying life of feeling. The psychologist Rignano goes so far as to maintain, as regards various forms of insanity, that these disorders of the intelligence are fundamentally disorders of feeling.[1] The assertion may be regarded as paradoxical, but it has none the less a far-reaching significance. If feeling thus helps us to understand the working of the intelligence, it is all the more necessary to have recourse to a study of feeling when we wish to understand that more primitive and spontaneous form of intelligence which is known as imagination.[2]

In addition to describing condensation, Ribot gives an excellent account of what he terms the *transference*[3] of a feeling. Transference may, in a sense, be regarded as the inverse of condensation. Here a feeling, instead of grouping round itself a number of separate images, is itself dispersed over a number of associated images. Ribot writes : " Transference may result from similarity. When an intellectual state has been accompanied by a strong feeling, a similar state tends to arouse the same feeling. It may result from contiguity. When intellectual states have coexisted, the feeling linked with the primary state tends, if strong enough, to be transferred to the others. The lover transfers the feeling which is at first associated with the person of his mistress to her clothing, her furniture, her dwelling. In an absolute monarchy, reverence for the person of the king is transferred to the throne, to the insignia of power, to everything which is more or less closely connected with the monarch." [4]

Anyone, however, who attempts to unravel phenomena of such a character—condensation or transference, for example—is likely to be led astray unless he knows that in many cases this interplay of feelings and images goes

---

[1] Psychologie du raisonnement, 1920.
[2] Baudouin, The Affective Basis of Intelligence, 1920.
[3] See Baudouin, Studies in Psychoanalysis, 1922, pp. 41, 51, etc.
[4] Logique des sentiments, p. 4.

on unawares. Everything happens as if such links were effected, but as if they were effected in the subconscious (unconscious). Only part of the phenomenon occurs within the realm of consciousness; another part is unknown to the conscious mind, or seems to be lacking. In a transference, therefore, the origin may be forgotten; the cult of a relic may no longer be superadded to the cult of the saint, but may take the place of the latter. Such substitutions frequently occur in the personal life. The apparently irrational preferences we have for certain flowers or certain colours often depend on the fact that the flowers or the colours in question became, in our early childhood, associated with some beloved personality, now forgotten. Irrational fears may have a like origin. Similarly, a condensation of images may arise in consequence of a feeling which we do not avow to ourselves, and which is hidden from the conscious mind. But if we turn our attention to the way in which the images are grouped, we may now become aware of the feeling which we had hitherto ignored. Such secret incubations are a familiar experience to those who are falling in love.

Ribot, therefore, is perfectly right when to the " affective factor" he adds the "unconscious factor," which is fundamentally a form of latent affectivity. Thus " at first we have an unconscious working, equivalent to a series of judgments of value, and proceeding by analogy. Subsequently, and mainly, we have an imaginative construction, consisting of associations radiating in various directions, but unified by the unconscious selective process of a dominant desire." [1]

Such inferences from the new psychology seem self-evident to anyone whose inner life is fairly vigorous and imaginative. What surprises us is, not that they have been drawn now, but that they were not drawn long ago. Nevertheless, the previous failure was quite natural.

[1] Logique des sentiments, p. 4.

Until our own time, psychology, like science in general, was purely intellectualist. Science had to make an effort before it could turn its attention towards the affective and instinctive life. This effort has been resolutely achieved; it is parallel with that made by the philosophy of intuition, and it is part of the general trend of contemporary ideas. We discern in it a happy symptom of the need for synthesis which is now widely felt; in this instance, we are concerned with a synthesis of feeling and intelligence. Yet the effort entails dangers for science, for there is a risk that science may forfeit its essential qualities of clarity and method. Perhaps there was no danger for a Ribot, whose genius was cautious and methodical; but the danger becomes apparent as soon as we turn to Freud and to the doctrines of his school, as soon as we turn to consider psychoanalysis. Still, while caution has its place in science, there is also a place for boldness—even if boldness must be paid for by a few mistakes. Nothing can be more injudicious than the way in which many French men of science continue to pour derision on Freud and psychoanalysis. The new doctrine requires criticism; but it is absurd, at this date, to regard psychoanalysis as null and void.

No one who undertakes an impartial study of the psychoanalytical conception of the imagination, can fail to notice how closely akin this conception is to that of Ribot. Freud examined the working of the imagination in dreams, and the chief laws he deduced for the dream imagination run parallel with those formulated by Ribot for the waking life. Condensation, displacement, and the role of the subconscious, form the foundations of the psychoanalytical theory of dreams.[1]

Let us first consider condensation, the *Verdichtung* of

---

[1] Freud, Die Traumdeutung (The Interpretation of Dreams); Régis and Hesnard, La psychoanalyse des névroses et des psychoses, 1914, pp. 97 et seq.

Freud. Ribot, in the passage previously quoted, states that this form is " common in dreams " ; and he points out that, through condensation, the images, not content with being juxtaposed, are linked. The psychoanalytical view is that this intimate linking may be regarded as normal in dreams, a combination so close that keen scrutiny is requisite before the combined elements can be distinguished. Our dreams resemble the " composite photographs " obtained by partial exposures of a photographic plate to the image of a number of different persons of the same family, in order to bring out " family traits." In the case we are now considering, the family trait is a likeness of feeling or emotion which serves as a link between separate memories. Thus it is that in a dream the landscape we have never seen, but which nevertheless we seem to recognise, is an amalgam of a number of landscapes which we actually have seen. Peculiarly applicable to these dream landscapes is Amiel's saying : " A landscape is a state of mind." In like manner, in a dream, several persons may fuse into one, because of a common impression they have made on us, or because they all have the same significance for us. This is why we often feel that we have dreamed of a person or a thing " which all the same was not precisely that person or that thing." It explains, again, the amusing phrases of Marinette (six years old), relating a dream which she had after I had told her the story of Hercules : " I had a dream about the lion man. He wasn't father, but he was a man who was father. There wasn't any lion, but all the same it seemed as if there was a lion." Here we have an obvious and simple condensation of father and Hercules.

In a dream we may condense, into an integer, objects to which we have reacted in similar fashion, although these reactions may have differed greatly in intensity. We condense the starting on a railway journey with an anticipated change in our mode of life. Or we condense an examination we had to pass in early youth with some trial we are undergoing in our adult life, and perhaps we add to the condensation a real feeling of physical distress from which we are suffering during sleep. Or we may condense a pleasure of the table with an erotic pleasure. In such condensations, which are composed of elements varying in importance, there frequently occurs a *displacement of affective stress*. In the dream, the most important element may become secondary, and an element of minor importance may assume the leading role. When dreaming of an examination, for example, we may cease to think of the matter which is troubling us in our waking life; when relating the dream, we do not think we have been dreaming about this present trouble, but only about the examination of long anterior date; we are astonished that the examination seemed so important to us in the dream. Such a displacement of stress is conspicuous in most nightmares. On awaking we feel it was absurd to have been terribly frightened by some object which was hardly important enough to arouse alarm. The reason for the alarm was that we had displaced on to this harmless object the affective stress properly attaching to a real cause of anxiety. I knew some one who dreamed of being attacked by a yellow dog. This dream was founded upon the reminiscence of an attack actually made by a dog during childhood, but the peculiar yellow colour of the dream dog was the colour of the waistcoat of a doctor who had recently attended the patient. Condensation had been effected, so that the attack by the dog had been fused with the attack by the doctor (the patient's dread of the medical treatment). But, in the dream, the recent cause of distress was almost hidden in the image of the dog which had been the old cause of trouble. Here is another case which came under my notice. A young woman who was pregnant fell asleep obsessed with the fear that the birth of her baby would take place on a Sunday, and that she would not be able to get a doctor. She dreamed that the stove-pipe was blocked, that it was Sunday, and that no chimney-sweep was available.

We may add that, in dreams, the association of images plays a part as well as condensation. Thereby images of minor importance are introduced, and the affective stress may be transferred to these. This is the chief reason why dreams seem so incoherent. If, for instance, we dream that we are feeling for a cat emotions which we really feel for the cat's owner, we are nonplussed. Yet there has been nothing more than a transference whose starting-point has been forgotten. Thus the law of displacement (*Verschiebung*, in Freud's terminology) strongly reminds us of Ribot's law of transference. But the notion of displacement is more complex, for it involves the simultaneous working of condensation, transference, and subconscious activity. Given an integration of images tinged with the same affective shade whether by condensation or by transference, displacement is the work which tends to thrust down into the subconscious the more important among these images (those to which the feeling or the emotion really attaches), and to bring into relief images of minor importance.

In some instances, the forgetfulness of the real object of the feeling is only partial; the repression into the subconscious is incomplete. In other instances, however, the real object is completely forgotten. Frequently, in the latter case, we are not concerned with simple oblivion, but with a process of repression whereby we automatically disembarrass ourselves of something disagreeable. This explains why we so rarely dream of our major preoccupations. In reality we do dream of them, but they appear under a mask. It is needless to follow Freud in all his explanations of the determinants of repression, or to accept his contention that these determinants are almost invariably sexual. Nor need we suppose that "repression" is at work wherever "displacement" occurs. We have to recognise that the Freudian concept of repression is an invaluable contribution to our understanding of the laws of the subconscious. But we must avoid giving to this idea of repression (I speak especially of sexual repression) the privileged, not to say unique, role which the exponents of psychoanalysis are apt to assign to it. By adopting condensation and transference as our points of departure, we shall make our ideas more digestible, so that they will prove acceptable even to those who are strongly opposed to Freudian doctrine.

In like manner, we should avoid speaking of the "symbolism" of dreams until we have finished our exposition of the laws of condensation and transference. There is justification for the alarm which the word "symbolism," the term "dream interpretation," and many other Freudian phrases, is apt to arouse in the circumspect. Freud is fond of paradox; he loves to startle the imagination, whose innermost secrets he has probed. The terms in question often suggest that we are being offered a "key to dreams," or some other product of a fantastic mysticism. But behind the words we must seek the things they represent, and the things are less disturbing. The foregoing exposition will have made it easy to understand in what sense dreams are symbolic. A dream landscape, resulting from the condensation of several real landscapes whose memories are tinged with a common affect, is a symbol of that affect. In a displacement, the accessory element symbolises the chief element. That which remains in consciousness is the symbol of that which is repressed; for example, in the cases previously recorded, the yellow dog symbolises the doctor, the chimney-sweep symbolises the accoucheur, and the stove-pipe symbolises the pelvic outlet.

There can be no doubt that the dream represents the most spontaneous play of the imagination, and it is from a study of dreams that we can best ascertain the inner laws of that faculty. The same laws are at work in the imagination during the waking life. In the latter case, however, their working is better hidden ; it is less simple, being partly neutralised by voluntary and rational activity. Hence it is essential to begin our study of imagination in the dream, where we encounter it in the pure state. To have done this was Freud's supreme service, whatever we may think of the rest of his teaching. Moreover, contemporary psychology stresses the resemblance of the dream, not only with the day-dream (this is familiar, and is implicit in the respective names), but also with works of art and above all with poetry.

Otto Rank,[1] in especial, draws attention to the relationships of the dream with poetry and myth. He quotes from Wagner's *Meistersinger* :

> Mein Freund das grad' ist Dichters Werk,
> dass er sein Träumen deut' und merk'.
> Glaubt mir, des Menschen wahrster Wahn
> wird ihm im Traume aufgetan :
> all' Dichtkunst und Poeterei
> ist nichts als Wahrtraum-Deuterei.
>
> [My friend, the whole task of the poet
> is to explain and to note what he dreams.
> Believe me, man's truest illusion
> is revealed to him in dreams :
> all the poetry in the world
> is nothing more than the interpretation of dreams.]

He quotes Schopenhauer, who considered that the greatness of Dante consisted in his having given expression to all the reality of the world of dreams, and who held that a great poet like Shakespeare was one capable of doing in the waking state that which lesser men do in a dream. Finally, he quotes Kant, who in his *Anthropologie* speaks of the dream as " involuntary poetry."

In France, Paul Souriau, though he has no affiliations

---

[1] Traum und Dichtung, Traum und Mythus (Supplements to Freud's Traumdeutung, 1919) ; Der Künstler, 1907.

with Freudism, has perhaps gone a step further. He, too, discerns the kinship between the work of art and the dream.[1] But he shows, in addition, that part of the artist's task is to induce by spontaneous or voluntary methods (among which rhythm is the most conspicuous) a quasi-equivalent of sleep, a state of slight hypnosis. For the auditor or the spectator in whom this state is induced, the artist's dream becomes more vivid and more absolute.

A British psychologist, Prescott,[2] maintains that poetry and dreams are equally the product of emotion. We, who have recognised that the affective life is the foundation of the imaginative life, shall not be surprised at this assimilation. Prescott further remarks that the poet and the dreamer alike enjoy a sense of deliverance from social constraints. The poet, like the dreamer, returns to childhood, shakes off the yoke of authority, and freely affirms his individuality.

Doubtless such resemblances, and others which might be mentioned, should not lead us to assimilate the dream and the poem without qualification. A good many dreams have little of the aesthetic in them; and when we compare the work of art with the dream we cannot fail to see that the former contains both more and less than the latter, that the work of art has more order and less litter. The dream is a bazaar, a curiosity shop; and the supreme task of the artist is to select. "Art," writes Alfred de Vigny, "is selected truth." In what, then, lies the interest of the assertion that the poem and the dream are akin? Does this mean no more than that both are products of the imagination? If this were all, we should merely have formulated a truism. What we have to understand, when we speak of such a kinship, is that the play of the imagination is *identical* in the

[1] Especially in his two books, La suggestion dans l'art, 1893, and La rêverie esthétique, 1906.
[2] Poetry and Dreams, "Journal of Abnormal Psychology," 1912.

dream and the poem (to take the poem as a typical work of art). What we have to understand is that, properly speaking, *there is no such thing as aesthetic imagination or poetic imagination—but simply imagination.* In other words, the difference between the dream or the day-dream, on the one hand, and the poem, on the other, must not be sought in a *difference of kind* in the imagination at work in the respective instances.

Where then is the difference to be found? He who speaks of imagination, speaks of sensibility; and we know that images are aroused and explained by the subjacent sensibility. This suggests that we may expect to find in sensibility the reasons for the differences in the work of the imagination. Perhaps we may say that a dream is the outcome of the imagination set to work by a common-place sensibility, and that a poem is the outcome of the imagination animated by a refined sensibility. Another difference, to which we have already alluded, is that the poem is, as it were, a dream organised by the voluntary activity of choice—of a choice determined by the sense of the beautiful. Undoubtedly the poet is endowed with a vigorous imagination, but not with a specific form of imagination. That whereby the poet is dis-tinguished from the child, the neuropath, the dreamer, and the day-dreamer, and from those who are exercising any kind of non-artistic imagination, consists of qualities which do not belong to the imagination, but to sensibility on the one hand, and to will on the other.

The main characteristic common to the poet's imagina-tion and to the dreamer's imagination may be expressed in a single word. Both the poet and the dreamer work constantly through *symbols.* The symbol (in the sense previously defined—a result of condensations, displace-ments, and repressions) is the very essence of imaginative activity. It matters not whether the subject is or is not aware that he is thinking symbolically; the symbol is often the expression of the subject's "unconscious."

Psychology has thus led us to a remarkable result, which confirms one of the intuitions of language. The word *image* is sometimes used to denote any kind of evocation arising in the mind and resembling a perception of reality, as when we say " I cherish the image of my mother." Sometimes it is used to denote a symbol, a poetical comparison, as when we say " the lily is the image [emblem] of purity." Modern psychology has taught us that these two senses of the term " image " overlap. We may say that every spontaneous mental image is to some extent symbolical.

A poem, therefore, presupposing as it always does a certain spontaneity of the imagination, is invariably more or less symbolical. It is more symbolical in proportion as the work of the imagination is more spontaneous, in proportion as the work of the imagination is less modified by the interference of the conscious mind—a necessary interference, but one which involves some sacrifice of the inner truth contained in the reverie as it welled up in the unconscious. " The sweetest verses are those which remain unfinished."

One school of poetry would jealously preserve all the spontaneity that is compatible with the necessities of expression. Rejecting, therefore, the rigid rules of versification, but obeying an intuitive logic which the foregoing considerations will enable us to understand, the members of this " symbolist " school have insisted that the symbol constitutes the essence of poetry. As we should expect, it is to symbolist poems that the laws of the dream are especially applicable ; and it is symbolist poems which, even to the eyes of the profane, seem to resemble dreams most closely.

Whatever we may think of the creations of symbolist art, we must admit that this school has had remarkable intuitions—intuitions which psychological study is able to confirm. We may also note that psychoanalysis, like symbolism, has one of its roots in the philosophy of Schopenhauer. Were it not that broadly conceived parallelisms tend always to err in the direction of undue simplification, we might say that psychoanalysis and symbolism are respectively the psychology and the aesthetics to which Schopenhauer's philosophy has given birth.

Edouard Dujardin has drawn attention to Schopenhauer's influence upon the French symbolists. He writes: " The first important study of Schopenhauer in the French tongue, that by Ribot, was not published until 1874. Burdeau's translation of *The World as Will and Idea* appeared in 1888. Quite a number of us had studied philosophy under Burdeau. At length, in 1885, ' La revue Wagnérienne ' began to make the work of the great German philosopher widely known to the younger generation." [1]

What did Schopenhauer teach these young people ? First of all he taught the unreality of the world, which is nothing but " unsere Vorstellung," our idea, and not a reality in itself ; this doctrine, or its reflection in the poet's mind, tends to take the form of an identification of reality with a dream. Next, Schopenhauer taught them of the mysterious and mystical " unconscious," the " night side of the soul " ; he thus gave them a desire to express it. Music and the symbol, for both of which these poets had a cult, were regarded by them as means for giving expression to the unconscious.

" The symbol as means for giving expression to the unconscious." Since then the idea has become a scientific theory, a part of modern psychology. Upon this matter, the intuitions of the symbolists were truly remarkable. The idea they formed for themselves of the symbol was as psychological as it could possibly be. The spontaneous symbol of the dream, as we learn from psychological study, is not as a rule a system of two terms (a parable), but a system of three or more terms. A condensation

[1] De Stéphane Mallarmé au prophète Ezéchiel.

is often tightly packed; the resulting symbol may be usable in two different ways, like a sheepskin coat; the inside symbolises the outside, and the outside the inside. We may say that each term of the condensation symbolises one of the other terms, and conversely; and further we may say (though even then we doubtless fail to probe the matter to its depths) that all the terms symbolise the subjacent affective reality. This is why divergent "interpretations" of a dream can be given without these interpretations being mutually exclusive. Returning to a previous example (p. 22), we may say that the dream of the examination symbolises the extant moral difficulty, or that it symbolises the physical distress from which the sleeper is suffering at the time, or simply that it symbolises his emotional distress. This multiple parallelism is characteristic of symbolism; we are reminded of a polyglot Bible, in which the text is printed in parallel columns in numerous languages. Mallarmé had an intuition of this multiple parallelism, of this complexity of the symbol, in virtue of which the chief image emits numerous overtones. Writing of Mallarmé, Théodore de Wyzewa says:[1] "To each of his verses he has tried to give several superimposed meanings. His aim has been that each verse should be simultaneously a plastic image, the expression of a thought, the utterance of a feeling, and a philosophical symbol."

In like manner Jean Ott, in a study of Han Ryner, writes: "This author's favourite form is the symbol, which to the crowd seems an ordinary fable, whereas to the intelligent it is an inverted truth, highly enigmatic, beneath whose hidden meaning there may lie a further meaning yet more deeply hidden. The enigma of the smile will discourage the ignorant, but will lead the wise to think more deeply; both these results are equally desirable."[2]

---

[1] Nos maîtres, 1895.
[2] Enquête sur Han Ryner, "Le Rythme," 1912.

INTRODUCTION 31

According to Dujardin,[1] Mallarmé would fain " expunge the word 'like' [comme] from the dictionary." The condensation that occurs in the dream, with its identification of analogies, does this very thing.

The symbolist poet is animated with the conviction that he is expressing his "unconscious." Beneath the parallel and superimposed strata which make up his poem, he senses something which remains obscure even for himself, and is therefore still more obscure for his readers. He does not know exactly what he wishes to symbolise ; just as the musician, who hears a melody singing within him, does not concern himself to know precisely what the melody signifies. It is amusing enough to note into what mazes this symbolist theory of the unconscious may lead. The theory is sometimes used to justify incoherence and even humbug. But we shall find more interest in emphasising the psychological truth which it embodies. Psychological analysis discloses that the poet, even when he believes himself to be objective, is usually expressing something more than he imagines himself to be expressing—something different. His work, apparently objective, is likewise the involuntary symbol of a subjective reality more or less unconscious.

Thus the idea which the symbolists have formed for themselves regarding the symbol is not arbitrary. They have had an intuition of condensation, and of the unconscious substratum of the symbol. Therein they have displayed a profound knowledge of the nature of their art. It is a grave error to look upon them as morbidly impulsive, to regard them as persons lacking clarity of intelligence. Indeed, in some instances, their fault is rather that their knowledge tends to remain at the level of pure knowledge, so that the intellect of the theorist is apt to hamper the expression of the poet. This is what has happened to Mallarmé, whose intelligence and lucidity are manifest to all that have studied his writings.

[1] Op. cit.

"To each of his verses," as de Wyzewa says, "he has tried to give several superimposed meanings." No doubt this was where he went wrong; he deliberately *tried* to arouse the involuntary and the unconscious, and to make his poem fit his theory.

Verhaeren, on the other hand, is one of the simplest of writers, one of those who most conspicuously exhibit the hallucinatory spontaneity of the dream. He is subject to the influence of the art of his day, but he vivifies what he assimilates. He is not encumbered with theories, but contemplates art and life with the naive outlook of the genius. Consequently his symbolism, being pre-eminently spontaneous, is preeminently favourable for the application of the analytic method of contemporary psychology. The essence of this analytic method, as might be foreseen, is found in unravelling the condensations of an imaginative creation, in disentangling displacements and repressions. To achieve this, we must seek to discover the ideas, the feelings, and the memories to which each element of the condensation is linked in the poet's psyche. The method will reveal, with a clearness that is often amazing, the inner psychological meaning of the most obscure symbols.

No detailed description of the method is requisite, for its theory is implicit in the laws of the imagination which have just been considered. As to the practice of the method, this can only be understood by studying it in actual use, and it will be seen in application throughout the present volume.

The method is partly derived from the school of Freud, and many of the teachings of this school are fiercely contested. But when we speak of Freudism we must never forget the distinction between theory and practice. Whereas the theory (still unstable in its outlines, and variously modified by dissident sects) is in many respects open to stringent criticism, the practice, harmonising as it does with the most concrete data of psychology, is entirely acceptable.

INTRODUCTION

Nor need the medical origin of our method of investigation give us pause. The analysis of the dreams or fantasies of a neuropath is curative, in that it disentangles the obscure affective troubles which underlie the neurosis. A similar analysis, when applied to the fantasies of the normal imagination, reveals the normal sensibility. Applied to the creations of the man of genius, it discloses the secret soul of the man of genius.

Such analysis is far from presupposing, as field of action, a morbid individual, towards whom the analyst assumes an air of medical superiority. So true is this, that a noted pastor, Georges Berguer,[1] has applied the analytic method to the personality of Christ without feeling himself to be in the least irreverent.

Théodore Flournoy [2] and Ferdinand Morel [3] have applied the same method to the study of certain mystics. A number of foreign authors have made use of a like method in the study of art and literature.[4] French writers are only now beginning to undertake criticism of this character. I may mention an essay by Maeder [5] upon the painter Hodler ; and a work in which J. Vodoz [6] studies the symbol of Roland, first in the medieval French epic, and subsequently in Victor Hugo's *Le Mariage de Roland*—a poem which seems to reveal one of the mental conflicts of the poet. But these first steps, tentative though they be, are rich with promise. They show that we have laid the foundations of the psychology of art, of a science of aesthetics which shall be genuinely scientific without thinking itself bound for that reason to approach art as a psychological " case " or as a " subject " to be catalogued, without succumbing to the danger of manifesting a sterile erudition, without losing contact with

---

[1] Quelques traits de la vie de Jésus, 1919.
[2] Une mystique moderne, " Archives de Psychologie," 1915.
[3] Essai sur l'introversion mystique, 1918.
[4] Cf. bibliography in Régis and Hesnard, op. cit.—See also, Pfister, Der psychologische und biologische Untergrund expressionistischer Bilder, 1920.
[5] Hodler, 1917.   [6] Roland, un symbole, 1920.

life, and without forfeiting the sense of beauty. We have here a manifestation of the endeavour towards synthesis to which reference has already been made, the endeavour to achieve a mutual understanding between art and science. There has been too much tendency of late years for art and science to regard one another with sovereign contempt—a somewhat puerile contempt which would have made Goethe or Da Vinci smile.

CHAPTER ONE

LES TENDRESSES PREMIERES [1]

REMINISCENCES of childhood are of great assistance in the analysis of imaginative creations. They are valuable, not only for the obvious and trivial reason that first impressions are among the most influential, but also for more subtle reasons which we have learned from the contemporary psychological study of the imagination and of memory. First of all, we perceive in reminiscences of childhood the formation of certain associations of ideas, exceptionally strong and stable, which will recur again and again throughout life, and to which their origin gives us a key. Secondly, a reminiscence is not a mere fragment of the past; it is a confluence of the past and the present.

" In every past event," writes Ribot, " the interesting elements revive alone, or revive with more intensity than the others. When we speak of being interested in a thing, we mean that it affects us agreeably or disagreeably. I may mention that the importance of this fact was pointed out, not only (as might have been expected) by the associationists, but also by writers who had nothing to do with the associationist school—by Coleridge, by Shadworth Hodgson, and by Schopenhauer. William James speaks of this law as the law of 'ordinary or mixed association.' [2] Doubtless the 'law

[1] Early affections.
[2] Psychology, vol. i. pp. 571 et seq.

of interest'[1] lacks the precision of the intellectual laws of contiguity and similarity. Nevertheless, it seems to penetrate farther into ultimate reasons."[2]

We remember the things which interest us. The interest may be mainly practical or mainly intellectual, but it always has an affective tinge. Ribot has pointed this out. The interest, as Freud shows, is more strongly affective in the case of reminiscences of childhood. These are heartfelt. The interest which evokes them is, in this case above all, a state of feeling. The state of feeling achieves a "condensation" of a present and a past tinged with the same affect—the process being analogous to that which we have seen at work in dreaming and imagination. *A reminiscence of childhood is such a condensation of the present and the past.* Sometimes our reminiscence condenses into a single picture several scenes of childhood charged with the same affective significance, so that the reminiscence becomes more loaded with meaning than was any one of the individual scenes. Above all, however, it is charged with a present meaning, for it consists of elements from the past which apply as closely as possible to an extant situation. Thus the reminiscence of childhood is a "symbol" of the present, and throws light on the present. Of course the reminiscence is a representation of the past, but one lacking in objectivity; a portrait rather than a photograph; a portrait in which the artist (the mind of to-day) following up certain lines and neglecting others, uses this particular form as a means of self-expression. It has been said that a portrait painter is always painting his own portrait. If the child explains the adult so well, this is not merely because, in the child, the adult already existed in the germ; it is also because the adult makes use of memories of childhood as a means of self-expression.

---

[1] This is Ribot's name for the law.
[2] Essai sur l'imagination créatrice, p. 31.

"Art is selected truth." In the same sense we may say that a reminiscence is a selected past—the past selected by the present.

Obviously, then, Verhaeren's *Les tendresses premières* will be of great interest to us, for in this book, which opens the series *Toute la Flandre*, the poet calls up in verses at once tender and impassioned the scenes of his childhood. He calls them up, or rather allows them to call themselves up, with his characteristic spontaneity. Verhaeren hardly troubles to tell us the story of his childhood. He has no definite plan, nor any concern for completeness. So true is this, that I think he does not give as much as three lines to reminiscences of his parents—a fact to which we shall return. Indeed a pedant would put his finger upon it as a sign of disorder and of aimlessness, referring to the terrible hiatus in a composition wherein a pupil was professing to give an account of his childhood. No writer who took up the theme as a task would fail to pay his respects to the memories of his father and his mother. But Verhaeren has not set himself a task, and that is why he remains so perfectly sincere. His reminiscences take the form of imagery, appropriately childish, trivial for those who look upon them only from without, but pregnant with meaning for anyone who grasps them from within. We are shown Saint-Amand, a village on the Scheldt; the minor craftsmen, such as the ropemakers, curriers, and blacksmiths; the old bellringer and the watchmaker; the juicy apples that looked so tempting. The value of these evocations to us depends upon their spontaneity and subjectivity.

Salient points of a more objective character are supplied by the biographers. Suffice it to mention, once for all, that Verhaeren was born at Saint-Amand, fifteen miles from Antwerp, on May 22, 1855. The following details are quoted from Léon Bazalgette : [1] " Verhaeren was a child of the Scheldt. The approaches to the North Sea were his consecration. The household consisted of his father ; his mother, Adèle, whose maiden name was Debock ; the latter's brother, whose factory belched forth its smoke hard by ; and an aunt, Amélie Debock, for whom Emile had a strong affection. The Debocks belonged to this countryside, and were proud of the fact. Their mother came from Herenthals ; her name had been Lepaige, which suggests a French origin. The Debocks gave a friendly reception to the 'foreigner' Gustave Verhaeren, Emile's father, who was from Brussels. Gustave's father had been a cloth-mercer in the rue de l'Ecuyer, and, having retired with a modest competence, had come to live at Saint-Amand. It is probable, however, that the Verhaerens were of Dutch origin."

With regard to Emile Verhaeren's parents, one of the poet's intimates has been good enough to supply me with additional details : " Emile cannot really be said to have been educated by his parents. They were too much occupied. He was mothered by his aunt, who devoted herself exclusively to the child. Verhaeren's first great sorrow was the death of this relative. He wrote a prose poem, which will show you better than anything the intensity of Emile's affection for his aunt, and his despair at losing her." [2]

We understand, now, why the father and the mother play so small a part in the *Les tendresses premières*. It is the aunt whom Verhaeren depicts at his bedside when he falls ill. He speaks of her as " my dear aunt," whereas he says merely " my worthy old parents."

Before examining *Les tendresses premières* let us pause for a moment to consider the *Liminaire*, which introduces

[1] Emile Verhaeren, 1907.
[2] This poem is printed as an appendix to the present volume.

the series *Toute la Flandre.* Here we have "the good season" [halcyon days], the old life, the garden, "the talks in summer on the doorstep." Contrasting with this picture of still life, there suddenly comes another picture giving expression to the bustle of modern times:

> Je me souviens de l'usine voisine,
> —Tonnerres et météores
> Roulant et ruisselant
> De haut en bas, entre ses murs sonores.—
> Je me souviens des mille bruits brandis,
> Des émeutes de vapeur blanche
> Qu'on déchaînait, le samedi,
> Pour le chômage du dimanche.

> [I recall how, from the factory hard by,
> Thunders and meteors
> Came rolling and streaming
> From above downwards between its reverberating walls.
> I recall thousands of wild noises,
> Riots of white steam,
> Let loose on Saturday
> In preparation for the Sunday rest.]

The factory plays a great part in Verhaeren's imagery. We have just learned from Bazalgette that it belonged to the poet's uncle Debock. We shall see later how it thrusts itself roughly into Emile Verhaeren's life. Bazalgette writes: "The Verhaerens and the Debocks had a great wish to see young Emile succeed his uncle some day at the oil-mill. Unfortunately the youth was by no means allured by the prospect of spending his life at the head of a factory in a petty township, and had other views. He was just twenty, and his education was regarded as finished. Provisionally, he yielded, and worked for a year at a desk in his uncle's office, where he was initiated into the mysteries of book-keeping. In the end, however, he got his own way."

We see how important the factory was in Verhaeren's

life. It became linked with the memory of the uncle to whom it belonged and with that of the father who wished his son to make it a career. In a word, it became linked with the memory of the two figures embodying paternal authority. In Emile Verhaeren's youth it was an object of conflict. But the day was to come when he would no longer feel any hostility towards the factory; when he would sing it in poems which were to be numbered among his masterpieces. This was to happen at the instant when, after a painful and momentous crisis, he came to accept reality, even brutal reality; when he came to accept modern life, the life of action. For him, the factory was the emblem of this reality and of this active life. We must endeavour to secure a full understanding of the conversion, which was the great event in Verhaeren's life and art. Symbolically it may be termed "the acceptance of the factory." At this point we have to note that for him the image of the factory is a condensation. First of all, it may be said to be the father, authority; next, it is material reality and action. The condensation of these two elements, the father and reality, is no chance matter.

C. G. Jung introduced the convenient terms "extroversion" and "introversion" to denote two contrasted tendencies: towards reality, the outer world, and action, on the one hand; and towards the inner life, and dreaming, on the other. The words have been adopted by Flournoy and Morel, but their significance remains ill-defined and varies considerably from author to author. We must avoid, therefore, making entities of them; and yet we have to recognise that they are something more than empty abstractions. Each of the trends in question is associated with certain characteristic psychological phenomena. Above all, psychoanalysts have been able to show that, in the mind of the youth, the introvert tendency is linked with the idea of the mother, and the extrovert tendency with that of the father. An attitude of protest against the father and against authority, an individualist character, is generally found in the introvert. This phenomenon is well marked in Verhaeren, who was extremely introverted until the crisis in his mental development.

It has been shown that anyone's earliest reminiscence of childhood is apt, by condensation, to symbolise a notable feature of his life.[1] The same may be said of the reminiscence, whether it dates from earliest childhood or not, by which a poet thinks fit to begin the story of his childhood. However this may be as a generality, the image of the factory introduced as an exergue into *Les tendresses premières* is full of significance in the case of Verhaeren. More noteworthy still, as we shall see, is the contrast by which we have already been struck between the garden and the factory. This corresponds intimately with the contrast between dreaming and action, between introversion and extroversion. The abrupt contrast between the garden and the factory is a miniature emblem of the great conflict in the poet's life. The struggle against the father and against the factory when Verhaeren was twenty is one of the episodes of this conflict; the crisis which came later was an acute expression of it; the final conversion was its denouement.

In Verhaeren's imagery, the significance of the garden is no less clear than that of the factory. The garden of his childhood is fully described in one of the poems in *Les tendresses premières*. We become sufficiently well acquainted with it to recognise it when it reappears in *Les rythmes souverains* as the *paradise* where Adam and Eve lived before the fall. Moreover, in the child's imagination the garden was already identified with the earthly paradise:

    Un amateur d'Anvers m'ayant offert, dûment,
    Deux oiseaux fiers qui s'en venaient de Numidie,

[1] Bovet, Preface to Artus-Perrelet's Le dessin au service de l'éducation.

> Et trois paons fous dont les plumes, soudain brandies,
> Ouvraient dans l'ombre, avant le soir, un firmament,
> > On les lacha, l'été, pendant tout un semestre,
> > > Libres et familiers, parmi les gazons roux,
> > Si bien que le jardin se changea tout à coup,
> > Pour mon esprit naïf, en paradis terrestre.[1]

> [A bird-lover in Antwerp having kindly offered me
> > Two stately birds from Numidia,
> And three gay peacocks whose feathers, suddenly brandished,
> Opened, in the gloaming as night fell, a firmament,
> > They were let loose for the whole summer,
> > > Free and friendly, to roam upon the parched turf,
> > So that the garden was changed all at once,
> > To my simple fancy, into an earthly paradise.]

It is easy, now, to establish detail by detail that the garden of childhood

> Avec des fleurs, devant, et des étangs, derrière

> [With flowers in front and ponds at the back]

is really the prototype of the *paradise*. It is easy to compare the imagery and the phraseology of this *paradise* with those of the *garden* in *Les tendresses premières*. We recognise even the insects. In *Le jardin* we read,

> Et le vol jaune et vert des insectes fragiles ;

> [And the yellow and green flight of frail insects ;]

while the corresponding passage in *Le paradis* runs,

> Et d'y regarder luire et tout à coup bouger
> > Les insects fragiles.

> [And to watch there shining and suddenly moving
> > Frail insects.]

We find once more in the paradise the very peacocks which were let loose in the garden. The fantastic beasts which the child's imagination fashioned out of the massive rocks.

[1] From Le jardin, in Les tendresses premières.

LES TENDRESSES PREMIÈRES 43

Comme on en voit sur le fond d'or des broderies,

[Such as one sees on the golden groundwork of embroideries,]

reawakened to life after the lapse of half a century in the transfigured garden. The imaginary panther of which he had been afraid one evening reappears beside the peacocks :

Le vent jouait avec l'ombre des lilacs clairs,
Sur le tissu des eaux et les nappes de l'herbe.
Un lion se couchait sous les branches en fleurs ;
Le daim flexible errait là-bas près des panthères ;
Et les paons déployaient des faisceaux de lueurs
Parmi les phlox en feu et les lys de lumière.[1]

[The wind was playing with the shadow of the bright lilacs,
On the web of the waters and the surface of the grass.
A lion was lying beneath the blossoming boughs ;
The lithe buck was wandering over there near the panthers ;
And the peacocks were spreading sheaves of light
Amid the flaming phloxes and the radiant lilies.]

What was the sin for which Adam and Eve were driven from this paradise ? It was love : that love which is, we are told, preeminently a manifestation of extroversion ; the love which was revealed to Verhaeren when he had passed through his crisis, simultaneously with the revelation of the beauty of the real universe and of human action ; the love which contributed greatly to his deliverance. In Adam's case, likewise, that which seen from the garden had been punishment and exile, disclosed itself to him after the expulsion as a joyful revelation. The two who had been banished from paradise felt themselves impelled, like the poet on the morrow of his crisis,

Vers les mondes nouveaux de la ferveur humaine.

[Towards the new worlds of human passion.]

It is the beauty of extroversion discovered amid a

[1] From Le paradis, in Les rythmes souverains.

sense of wonderment comparable to that of *La multiple splendeur.*

It is love for earthly reality:

> L'homme sentit bientôt comme un multiple aimant
> Solliciter sa force et la mêler aux choses ;
>   .   .   .   .   .
> Son cœur naïf, sans le vouloir, aima la terre.

[Soon the man felt as though a multiple magnet
Were drawing forth his energy and mingling it with things ;
  .   .   .   .   .
His simple heart, involuntarily, loved the earth.]

Faith in action, faith in human effort, suddenly exalts Eve's soul :

> Elle songeait, vaillante et grave, ardente et lente,
> Au sort humain multiplié par son amour,
> A la volonté belle, énorme et violente,
> Qui dompterait la terre et ses forces un jour.

[She, brave and serious, ardent and deliberate, pondered
On human destiny multiplied by her love,
Upon the will, lovely, titanic, and passionate,
Which would one day tame the earth and its forces.]

Despite the welcoming gesture of the angel, Eve refuses henceforward to reenter paradise, the closed garden of the introverted spirit. We perceive how original a trend Verhaeren gives to the ancient myth, endowing it with a meaning at once intimate and profoundly human. We recognise, too, the overtones of the emblem of the "garden." It is a life self-enclosed ; it is a dream. That which the garden induced in the child poet, was it not in fact a dream ?

> Tout m'apparut énorme, étrange et merveilleux. . . .
> Depuis ce temps, mon rêve à mon désir tressé,
>   Illumina tout le jardin de féeries. . . .
>   Et ce rêve dura autant que les beaux jours.[1]

[1] From *Le jardin*, in *Toute la Flandre*.

LES TENDRESSES PREMIERES 45

[Everything seemed to me huge, strange, and wonderful. . . .
Thenceforward my dream, interwoven with my longing,
    Illumined all the garden with scenes of faëry. . . .
And this dream lasted the whole summer.]

The "garden" and the "factory" are here made equally intelligible to us. Resuming the language of symbolism, we may say that "the flight from the garden" is equivalent to "the acceptance of the factory."

Les tendresses premières begins with the poem *Ardeurs naïves*, the poem of a child's love:

> J'entends là-bas sa voix, sa voix—
> Oh ! la petite amie espiégle et blonde
> Qui s'en alla, vers l'autre monde,
> Toute fragile, alors qu'elle ni moi
> Ne soupçonnions encor
> Ce qu'est la mort.

> [I heard over there her voice, her voice—
> Oh ! the little friend, roguish, fair-haired,
> So soon to set out for the other world,
> A frail being, although neither she nor I
> Had an inkling as yet
> Of what death is.]

Those who know the famous poem *Le passeur d'eau* will perhaps immediately trace a resemblance between this "voice over there" and the voice of the woman who, from the other side of the impossible, hails the symbolical ferryman, the ferryman who is striving to make his way up-stream, and wishes to relive his life :

> Le passeur d'eau, les mains aux rames,
> A contre flot, depuis longtemps,
> Luttait, un roseau vert entre les dents.

> Mais celle hélas ! qui le hélait,
> Au delà des vagues, là-bas,
> Toujours plus loin, par au delà des vagues,
> Parmi les brumes reculait.[1]

[1] From *Le passeur d'eau*, in *Les villages illusoires*.

[The ferryman, his hands on the oars,
Up-stream, for a long time,
Had been battling, a green reed between his teeth.

But she, alas, who was hailing him
From across the waters, over there,
Ever farther off across the waters
Receded into the mists.]

In *Ardeurs naïves*, the poet talks to his little friend, who is dead:

De ceux que nous avons connus, c'est ton aïeule
  Qui me parle le plus souvent,
  Avec son cœur et son esprit fervents,
Des ans inoubliés qui furent notre enfance.
  A l'entendre, je revois tout.

[Of those whom we knew, it is your grandmother
  Who speaks to me most often,
  With her loving heart and mind,
Of the unforgotten years of our childhood.
  As I listen, it all comes back to me.]

Next come some pictures of their childhood together, images which stand forth in his mind. One of them is that of

Le bourg de Saint-Amand, avec le fleuve au bout.

[The township of Saint-Amand, with the river beyond.]

Shortly afterwards he speaks of "the voices of the ferrymen." This river which is the end of the world for the two children, the ferrymen on the river—in these we have been led back to the poem in *Les villages illusoires*, and thus the kinship between the two reminiscences is fully established. We cannot doubt that in the voice which hails the ferryman there is much of the voice of the little friend of childhood's days, who has crossed the river and entered the other world.

LES TENDRESSES PREMIERES 47

> Un jour on m'assura qu'en des pays d'étoiles
> Elle s'était perdue, avec des voiles
> Et des roses, entre ses doigts petits;
> Son image resta fixé en mon esprit
> Si belle,
> Que tout mon cœur partît vers elle.

[One day they told me that in the lands of the stars
  She had lost her way with veils
  And roses between her little fingers;
  Her image remained fixed in my mind,
    So lovely
That my whole heart went out towards her.]

"Went out towards her," just as the ferryman went out towards the impossible, the reminiscence of childhood against the current of life. This "up-stream" of *Le passeur d'eau* gives admirable expression to what psychologists have termed the "regressive" tendency which appears to be one of the regular characteristics of introversion. As we noted in the case of the term introversion, the words regression and regressive are used in slightly varying senses by different authors. Let us accept them for the nonce in their simplest meaning, in a purely temporal significance, to denote a marked tendency to revive the past, and especially the days of childhood. We will not enquire at present what other phenomena may be presupposed by or involved in this tendency. Enough to say that it manifests itself in one whose vital energy has remained moored to unduly powerful "early affections," so that it leads to the spontaneous revival of the images and states of childhood's days. One with such a tendency turns towards dreams of childhood rather than towards the realities of life. We see in it a stage on the way to introversion.[1]

Underlying this tendency, in the youth, there is

---

[1] Freud's concept of regression is unduly complicated. For him the term subsumes quite a number of phenomena (including, apparently, introversion itself)—phenomena which it would certainly be better to name and study separately.

commonly supposed to exist a first love, one of great intensity, for the mother, or for some person who acts as substitute for the mother. Such a cause of introversion probably existed in Verhaeren; but as far as the revelations in *Les tendresses premières* are concerned, we have direct evidence of a childish passion for the girl friend who died. The "naive ardours" of children are sometimes the most passionate of feelings. This sentiment turns the poet's gaze towards his childhood, and towards the inner life in which his childhood is revived. Psychoanalysts are fond of discerning in a regressive love for the mother one of the mainsprings of the mystical life, and above all of the cult of the Virgin Mary. Verhaeren himself informs us that his love for the little girl who died gave him a similar trend, his case being paralleled by that of Dante, whom Beatrice leads to heaven :

> Je conservais longtemps son souvenir pieux,
>   Dans mon étroit livre de messe ;
>   On y lisait la bonne promesse
>   De se retrouver tous aux cieux ;
> Et c'est ainsi que je fis plus douce connaissance
> Grâce à sa mort, avec la Vierge et le bon Dieu.

> [I preserved for a long time an affectionate memory of her
>   In my little mass book ;
>   There could be read the good promise
>   That we shall all meet again in heaven ;
> And it was thus that I came to know better,
> Thanks to her death, the Blessed Virgin and God.]

An analysis of the verses which follow those just quoted would take us a little away from our subject :

> Depuis—Oh ! que de morts et de naissances
> Et que de gens défunts—ses parents et les miens—
>   Et le curé de Marikerke et le gardien
>   Du tir à l'arbalète où nous allions ensemble !

[Since then, how many deaths and births,
And how many people have died—her parents and mine—
    And the parish priest of Marikerke, and the keeper
Of the cross-bow shooting range whither we were wont to go together!] [1]

Nevertheless, this childish passion made no pretension to be platonic. A confused sensuality was awake in it.

Mais vers le soir, quand seul j'étais tapi,
Entre mes draps et que je m'endormais,
    Je me souviens t'avoir alors
    Si doucement serrée et embrassée,
Avec les bras et les lèvres de ma pensée
    Que j'en frissonne encor :
La lampe était ton front et l'édredon ton corps
    Et le coussin ta joue.

[But at night, when I was alone, curled up
Between the sheets, and when I was going to sleep,
    I recall having then
    So gently clasped and caressed you
With the arms and the lips of my thought
    That I am still thrilled at the memory :
The lamp was your forehead, the quilt your body,
    And the pillow your cheek.]

Death supervened to give a mystical trend to this passion.

We shall be struck more than once, in the course of our study, by the sudden and violent transition in Verhaeren's writings from the sensual life to the mystical life and from love to death. One of the causes of the abrupt transition may perhaps be discovered in the ruthless way in which death came to put a term to his childish love. But at this stage we can already see that there must have been other and deeper causes ; for even

---

[1] One accustomed to analyse symbols will discover an idyllic emblem in " the cross-bow shooting range whither we were wont to go together." The relatives and the keeper of the shooting range are authorities who exercise a censorship against the childish passion. This passion takes its revenge in an unconscious delight at the idea of the dying off of all these people with their obstructive morality.

while his little friend was still alive, the boy's imagination was fond of playing with gloomy fancies in which love mingled with death:

> Je me souviens aussi de cette histoire
> Où deux enfants, les doigts unis, mouraient
> D'un même coup de hache, un soir, dans la forêt ;
> Et je voulais mourir ainsi, et je voulais
> Dormir ainsi, avec toi seule,
> Loin du monde, sans qu'on le sût jamais.

> [I recall, further, the story
> In which two children, hands clasped, died
> From a single blow of an axe, one evening, in the forest ;
> And I wanted to die thus, and I wanted
> To sleep thus, alone with you,
> Far from the world, with never a soul to know.]

Let us consider the " axe " which, in the child's mind, is so intimately associated with the idea of the death he longs for. In the same poem *Ardeurs naïves* we read a little farther on :

> Quand je ferme les yeux,
> J'entends encor
> Le choc des fers et des essieux,
> Et les lourds camions sur les routes profondes.

> [When I close my eyes,
> I can still hear
> The clank of the irons and of the axles,
> And the heavy drays on the sunken roads.]

We fail to understand at first why this reminiscence of irons and of axles should revive at such a moment, or what concern it can have with the lad's girl friend. But it is precisely when the images appear in such a fashion, devoid of any logical tie with their context, that they are of the utmost value for the analysis, since they have in truth a more secret and often a more intimate tie. The next poem, *Les pas*, supplies the clue to the enigma, for now the clash of the irons and of the axles is con-

LES TENDRESSES PREMIERES

joined with the image of the axe in association with the idea of death :

> *Un soir, qu'avaient passé des attelages,*
> *Avec des bruits de fers entrechoqués,*
> On trouva mort, le long du quai,
> Un roulier roux qui revenait de Flandre.
> On ne surprit jamais son assassin.
> Mais certes, moi, oh ! j'avais dû l'entendre
> Frôler les murs, avec sa *hache* en main.

> [*One evening, when some teams had passed*
>   *With a clash of iron,*
>   There was found dead, by the quayside,
> A red-haired wagoner who was on his way back from Flanders.
> The murderer was never discovered.
> But I am sure I heard him,
> Brushing against the walls, *axe* in hand.]

We see that the clashing iron of the axles is condensed with the iron of the axe to express the anguish of death—an anguish vaguely associated with longing. These are powerful and intimate associations which will retain a tragical significance throughout the poet's life. Moreover, the significance undergoes extension to all the clashes of metal, to the heavy clatter of the axles and other ironwork of the *trains* which, in Verhaeren's writings, invariably seem to produce a nightmare impression as they pass. This generalisation is a perfectly natural one. It is a transference, in which some of the new elements are stressed at the expense of the old. In the following passage, Auguste Forel gives a typical instance of such a transference, which he terms " conversion ; " it affords at the same time an excellent example of the strange way in which the emotions of childhood preserve a latent activity in the subconscious : " Breuer, Freud, and others, have proved that the emotions or passions pent up may remain latent, whether forgotten or not, in the subject's brain for ten, twenty, thirty, or forty years, and even longer. A fright, for example a sexual assault, experienced at the age of five, may continue to produce effects at the age of fifty or more. I am personally acquainted with a woman of sixty-four who was bitten in childhood by a vicious horse. She lives in Stockholm, and always makes her way about the town on foot, being affected with a latent terror, not merely of horse-drawn vehicles, but also of electric trams (conversion)." [1]

The case recorded by Forel has little to do with the science of aesthetics, but it belongs to the same psychological family as the more impressive case of Verhaeren, who transferred to the trains which always "hallucinated" and fascinated him, the fear and the dread delight of the death from the axe-blow that in childhood he had dreamed of undergoing in company with his little friend. We shall study the evolution of these symbols. Suffice it now to select, from among a number, some of the gloomy visions of frenzied trains. They will serve to show us how terrible is destined to become the emblem whose simple origin has just been disclosed.

> Et stride un tout à coup de cri, stride et s'éraille :
> Et trains, voici les trains qui vont plaquant les ponts,
> Les trains qui vont battant le rail et la feraille,
> Qui vont et vont mangés par les sous-sols profonds
> Et revomis, là-bas, vers les gares lointaines,
> Les trains, là-bas, les trains tumultueux—partis.[2]

> [The air is riven with a sudden and harsh noise :
> Trains, here are the trains jolting over the bridges,
> The trains which clatter along the rails and the ironwork,
> Which go and go, swallowed by the deep tunnels,
> And revomited, over there, towards the distant stations,
> The trains, over there, the noisy trains, have gone.]

This vision is from the poem *Les villes* in *Les flambeaux noirs*. That which follows is from *La ville* in *Les campagnes hallucinées*.

[1] La psychanalyse et la guerre, "Le Carmel," 1917.
[2] From Les villes, in Les flambeaux noirs.

LES TENDRESSES PREMIERES 53

Des quais sonnent aux *entrechocs* de leurs fourgons. . . .
Des ponts s'ouvrant par le milieu,
Entre les mâts touffus dressent un *gibet* sombre. . . .
Par au dessus, passent les cabs, filent les roues,
Roulent les trains, vole l'effort,
Jusqu'aux gares, dressant, telles des proues
Immobiles, de mille en mille, un fronton d'or.

[The quays resound with the *clashings* of the wagons. . . .
Bridges opening in the middle,
Among the thickly clustered masts, look like gloomy *gibbets*. . . .
Above pass the cabs, turn the wheels,
Roll the trains, flies effort,
Towards the stations, rearing, like motionless prows,
Thousands upon thousands, a golden front.]

I underline two words in this extract. First of all "clashing," the same clashings that we have heard in *Les tendresses premières*, that of the axles and other ironwork of the drays. Next I underline "gibbets," which call up the idea of death—a death the thought of which is closely associated with that of death by the executioner's axe. Numerous instances of such juxtapositions could be selected to confirm our conviction of the kinship of these images.[1]

One of Verhaeren's strongest memories of childhood was that of the watchmaker who stimulated the curiosity of the little boy peering at him through the window after nightfall:

Et tout à coup, comme un vieux fou,
Face pâle, levait vers nous
Son œil géant, avec sa loupe.
Mes compagnons fuyaient : ils avaient peur.
La crainte également serrait mon cœur,

---

[1] Confining our analysis to the passages already quoted, let us recall, in connexion with the reminiscence of the axles, the vision of the wagoner who was found dead on the quayside. We could hardly discover a word more intimately associated with trains. [In French the word "quai" denotes a railway platform as well as a quay.]

> Mais, néanmoins, je restais là, planté
> Quand même à la vitrine.
> L'œil noir de l'horloger
> Plânait de tous côtés.[1]

> [And suddenly, like an old madman,
> His face pale, he lifted towards us
> His huge eye, with its lens.
> My companions fled, they were afraid.
> Fear seized my heart, likewise,
> And yet I stayed there, glued,
> In spite of myself, to the windowpane.
> The black eye of the watchmaker
> Swivelled in every direction.]

One day the child plucked up courage and made up his mind to cross the threshold of this human enigma, at once alarming and fascinating.

> Il était ma folie et déjà mon tourment.

> [He was my madness and already my torment.]

But as soon as he ventured into the shop, the inquisitive little hero was spellbound by an image seeming to multiply to infinity the haunting power of the solitary round eye which a moment before he had been looking at through the windowpane:

> Les ronds joufflus des gros cadrans
> Ornaient d'un lunaire sourire
> La chaux des grands murs blancs.

> [The great, round, chubby clock-faces
> Decked with a full-moon smile
> The whitewash of the vast walls.]

In this round eye of the watchmaker and in these full moons of clock-faces we can certainly discover the prototypes of a visionary image which continually haunted Verhaeren, and which, somewhat like the trains, was his madness and his torment. It is the image of the

[1] From L'horloger, in Les tendresses premières.

dials in the clock-towers, or that of the round dormer-windows (sometimes, by transference, of any window)—dormer-windows and clock-faces in which he sees " eyes " and " moons."

Les cadrans blancs des carrefours obliques,
Comme des yeux en des paupières,[1] . . .
[The white clock-faces, where the slanting cross-roads meet,
Like eyes in eyelids, . . .]

These affrighted eyes watch the futile efforts of the ferryman to reach the woman who hails him :

Les fenêtres, avec leurs yeux,
Et le cadran des tours, sur le rivage,
Le regardaient peiner et s'acharner.

[The windows, with their eyes,
And the clock-face of the towers on the bank,
Watched him toiling and straining.]

It is they which will impassively contemplate his defeat :

Les fenêtres et les cadrans,
Avec des yeux béats et grands
Constatèrent sa ruine d'ardeur.[2]

[The windows and the clock-faces,
With their large and impassive eyes,
Noted the ruin of his ardour.]

And these moon-faced dials are mad, like the eye of that "old madman," the watchmaker. During the crisis they will be the obsessive emblem of madness :

Je veux marcher vers la folie et ses soleils
Ses blancs soleils de lune au grand midi, bizarres.[3]

[I would fain walk towards madness and its suns,
Its strange white moon-suns shining at high noon.]

[1] From La révolte, in Les villes tentaculaires.
[2] From Le passeur d'eau, in Les villages illusoires.
[3] From Fleur fatale, in Les soirs.

> Je sens pleurer sur moi l'œil blanc de la folie.[1]
>
> [I feel the white eye of madness weeping over me.]

Again, the Lady in Black of the cross-roads will say:

> Vers les lunes de mes deux yeux.[2]
>
> [Towards the moons of my two eyes.]

Indubitably, of all the symbols in Verhaeren's writings, this is one of those most fraught with meaning and with anguish. The reason is that from the first it contains something over and above the child's dread of the watchmaker, for on this very day the watchmaker told the little boy the tale of the gnome and the three lady gnomes. Young Emile must have been greatly impressed thereby, for he relates the story in every detail, making of it the centre-piece of his poem. The gnome used to bustle all over the world (this meaning Flanders!) setting the clocks in the church-towers and the belfries. His heart kept perfect time, so that he could set the clocks by it. Of a sudden, all the clocks in the country went wrong, and the right time was lost. The watchmaker, who used to keep the invaluable little creature in a boxwood clock-case, found that the cage was empty and that the gnome had vanished:

> Bien plus. Là-bas, sur la pelouse humide,
>   Se trémoussait
> Une troupe en or de gnomides.
> Le silence souffrait, ployait et se cassait.
>   Quand au gnome, vautré au centre
> D'un tourbillon de mains, de bras, de seins, de ventres,
>   Son cœur régulateur des jours
> Battait et sursautait, comme un tambour.
>
> [Nay more. Over there, on the dewy lawn,
>   Were disporting themselves
> A number of golden lady-gnomes.

---

[1] From Inconscience, in Les débâcles.
[2] From La dame en noir, in Les flambeaux noirs.

The silence suffered, bent, and broke.
As for the gnome, wantoning amid
A whirlwind of hands, arms, breasts, and bellies,
His heart, the regulator of the days, the timekeeper,
Was beating and throbbing like a drum.]

The watchmaker grasped the situation, and knew what to do. At nightfall he put the gnome to sleep with a poppy draught. Then, with a magic flute, he lured the three little ladies into his shop, and locked each of them up in a separate clock-case. Thereupon the gnome's heart grew calm again, and the clocks began to keep time once more in all the church-towers and belfries.

Here, then, in association with the round eyes of the clock-dials, we have a strange story of escapades which "lead to madness." At the time of the crisis, when Verhaeren is haunted by the idea of madness, we rediscover similar themes, in which there is an obvious condensation of the grown man's crisis with the child's reminiscence.

But what are these escapades which lead to madness? Are we to think of the miscellaneous revels characteristic of a student's bohemian life such as Verhaeren led for a time—a life which certainly played its part in causing the moral and nervous depression of the ensuing years. Obviously this is the first element to be considered. If, however, we have recourse to an analysis of the " collective unconscious " (remembering that such an analysis must be made with due caution, and that its results can only be accepted with reserve), we shall find it possible to attune the foregoing interpretation with one having a more general application.

The story of the gnome and the three lady-gnomes recalls a common mythological motif, that of the three women from among whom a man has to choose. We have Paris and the three goddesses; Lear and his three daughters; Cinderella and her two sisters; the Parcae of classical antiquity, or the three Norns of Scandinavian mythology. The analysis of this motif has led Freud to admit that it is the manifestation of a spontaneous and widely diffused working of the human imagination. The three feminine figures, he says, respectively symbolise the mother, the wife, and death.[1]

If we accept this interpretation, in Verhaeren the vision of the clock-faces will be found linked to the drama of love and death, and we shall have no reason for surprise because it arouses the same prophetic anguish as the image of the trains. We have to admit that it is a risky matter to interpret an individual symbol with the aid of a collective myth. I should not myself take the risk unless I had been led to the same conclusion by the direct analysis of this image throughout the poet's works, before I had studied *L'horloger*, and before I had even thought of this poem or of the lady-gnomes. We shall see, in fact, that in Verhaeren's writings, " gold " is constantly used as a symbol of the impassioned life in its aspects of fertility and love ; " blackness " is a symbol of death ; the clash between black (or ebony) and gold is a symbol of the clash between love and death. The clock-faces, now lighted and now unlighted, appear to him by turns as golden or as black ; now they are burning eyes, and now again the black eye-sockets of a skull. The transition is abrupt and startling like those of a nightmare. For the moment, one example will suffice :

Vers les lunes de mes deux yeux,

[Towards the moons of my two eyes,]

cries the Lady in Black of the cross-roads. Then, suddenly :

Vers les lunes de mes deux yeux *en noir*.

[Towards the moons of my two eyes *showing black*.]

[1] Cf. " Imago," No. 3, 1913.—Summarised in French by Régis and Hesnard, op. cit., p. 172.

Then :
>Mes dents comme des pierres *d'or*
>Mettent en moi leur étincelle :
>
>[My teeth, like stones *of gold*,
>Put their sparkle into me :]

Then, without transition :
>Je suis belle comme la mort
>Et suis publique aussi comme elle.
>
>[I am as beautiful as death,
>And I am public too, like death.]

The emblem of the *clock-faces* is closely connected with that of the *clock-towers*. Flanders is a land of church-towers and belfries, and it is therefore natural that their image should have impressed itself on Verhaeren's mind. But the dramatic significance of these images was underlined by an incident of his childhood, the burning of the village clock-tower, related in *Les tendresses premières*. " I was proud of my clock-tower," says the poet.

>Aussi de quelle angoisse et de quelle douleur,
>>Mon âme en deuil fut atterrée,
>
>La nuit que je le vis tout ruisselant de feux
>S'affaisser mort, dans l'ancien cimetière,
>>Le front fendu par le milieu,
>>À coups d'éclair et de tonnerres.[1]
>
>[With what anguish, then, and with what sorrow
>>My mourning spirit was crushed
>
>The night when I saw the tower, lapped in flames,
>Crumble to death in the old churchyard,
>>Its front split down the middle,
>>While the lightning flashed and the thunder rolled.]

The clock-towers, like the clock-faces, will continue to be charged with prophetic anguish. Moreover, again and again we shall see this reminiscence of the burning

---

[1] From Mon village, in Les tendresses premières.

tower revive. In *Les villages illusoires* the whole scene is reconstructed :

> La tour,
> Avec, à son faîte, la croix brandie,
> Epand vers l'horizon halluciné,
> Les crins rouges de l'incendie.
> Le bourg nocturne en est illuminé.
> Les visages des foules apparues
> Peuplent de peur et de clameur les rues,
> *Et, sur les murs soudain éblouissants,*
> *Les carreaux noirs boivent du sang.* . . .
>
> La tour,
> Un décisif fracas,
> Gris de poussière et de plâtras,
> La casse en deux, de haut en bas.
> Comme un grand cri tué, cesse la rage,
> Soudainement, du glas.
> Le vieux clocher
> *Tout à coup noir* semble pencher.[1]
>
> [The tower,
> With the cross displayed at its summit,
> Extends towards the hallucinatory horizon
> The red mane of the conflagration.
> The darkling village is lighted up thereby.
> The crowds that have gathered
> People the streets with fear and clamour,
> *And on the walls suddenly flashing into light,*
> *The black window-panes drink blood.* . . .
>
> The tower !
> A final uproar,
> Grey with dust and plaster,
> Rends it in twain from top to bottom.
> Like a great cry strangled, the fury of the knell
> Suddenly ceases.
> The old clock-tower, *black all at once*, seems to lean over.]

The two passages I have italicised present to us once again the abrupt contrast between black and gold which was described in the case of the clock-faces, alternately

---

[1] From Le sonneur, in Les villages illusoires.

glowing and dark. The clock-tower only thrusts upward amid the conflagration to die " black all at once." These brusque reversals of value in the picture, contribute greatly to the hallucinatory aspect of Verhaeren's clock-faces and towers.

We shall meet with the towers again, pinning up " the garland of the dunes." Just as in childhood the poet was proud of his clock-tower, so in later life he felt a pride in all the towers of Flanders :

> O que mon cœur toujours reste avec vous d'accord !
> Qu'il puise en vous l'orgueil et la fermeté haute,
> Tours debout près des flots. . . .[1]

> [Oh that my heart may always be in harmony with you,
> That it may derive from you pride and lofty firmness,
> Towers erect near the waves. . . .]

They bear witness to the lost glory of Flanders. In the days of that glory, beacon fires flared from them :

> Jadis on allumait des feux
> Sur leur sommet, dans le soir sombre ;
> Et le marin fixait ses yeux
> Vers ce flambeau tendu par l'ombre.

> [Of old they used to light fires
> On the top, at nightfall ;
> And the sailor kept his eyes fixed
> Upon this torch held out to him by the night.]

Now the fires have been quenched and the towers are in mourning :

> Et d'autres blocs et d'autres phares,
> Armés de grands yeux d'or et de cristaux bizarres,
> Jettent, vers d'autres flots, de plus nettes clartés.

> [And other blocks of masonry and other lighthouses,
> With great golden eyes and with strange crystals,
> Throw, towards other waves, clearer lights.]

[1] From Les tours au bord de la mer, in La guirlande des dunes.

But it is in his pictures of revolt that Verhaeren shows his fondness for flaming towers, from which, as from the burning clock-tower, the tocsin continues to sound. They play a part in the rising of the people against Jacob van Artevelde :

On le tua à l'heure où les tours étaient rouges
Et comme en feu, de loin en loin, sous le couchant. . . .
Cœurs tragiques, fiévreux et haletants dans l'ombre,
Là-haut, sans qu'on les vît, battaient les tocsins sombres.[1]

[He was killed at the hour when the towers were red,
As if flaming, from point to point, in the light of the setting sun. . . .
Tragic hearts, feverishly panting in the darkness,
Up there, unseen, were sounding the dismal tocsins.]

The towers have a similar aspect in the poem specifically named *La révolte* :

La rue, en un remous de pas,
De corps et d'épaules d'où sont tendus des bras
Sauvagement ramifiés vers la folie,
Semble passer volante. . . .
Toute la mort
En des beffrois tournants se lève. . . .
Tappant et haletant, le tocsin bat,
Comme un cœur dans un combat,
Quand, tout à coup, pareille aux voix asphyxiées,
Telle cloche qui âprement tintait,
Dans sa tourelle incendiée,
Se tait.[2]

[The street, in an eddy of footsteps,
Of bodies and shoulders from which are stretched forth arms
Waving wildly towards madness,
Seems to pass on the wing. . . .
Death rises
In the spinning belfries. . . .
Pulsating and panting the tocsin sounds,
As a man's heart beats in the fight.

[1] From Jacques d'Artevelde, in Les héros.
[2] From La révolte, in Les villes tentaculaires.

LES TENDRESSES PREMIERES

Now, all at once, like a voice that has been strangled,
Some bell, which has been harshly clanging
In its burning tower,
Is silenced.]

These visions of towers in the pictures of revolt are instructive. Our fantasies of revolt are apt to give expression to that which is *in revolt within ourselves*. In especial they give expression to the mob of our instincts. These, after being held in leash by some moral or religious scruple, after having been restrained by our judgment and our will, in a word by the " front," [1] take sudden and brutal revenge. The clock-tower just now looked like a " front " suddenly split. In like manner, Artevelde is a " front " against the assaults of the revolt:

Et ce torride amas de rages populaires
Montait battre le seuil d'Artevelde—debout.
Il était là, le front tourné vers la marée
De ces âmes, par sa présence, exasperées.[2]

[And this hot wave of popular wrath
Rose to assault the threshold of Artevelde—standing there.
There he stood, confronting the tide
Of these souls infuriated at the sight of him.]

Again, we shall encounter in *Les moines* the heretic who, having lost his faith, rears himself up like a " tower," and like a scarlet and lightning-riven façade [front]. To the last the poet will tell us:

. . . j'éduque aussi ma volonté
A me bâtir un front qui doit rester mon maître.[3]

[. . . moreover I train my will
To build me a front which shall be my master.]

[1] There is an untranslatable word-play, a " condensation " in fact, in the French original here. " Front " means forehead as well as front or façade. The forehead or brow is symbolical of the judgment or intellect which holds the mob of instincts in leash; this forehead or façade is split, is rent in twain, by the revolt of untamed instincts.—TRANSLATORS' NOTE.
[2] From Jacques d'Artevelde, in Les héros.
[3] From La vie ardente, in Les flammes hautes.

The front or façade of the towers and belfries—representing will and religious scruple—is exposed to the assaults of the lower nature. This is why, in *Le sonneur*, the fierce conflagration vents its rage upon the symbol of the Christian faith :

> Et, dans l'effondrement du faîte entier, la croix
> Choit au brasier, qui tord et broie
> Ses bras chrétiens, comme une proie.
>
> [And when the summit crashes, the cross
> Falls into the furnace, which twists and brays
> Its Christian arms as if they were prey.]

The same gesture of rage is seen in *La révolte* :

Telle une neige, on dissemine les hosties
Pour qu'elles soient, sous des talons rageurs, anéanties.

[The consecrated wafers are scattered like snowflakes
So that they may be ground to powder beneath the raging heels.

We must, moreover, link this image with another in the same poem :

> Les cadrans blancs des carrefours obliques,
> Comme des yeux en des paupières,
> Sont défoncés à coups de pierre.
>
> [The white clock-faces, where the slanting cross-roads meet,
> Like eyes in eyelids,
> Are smashed with hurtling stones.]

It would seem that the white clock-faces, like the consecrated wafers, arouse the fury of the mob.

The towers, like the clock-faces, bring us back to a contrast, to the way in which the higher life, for the very reason that it is higher, suddenly destroys itself and collapses into negation. We shall see how Verhaeren was impressed by this contrast in the hour of crisis, when giving up the gluttonous and fleshly life into which he had wildly plunged, he fell into an abyss of depression.

LES TENDRESSES PREMIERES

The paroxysm of frantic enjoyment had originated in the loss of religious belief occurring in a man of strong character, a man made for an ardent life but from whom the old reason for ardour had been snatched. Thereupon, for a space, he threw himself blindly into the furnace of purely sensual delights, with which persons of fine endowment cannot long rest content. Now, whereas other symbols used by the poet seem to allude to the crisis in general terms, the emblem of the tower and that of the burning tower stress one of the causes of the crisis. We can divine this cause from our study of Verhaeren's life, and an analysis of the emblem of the burning tower confirms our judgment. This *destruction* of the *bell-tower* in his *native village*—could there be a clearer and more exquisite symbol of the *loss* of the *faith of childhood*? The disaster leaves the soul lonely and stifled. We have the bell which has been silenced " like a voice that has been strangled " in La révolte ; and we have also the bell-ringer buried under the fallen bell :

> Le vieux sonneur n'a pas bougé
> Et la cloche qui défonça le terrain mou
> Fut son cercueil et fit son trou.[1]

> [The old bell-ringer had stuck to his post.
> And the bell, burying itself in the soft ground,
> Dug his grave and formed his coffin.]

We are told in Les tendresses premières how fervently religious Verhaeren had been since childhood's days:

> Je me cachais pour sangloter d'amour ;
> J'aurais voulu prier toute ma vie,
> A l'aube, au soir, la nuit, le jour,
> Les mains jointes, les deux yeux ravis
> Par la tragique image
> Du Christ saignant vers moi tout son pardon.[2]

---

[1] From Le sonneur, in Les villages illusoires.
[2] From Les Pâques, in Les tendresses premières.

> [I hid myself to sob out my love;
> I should have liked to pray all my life,
> At morn, at eve, by night, by day,
> Hands clasped, eyes rapt
> By the tragic figure
> Of Christ bleeding towards me his full forgiveness.]

But when the repast of the first communion degenerated into a blasphemous orgy of gluttony—one of those gross Flemish merry-makings which Verhaeren depicts in a later poem—" I was frightened," he says:

> ... et m'en allai je ne sais où
> Dans un recoin de la maison profonde,
> Prier pour ceux qui outrageaient mon Dieu.

> [... and crept away, I hardly know whither,
> Into some out-of-the-way corner of the house,
> To pray for those who were outraging my God.]

It was natural that in such a mind the loss of faith should cause one of those shipwrecks after which the sufferer long remains derelict. Such is the significance of the burning tower, and that is why its image is always so poignant.

This interpretation explains certain details which might otherwise have been overlooked, and whose significance is only made plain by the new light. For instance, in *La guirlande des dunes*, the darkened towers are replaced by modern lighthouses, which

> Armés de grands yeux d'or et de cristaux bizarres,
> Jettent, vers d'autres flots, de plus nettes clartés.

> [With great golden eyes and with strange crystals,
> Throw, towards other waves, clearer lights.]

Verhaeren is using the phraseology habitual to him when he wishes to convey the idea of modern science replacing the traditional creed. The lighthouses are closely paralleled by the observatories and laboratories in *La recherche*.

Cristaux monumentaux et minéraux jaspés. . . .
Instruments *nets* et délicats. . . .

C'est la maison de la science au loin dardée
Obstinément, par à travers les faits et les idées,
Vers l'infini et ses mystères
Et ses silences refractaires.

Avec des *yeux*
Méticuleux ou monstrueux,
On y surprend les croissances ou les désastres
S'échelonner depuis l'atome jusqu'à l'astre.
La vie y est fouillée, immense et solidaire,
En sa surface ou ses replis miraculeux,
Comme la mer et ses gouffres houleux,
Par le soleil et ses mains d'or myriadaires.[1]

[Huge *crystals* and veined minerals. . . .
Delicate instruments of *precision*. . . .

It is the house of science, persistently impelled,
Far athwart facts and ideas,
Towards the infinite and its mysteries
And its refractory silences.

With *eyes*
Microscopic or telescopic,
Those who work there detect growths and disasters
Ranging from the atom to the star.
Life, vast and integral, is rummaged there,
Both on its surface and in its wonderful recesses,
As the sea and its troubled depths
Are searched by the sun and its myriad golden fingers.]

The reader can study similar images in *Les penseurs* (*La multiple splendeur*).
Our interpretation can also take into account an apparently insignificant detail with which Verhaeren

[1] From La recherche, in Les villes tentaculaires.

concludes the poem *Mon village,* wherein he tells the story of the conflagration. Speaking of the clock-tower, he writes :

> Il lui fallut trois ans pour ressurgir au jour !
> Trois ans pour se dresser vainqueur de sa ruine !
> Trois ans que je gardai, dans ma poitrine,
> La blessure portée à mon naïf amour !
>
> [It took three years for the tower to rise again !
> Three years to rise victorious out of its ruins !
> Three years during which I harboured, in my breast,
> The wound inflicted on my simple love !]

From a literary point of view, this repetition of " three years " might be considered inelegant. But if it be the outcome of a spontaneous need for expression, we shall do well to search for the subconscious cause of the poet's insistence. However intense a fondness the child may have felt for the village tower, his love cannot justify the importance given to the fact that three years were needed for its rebuilding. It seems unlike Verhaeren to conclude a beautiful poem by stressing a minor detail. We have, therefore, to ask whether the term of " three years " has a personal significance. In fact, the only way in which it can possess such a significance is by way of condensation, so that the rebuilding of the clock-tower is not the only matter at stake. If we recall that the destruction of the clock-tower by fire has been condensed with the moral crisis in the poet's own life, that this crisis apparently lasted three years (1887–1890), and that it secured literary expression in the three stages of *Les soirs, Les débâcles,* and *Les flambeaux noirs,* we shall understand why the term of three years is so important—the three years that were requisite for Verhaeren himself " to rise again." Moreover, we can hardly avoid thinking of how Christ rose again on the third day, and how three days were needed to " rebuild this temple."

Such a train of thought is impressed on us all the more, seeing that Verhaeren, at the time of the crisis, imagines himself crowned with thorns and bleeding on the cross. It is verily the Christ who is dead in him, and who must be resurrected in the form of a new faith

CHAPTER TWO

LES FLAMANDES AND LES MOINES[1]

(DAYS OF YOUTH, DOWN TO 1886)

Les flamandes and *Les moines* were the two chief works of Verhaeren's youth—a youth slowly ripening in one who thus early attained to mastery. *Les flamandes* was published in 1883, when the poet was twenty-eight; *Les moines* in 1886, when he was thirty-one. In these interrelated works, vehement in their contrasts, are polarised the two opposing aspects of the vigorous Flemish nature, which is at once voluptuous and mystical. They likewise exhibit the two contradictory aspects of Flanders itself; Verhaeren is surrounded by scenes which are the concrete expression of his own duality. We are in the Parnassian [2] period of his art. He produces objective works, in which he delights to portray the luxuriance and vigour of the forms in his environment. But what Maeder [3] has established concerning Hodler, when analysing this artist's symbolism, is equally true of

---
[1] Flemish Women, and The Monks.
[2] The term " Parnassian," as applied to a Belgian poet, has a precise significance. " The Belgian poets are divided into two . . . camps with regard to metrical questions. The Parnassians . . . cling to the traditional forms of French verse . . . and to the time-honoured diction; whereas the verslibristes use the free forms of verse. . . . Verhaeren, who wrote in vers libres after his first two volumes, has in his last book, Les rythmes souverains, approximated to the regular alexandrine.'— Quoted from the introduction to Jethro Bithell's Contemporary Belgian Poetry, p. xv.—TRANSLATORS' NOTE.
[3] Op cit.

Verhaeren. Although the latter's aim seems to be nothing more than to limn in great frescoes the warm colouring and rude contrasts of his native land, he is simultaneously giving expression to one of the deepest conflicts within himself. The twofold Flanders is in Verhaeren. Stefan Zweig, one of the most perspicacious of Verhaeren's commentators, and a personal friend of the poet, sees this clearly, and puts the matter very well. He writes: " This conflict for a conception of the world pierces through the constant contrast between the acceptance and the denial of life in the poet. . . . The hostility which divides his country into two camps seems to have taken refuge in his soul to fight it out in a desperate and mortal duel ; past and future seem to be fighting for a new synthesis." [1]

Les flamandes is a rising of the sap, a paroxysm of carnal life, a festival of all the senses, a kermesse opened under the auspices of the old Flemish masters, the poet's models, whose way it was " to paint a masterpiece between two drinking bouts." The verses are not so much to be read as to be chewed and swallowed. They savour of orgies. In these poems, love is still " gormandising," and a funeral is an occasion for a debauch. Veuillot declared that in *Chansons des rues et des bois* Victor Hugo had procreated the most splendid beast in the French tongue. Now that *Les flamandes* has been written, the dictum is perhaps no longer true.

> Dites ! jadis, ripaillait-on
> Dans les bouges et dans les fermes :
> Les gars avaient les reins plus fermes
> Et les garces plus beaux tétons. . . .
>
> De grands buveurs compacts et forts
> Riaient, chantaient, gueulaient à boire,
> Bâfraient à casser leur mâchoire,
> Hurlaient à réveiller les morts.[2]

---

[1] Zweig, Emile Verhaeren, English translation, pp. 52–3.
[2] From Truandailles, in Les flamandes.

> [Tell me, did they guzzle in days of old
> In the hovels and in the farms?
> The lads had stouter loins
> And the girls, finer nipples. . . .
>
> Hard drinkers, well-knit and strong,
> Laughed, sang, bawled over their liquor,
> Stuffed their mouths so as almost to break their jaws,
> Shouted till they nearly woke the dead.]

These pictures, so aggressive in their frankness, in their effrontery, are veritable mines for the purposes of the present study. We shall profit by the crude realism with which they portray the world wherein the poet's childhood and youth were passed. For in this first work, much as in the reminiscences of childhood, we discover images whose objective origin is unquestionable. We know the definite things and memories with which these images were, from the beginning, linked in the poet's mind, and we shall therefore be able to detect the symbolic resonances of the images throughout all his later work.

Among such emblems, gold is one of those whose significance is fixed and obvious from the outset. It expresses wealth and plenty. It is the gold of the rich harvests which have rejoiced Verhaeren's eyes in the Flemish plains; it is love as one of life's elemental forces; it is the sensuous fertility of all things.

> *Les graines d'or.* . . .
> *Un tressaillement d'or* court au ras des moissons,
> La terre sent l'assaut du rut monter en elle,
> Son sol générateur vibrer de longs frissons,
> Et son ventre gonfler de chaleur éternelle.[1]
>
> [*Golden grain.* . . .
> A *golden shiver* runs athwart the crops,
> The earth feels the onset of the rut rising within her,
> Feels her fecund soil vibrating with long thrills,
> Feels her womb swelling with everlasting heat.]

[1] From Les plaines, in Les flamandes.

> Et telles, plus folles encor,
> Arrondissant leurs hanches nues
> Et leurs belles croupes charnues,
> Où cascadaient leurs *cheveux d'or*.[1]

[And others, even more frenzied,
Rounding their naked haunches,
And their beautiful fleshy buttocks,
Down which their *golden hair* cascaded.]

> Ses cheveux sont plus blonds que l'orge dans les plaines. . . .
> Ses mains sont de rougeur crue et rèche ; la sève
> Qui roule, à flots de feu, dans ses membres hâlés,
> Bat sa gorge, la gonfle, et, lente, la soulève
> Comme les vents lèvent les blés.
> Midi, d'un baiser d'or la surprend sur les saules.[2]

[Her hair is fairer than the barley in the plains. . . .
Her hands are raw and red and chapped; the sap,
Which flows in fiery waves through her sunburnt limbs,
Beats in her throat, swells it, and slowly lifts it
 As the breeze lifts the corn.
Noon, with a golden kiss, surprises her among the willows.]

Gold, then, symbolises this very exuberance of life, which in *Les flamandes* is pushed to an extreme. We are even tempted to say an exuberance of health. But in this ardour, this desperate ardour, for life, there is something hypertrophic which arouses our alarm. The cynical critic who stigmatised *Les flamandes* by saying, " M. Verhaeren seems to have just been opening an abscess," let his wit run away with his judgment. Nevertheless, in the foolish phrase there was a meaning which the critic may never have suspected. We know how this poet's imagination clashes the ideas of blackness and gold one against the other, and how for him an exuberant life is to be a life that is self-destructive. This superfluity of health embodies, in the germ, to-morrow's crisis;

---

[1] From Art flamand, in Les flamandes.
[2] From La vachère, in Les flamandes.

hidden in the lovely fruit is a gnawing worm. There is a presage of evil already in *Les flamandes*, but the foreshadowing grows much plainer in the beautiful *Méditation* —the second of the two *Méditations* in *Les moines*.

Toute science enferme au fond d'elle le doute,
Comme une mère enceinte étreint un enfant mort.
Vous qui passez, le pied hardi, le torse fort,
Chercheurs, voici le soir qui vous barre la route.

Toute chair est fragile et son déclin est tel
Que jeune elle est déjà maudite en ses vertèbres,
Quels crocs ont déchiré l'orgueil des seins célèbres.
Vous qui passez, songez au chien de Jésabel.

[All science encloses a hidden doubt,
As a pregnant mother clasps a dead child.
You who are passing by, robust of frame and firm of tread,
Seekers, lo nightfall blocks the way.

All flesh is frail, and its decay is such
That even in youth it is smitten in its very bones.
What fangs have torn the pride of far-famed breasts.
You who are passing by, remember the dogs of Jezebel.]

The last image leads directly to one of Verhaeren's chief poems, one we have already considered, *La dame en noir* in *Les flambeaux noirs*. Here we have the most concise expression of the drama in gold and black of carnal love which at the same time is death:

Les chiens du noir espoir ont aboyé, ce soir,
Vers les lunes de mes deux yeux,
Si longuement vers mes deux yeux silencieux,
Si longuement et si lointainement, ce soir,
Vers les lunes de mes deux yeux en noir. . . .

Dites, quel incendie et quel effroi
Suis-je pour ces grands chiens, qui me lèchent ma rage ?
Et quel naufrage espèrent-ils en mon orage
Pour tant chercher leur mort en moi ?

[The hounds of black hope were baying this evening
At the moons of my two eyes,
For so long a time at my two mute eyes,
For so long a time and so distantly this evening,
At the moons of my two eyes showing black.

Tell me, what sort of a conflagration and horror
Am I for these huge hounds which are licking my frenzy?
And what shipwreck do they look for in my storm
That they should thus seek their death in me?]

As for the golden eyes which "hallucinate" the hounds, we are not perfectly clear whether they are really eyes or breasts. The two images seem to be fused. Towards the end of the poem, with one of those sudden transitions which are common in dreams, and of which *La dame en noir* contains several examples, we read:

> La démence incurable et tourmentante
> Qui donc en lui la sentira
> Monter, jusqu'à mes *seins* qui hallucinent?

[Madness, incurable and torturing,
Who can feel in himself how it surges
Upwards towards my *breasts* which hallucinate?]

Such a vision of breasts which shine like eyes, or like the moon-faces in the clock-towers, is found in other poems by Verhaeren:

> Le soir quand, sur sa couche amoureuse, la chair
> S'illumine du large éclat de ses seins clairs.[1]

[At night when, on her amorous couch, her flesh
Is lighted up by the radiance of her lustrous breasts.]

> Les deux seins noirs, pareils à deux lunes funèbres,
> Laissent deux baisers froids tomber en des ténèbres.[2]

[The two black breasts, resembling two mournful moons,
Let two cold kisses fall into the gloom.]

[1] From La vie ardente, in Les flammes hautes.
[2] From Aprement, in Les bords de la route.

We are here at the very heart of the complex which we have more than once encountered: that of black contrasted with gold; that of life which exalts itself, and which by the very fact of its exaltation negates itself. The Flemish plains exhibit this double aspect and this abrupt contrast. They have been golden plains, but when autumn supervenes they become " sombre plains." All their fertility has been changed into barrenness. Something wretched, effete, and sickly has suddenly followed upon the fullness and richness of life. Hence these images of decay, mouldiness, torpor, inertia; of cripples; of things which grow flaccid and flutter in the wind:

> Villages et hameaux geignent au vent du Nord;
> L'humidité flétrit les murs de plaques vertes,
> La neige tombe et pèse et lourdement endort
> Les chaumes noirs groupant entre eux leurs dos inertes.
>
> . . . . .
>
> Sur les digues un nid d'oiseau ballotte encor.
>
> . . . . .
>
> Ils [les vents] s'acharnent au ras des champs planes et mous,
> Cinglant les nudités scrofuleuses des terres,
> La végétation pourrie—et leur remous
> Abat sur les chemins les ormes solitaires.
>
> . . . . .
>
> Et dans la plaine vide on ne rencontre plus
> Que sur les chemins noirs de poussifs attelages,
> Que des voleurs, le soir, le matin, des perclus,
> Se traînant mendier de hameaux en villages,
>
> Que de maigres troupeaux, rentrant par bataillons,
> Sous les soufflets du vent, avec des voix bêlantes,
> Que d'énorme corbeaux plânants, aux ailes lentes,
> Qu'ils agitent dans l'air ainsi que des haillons.[1]
>
> [Villages and hamlets moan in the north wind;
> The damp blights the walls with green patches. . . .

[1] From Les plaines, in Les flamandes.

LES FLAMANDES AND LES MOINES

The snow falls, and lies, and heavily puts to sleep
The black hovels humping their inert backs side by side.

. . . . .

On the dike, a bird's nest still swings. . . .

. . . . .

The winds rage across the flat and sodden fields,
Lashing the scrofulous nakedness of the ploughlands,
And the decayed vegetation; their gusts
Blow down the solitary elms across the roads.

. . . . .

And, in the empty plain, one meets with nothing
But, on the black roads, creaking carts,
Thieves, at nightfall, in the morning cripples,
Limping along to beg from hamlet to village,

Nothing but lean flocks coming home in troops
Bleating under the buffets of the wind,
Nothing but huge crows hovering on slow wings,
Which they flap in the air as one flaps a rag.]

Here we have all the emblems which will abound once more before the crisis; we can put a finger on their origin, and can thus learn their meaning. Such emblems, and the ideas they express, are not conspicuous in *Les flamandes*, but they lie in ambush, they are threatening. They seem to warn us that the health and the fertility which overflow from the poems were being furtively undermined. They warn us that the all-pervading thought of the *Méditation* is obscurely making itself felt:

> Toute chair est fragile et son déclin is tel
> Que jeune elle est déjà maudite en ses vertèbres.
>
> [All flesh is frail, and its decay is such
> That even in youth it is smitten in its very bones.]

It is not difficult to perceive the shadow cast by this threat upon the "golden" emblems of exuberant life.
The *cows*, for instance, the *mill* and the *miller*, seem

to be associated with coarse and rustic loves, with this flux of sensual and gluttonous life :

C'est sa besogne à l'aube, au soir, au cœur du jour,
De venir traire, à pleine empoignade, ses bêtes
En songeant d'un œuil vide aux bombances d'amour,
Aux baisers de son gars dans les charnelles fêtes,

De son gars, le meunier, un gros rustaud râblé,
Avec des blocs de chairs bossuant sa carcasse,
Qui la guette au moulin, tout en veillant au blé,
Et la bourre de baisers gras, dès qu'elle passe. . . .

Et c'est là qu'elle vit, la pataude, bien loin
Du curé qui sermonne et du fermier qui rage,
Qu'elle a son coin d'amour dans le grenier à foin,
Où son garçon meunier la roule et la saccage,

Quand l'étable profonde est close prudemment,
Que la nuit autour d'eux répand sa somnolence,
Qu'on n'entend rien, sinon le lourd mâchonnement
D'une bête eveillée au fond du grand silence.[1]

[It is her task, at dawn, at eve, and at high noon,
To milk, with vigorous hands, her cows,
While her thoughts wander to love orgies,
To the kisses of her lover in their feasts of the flesh,

Of her lover, the miller, a strong-loined rustic,
His body embossed with lumps of flesh,
Who waylays her at the mill, keeping his eye on the wheat all the time,
And smothers her with fat kisses as she passes by. . . .

And it is there that she lives, the hoyden, remote from
The curé who sermonises and the farmer who scolds,
There that she has her love nook in the hay-loft,
Where her lover, the miller, tumbles and rummages her,

When the great cowshed is discreetly closed,
When the night spreads its drowsiness around them,
When there is nothing to be heard, amid the profound silence,
Save the heavy chewing of one of the wakeful beasts.]

[1] From Kato, in Les flamandes.

LES FLAMANDES AND LES MOINES 79

Since Verhaeren has made so frank an avowal (one of those avowals which are as unashamed as some of Rousseau's confessions), we may suitably give ear to an overtone of this poem, may listen to the echo of emotions actually experienced by the poet during adolescence :

> Pendant des mois au jour le jour,
> Nos corps se sont aimés, dans la ferme lointaine,
> Ou rien, sinon les bruits monotones des plaines,
> Venaient mourir au soir tombant.
>
> . . . . .
>
> Les étables et, plus encor, les vieux greniers,
> Où l'on versait le grain, par sacs et par paniers,
> Nous invitaient et nous servaient d'asile.[1]

> [From day to day, for months,
> Our bodies were joined in love, at the remote farm,
> Where nothing save the monotonous noises of the plains
> Came to die at nightfall.
>
> . . . . .
>
> The cowhouses, and still more the old lofts,
> Where the grain was emptied in basketfuls and sackfuls,
> Beckoned us and served us as refuge.]

The passage gives a strangely enhanced meaning to all these emblems of gold, grain, and lofts. We may note, too, that "Kato," which is the name of the milkmaid in *Les flamandes*, becomes in *Les bords de la route* the name of the loved woman whose glories the poet sings, to tell us in the end of her death. For she, too, dies, like the little friend of his childhood's days. Suddenly she goes "to the cross-roads of death"; suddenly her luxuriant body is blighted. Who can doubt that this experience helped to create in the poet's mind the idea of an abrupt reversal of values, of a precipitate transition from love to death. Henceforward we shall understand how vigorous a condensation of manifold impres-

[1] From L'étrangère, in Les tendresses premières.

sions there is in this contrast ; we shall understand how strongly charged it is with meaning and with emotion :

Tes bras qui s'étalaient au mur de ta jeunesse,
Tel qu'un cep glorieux vêtu de vins et d'or,
Au long de tes flancs creux lignent leur sécheresse,
Pareils aux bras osseux et sarmenteux des morts.

Tes seins, bouquets de sève étalés sur ton torse,
Iles de rouge amour sur un grand lac vermeil,
Délustrés de leur joie et vidés de leur force. . . .

. . . . .

A voir si pâle et maigre et proche de la mort,
Ta chair, ta grande chair, jadis évocatoire,
Et que les roux midis d'été parsemaient d'or
Et grandissaient, mes yeux se refusent à croire

Que c'est à ce corps-là, léché, flatté, mordu,
Chaque soir, par les dents de l'ardeur d'une bête,
Que c'est à ces deux seins pâles que j'ai pendu
Mes désirs, mes orgueils et mes ruts de poète.[1]

[Your arms which were spread on the wall of your youth
Like the branches of a splendid vine clad with grapes and gold,
Are now drooping their withered length adown your hollow flanks
Like the bony and sapless arms of the dead.

Your breasts, nosegays of vintage displayed upon your body,
Islands of red love in a vast crimson lake,
Have now lost their lustre of joy and are emptied of their strength. . . .

. . . . .

When I see so pale and thin and near to death,
Your flesh, once so splendid and so stimulating,
Which the russet noons of summer strewed with gold
And magnified, my eyes refuse to believe

That it is upon this body, licked, stroked, bitten
Evening after evening by passionate animal teeth,
That it is upon these two pale breasts that I hung
My desires, my pride, and my poet's ardours.]

[1] From Au carrefour de la mort, in Les bords de la route.

LES FLAMANDES AND LES MOINES

Beside the golden grain, beside the miller, we find breadmaking associated with the emblems of carnal health:

> Les servantes faisaient le pain pour les dimanches. . . .
> La sueur les mouillant et coulant au pétrin. . . .
> Leur gorge remuait dans les corsages pleins,
> Leurs deux poings monstrueux pataugeaient dans la pâte
> Et la moulait en rond comme la chair des seins.[1]

> [The maids were making bread for Sunday. . . .
> They were damp with sweat, which ran down into the kneading-trough. . . .
> Their throats were moving in their well-filled bodices,
> Their huge fists were plunging into the dough,
> And were moulding it in rounds like the flesh of breasts.]

But the *grain* and the *flour* (emblems of fecund sensuality) are threatened by the *teeth* of the beast we have just seen, at "the cross-roads of death," biting and gnawing the flesh, "once so stimulating," of his doomed mistress. The teeth, and everything which gnaws and bites, are emblematic of a hidden ailment which is undermining health, fertility, and life:

> S'élargissaient, là-bas, les granges recouvertes,
> Aux murs, d'épais crépis et de blancs badigeons,
> Au faîte, d'un manteau de pailles et de joncs,
> Où mordaient par endroits les dents des mousses vertes.[2]

> [Over there extended the great barns,
> Their walls rough-cast and whitewashed,
> Their roofs thatched with straw or rushes,
> Bitten into here and there by the teeth of green mosses.]

These mosses bite the *barns* and their *thatched* roofs, emblems which immediately recall the golden harvests. The "green mosses," moreover, must be brought into relation with a verse previously quoted:

[1] From Cuisson du pain, in Les flamandes.
[2] From Les granges, in Les flamandes.

L'humidité flétrit les murs de plaques vertes.

[The damp blights the walls with green patches.]

The reader will remember that this was part of a description of one of the aspects of the sombre plains which, in autumn, suddenly replace the golden plains. All these invasions of green blight bring us back once more to " the cross-roads of death ":

La mort peindra ta chair de ce vieux ton verdâtre.[1]

[Death will paint your flesh with the greenish hue of decay.]

We readily recognise the corpselike tints of these mosses and green patches. All the emblems hang together, mutually strengthen one another, and enforce a definite interpretation.

The same menace of blight broods over the margin of the stagnant water of the ditches and ponds. When the noontide sun " sabred the water " of the ditches,

La ferme s'allumait d'un encadrement d'or.[2]

[The farm was lighted up by an enchasement of gold.]

But this charm was doomed to extinction, like everything " golden " ; and thenceforward the ditches presented nothing but emblems of dead torpor:

Ils s'étendaient, *plaqués* aux bords de *mousse verte*
Et de lourds nénuphars étoilant le flot noir.
Les grenouilles venaient y coasser, le soir,
L'œil large ouvert, le dos enflé, le corps inerte.

[They extended, *flecked* at the edge with *green moss*
And with great lilies starring the black waters.
The frogs came to croak there every evening,
Their eyes opened wide, their backs humped, their bodies inert.

[1] From Au carrefour de la mort, in Les bords de la route.
[2] From L'enclos, in Les flamandes.

LES FLAMANDES AND LES MOINES

The golden waters have become black waters. Once more life has been "flecked" with death.

In *Les flamandes* the funereal significance of *blackness* and of *ebony* are already growing manifest:

> Et sur fond de soleil, des barques toute noires
> Vont comme des cercueils d'ébène au fil des eaux.[1]

> [Against a background of sunshine, black barges,
> Looking like ebony coffins, float down the stream.]

Again we have been brought straight back to "the crossroads of death," to that poem in *Les bords de la route* which is highly charged with meaning—for so many emblems call it up to our minds and jostle one another in its verses:

> Et néanmoins je l'aime encor, quoique flétri. . . .
> Ce corps de pulpe morte et de chair effacée,
> Et je le couche en rêve au fond du bateau noir,
> Qui conduisit jadis, aux temps chanteurs des fées,
> Vers leurs tombeaux ornés d'ombre, comme un beau soir,
> —Trainés au fil des eaux et robes dégrafées—
> Les défuntes d'amour. . . .[2]

> [Yet I still love it, blighted though it be. . . .
> This body of dead pulp and faded flesh
> My fancy beds in the black barge
> Which, in days of old when fairies were sung,
> Conveyed, towards their graves decked with shadow like a fine evening,
> —Borne along by the current with gowns ungirdled—
> Maidens who had died of love.]

From time to time, in this beautiful poem, we note a somewhat repellent fondness for stripping and caressing a corpse; but we must not take it too much amiss in Verhaeren, who, in his student days, was strongly influenced by the excessive realism of Baudelaire and Zola.

---

[1] From Marines, in Les flamandes.
[2] From Au carrefour de la mort, in Les bords de la route.

This influence is felicitously illustrated in a study of Verhaeren by Georges Doutrepont, professor at the University of Louvain. Though the poet (writing under the pen-name of Rodolphe in the " Semaine des Etudiants " of which he was founder and editor) sometimes takes the liberty of caricaturing his masters, he continues to regard them as his masters. Concerning " Olivier " (Maurice Warlomont, alias Max Waller) he writes :

> Son cœur, les bêtes l'ont mangé.
> Qu'en reste-t-il pour sa donzelle ?
> Rien qu'un amas en vers changé,
> Rien qu'un paquet de vermicelle.[1]
>
> [His heart—the beasts have eaten it.
> What is left for his mistress ?
> Nothing but a heap of worms,
> Nothing but a packet of vermicelli.]

Of Baudelaire, Verhaeren says :

Et Charles Baudelaire, opiumesque ivrogne,
Qui demandait, tous les soirs, aux vents étonnés
De lui servir tout frais un parfum de charogne,
Et pour le respirer s'ouvrait les trous du nez.[2]

[And Charles Baudelaire, drunkard and opium-eater,
Who, every evening, asked the astonished winds
To serve him up, quite fresh, an odour of carrion,
And who, to inhale it the better, stretched his nostrils wide.]

However, this influence exercised by the school of literary sadism served merely to exaggerate the confused and disturbing instinct underlying the voluptuous sentiment—the algolagniac instinct which implants the germs of cruelty in every love. A frank mind will not hesitate to avow the existence of this instinct, which is indubitably

---

[1] Quoted by Doutrepont, Les débuts littéraires d'Emile Verhaeren à Louvain, p. 63.
[2] Ibid., p. 67.

the biological foundation of all those fantasies dear to the human imagination in which death rubs shoulders with love. Such an avowal, therefore, is quite appropriate to this poem which typifies love and death. The trees (and the rows of trees), which we shall find conspicuous in Verhaeren's subsequent works, make their appearance already in *Les flamandes*, being simultaneously associated with images of superabundant life and images of ruin and sterility:

Des arbres vieux, *moussus*, les branches étagées,
Baignaient dans le soleil de Mai, sur vingt rangées,
Leur domes élargis en toute leur ampleur.

Les bourgeons sous l'éclat de la jeune chaleur
Pointillaient les rameaux de rosâtres dragées,
Les verdures vêtaient les cimes de frangeés,
Les *vaches*, le pis lourd, vaguaient dans l'herbe en fleur.[1]

[Old trees, *moss-grown*, their branches in tiers,
Twenty rows of them, were bathing in the May sunshine,
Their domes expanded to their utmost width.

The shoots, under the stimulus of the early heat,
Were thrusting upwards their sprays of pink buds;
The verdure was fringing the summits;
The cows, heavy-uddered, were roaming in the flowery mead.]

In this picture, the trees, though old and moss-grown, are swollen with the sensual sap which rises and exudes throughout *Les flamandes*; and they are juxtaposed with the " heavy-uddered cows "—an emblem whose overtones we already know. But in the following picture, the row of trees will be encountered in association with the beggars of autumntide; and the trees, acquiring powers of locomotion, will march in file, as we shall see them marching soon in the company of the monks:

[1] From Les vergers, in Les flamandes.

La misère séchant ses loques sur leur dos,
Aux jours d'automne, un tas de gueux, sortis des bouges,
Rôdaient dans les brouillards et les prés au repos,
Que barraient sur fond gris des rangs de hêtres rouges.[1]

[In autumn days, a rout of beggars, coming forth from their hovels,
The rags of poverty drying on their backs,
Prowled through the fog and across the quiet fields,
Hedged in the grey distance by rows of ruddy beeches.]

The beggars who were passing through this sepulchral autumn landscape were making the sign of the cross:

> Puis reprenaient en chiens pouilleux, à l'aventure,
> Leur course interminable à travers champs et bois,
> Avec des jurements et des signes de croix.[2]
>
> [Then, like lousy dogs, haphazard, they resumed
> Their interminable tramp through meadows and woods,
> Cursing the while and making the sign of the cross.]

This sign of the cross is a sign of death:

> Un gars traça des croix sur le front de la vache.
> Et, le licol tendu, la mena vers la mort.[3]
>
> [A lad traced some crosses on the forehead of the cow,
> And, pulling the halter, led her to death.]

If we recall that the cow is one of the emblems of a fleshly and superabundant life, we shall grasp the full significance of these signs of the cross on the cow's forehead. It is the sign of doom, an omen, for it is the sign made by the simple folk of the Flemish plains, believing in the destiny which hazard or magic brings them. The cross is also associated with the death of Kato, and, just as upon the actual crossing of the ways, so its outline is projected upon "the cross-roads of death":

[1] From Les gueux, in Les flamandes.
[2] Ibid
[3] From La vache, in Les flamandes.

Et rien n'effacera jamais de ma mémoire
La croix que sur ton cœur dessineront tes mains.[1]

[And nothing will ever obliterate from my memory
The cross which your hands will form over your heart.]

Let me add that this sign of death is also the Christian and mystical emblem, the emblem of "cruciferous" monks. There is no contradiction here, for to be born to the mystical life is to die to the fleshly life.

In the sonnet entitled *Les greniers* several of the symbols just mentioned are amalgamated. In view of what we already know concerning the overtones of the loft, we need not be surprised to find this heaping up of symbols, as a sign of the heaping up of meanings:

> Sous le manteau des toits s'étalaient les greniers,
> Larges, profonds, avec des géantes lignées
> De solives, de poutres, de sommiers,
> Les *récoltes en tas* s'y trouvaient alignées :
> Les froments par quintaux, les seigles par paniers. . . .
> Un silence profond et lourd, tel une *mare*,
> S'étendait sur les grains. . . .
> Au reste les souris toutes se tenaient coites.[2]

> [Cloaked by the roofs, the lofts stretched
> Wide and deep, with huge lines
> Of rafters, cross-beams, and struts . . .
> *The crops* were ranged there *in heaps* :
> The wheat in sacks, the rye in baskets. . . .
> A deep and heavy silence, like that of a *mere*,
> Brooded over the grain. . . .
> The mice were all as still as could be.]

The *cross*-beams have already been mentioned in *L'étrangère*, the poem in *Les tendresses premières*, the poem which, a few pages back, threw light on the Kato of *Les bords de la route* :

[1] From Au carrefour de la mort, in Les bords de la route.
[2] From Les greniers, in Les flamandes.

Nos corps noués s'incendiaient l'un l'autre,
 Sous les angles et sous les croix
Que dessinaient l'arête et les poutres du toit.

[Our intertwined bodies lent fire each to the other,
 Beneath the angles and under the crosses
Traced by the groin and the beams of the roof.]

Knowing the prophetic significance attached to this symbol of the cross, which presents itself almost as an obsession in some of Verhaeren's other works (*Les campagnes hallucinées*), we can see once more, in these crosses described in the loft of his love-making, the familiar menace. Indeed, the whole sonnet is fraught with this foreboding : the mere, which is an emblem of the stagnant water that threatens the harvests at flood-time ; the little mice. We know the significance of something which gnaws and bites, of the "beast" which nibbles at the grain of fruitfulness. Mice are preeminently nibblers. As yet they are only a menace ; they are as still as can be, watching the golden grain—but later they will be loosed, and we shall hear them pattering, and nibbling with their little teeth, in nightmare poems.

Léon Bazalgette writes as follows concerning the origin of *Les moines* : " This sequence of poems was the outcome of impressions of childhood. At Bornhem, two or three miles from Saint-Amand, was a Cistercian monastery. Gustave Verhaeren . . . was in the habit of visiting the place once a month, as a pious pilgrim. The son, whenever he happened to be at home, accompanied his father, and the two would set out at half-past four in the morning for confession and communion. The early expeditions, and the figures of the monks, looking so tall and dignified as they moved through the cloisters in their voluminous habits, had greatly struck the child's imagination. Long afterwards, his mind was still haunted by the recluses of Bornhem. They were his models for *Les moines*. Brooding over the verses thus entitled, and wishing to revive his memories of the cloister, he went into retreat for twenty-one days at Forges monastery near Chimay."[1]

In works of fantasy, the cloister is apt to symbolise the idea of introversion. In Verhaeren's writings, such a meaning of this symbol is obvious. The interpretation will have to be considered once more when, in one of the plays, we see Dom Balthazar driven to the cloister by having committed parricide, just as young Verhaeren was led there by his father. Furthermore, when the poet went into retreat, it was in order to revive the memories of childhood, to plunge again into this distant past. The movement of regression does not surprise us in this connexion, for we know how close a tie there is between the regressive tendency and the tendency to introversion. Already we begin to realise the atmosphere of inwardness, and of the past, which must be breathed by those who would understand *Les moines*, and our analysis of the work will confirm this first impression.

In *Les flamandes* we see Verhaeren urged towards a carnal paroxysm whose very exaggeration discloses the sense of effort. Generally speaking, anyone who is aggressive in a profession of faith, as the poet is aggressive in this Rabelaisian evangel, is one who feels the need to preach to himself—for the very reason that he is not an enthusiastic convert. He cries so loudly, because he is attempting to drown another voice which would fain make itself heard within him. There is a good deal of doubt underlying fanaticism, and this applies to carnal fanaticism no less than to other forms.

In boyhood, Verhaeren was strongly religious; we have seen him weeping because, on the day of his first communion, the guests participated in an orgy; we have seen how, month after month, he accompanied his father on the pilgrimage to Bornhem. These things could not fail to make a deep impression on him. A grown person

[1] Bazalgette, op. cit.

may have lost the faith of childhood, and yet the vigorous sublimation imposed upon his instincts by that faith may none the less remain intact; there has been, as it were, an organic change, which must be reckoned with henceforward. A religious tendency has been born; it has the force of an instinct (in part, no doubt, it is inherited); it claims its rights.

In *Les flamandes*, the voice of this tendency had been stifled. In *Les moines*, it made itself heard once more, and was all the more clamorous because it had previously been stifled. Let me take this opportunity of pointing out that the psychoanalytical concept of repression is in need of amplification. We do not repress crude instincts merely; we repress, likewise, sublimated instincts. For instance, we repress a religious tendency when we lose our faith. This repression of sublimated instincts would appear to be subject to the same laws as the repression of crude instincts. Thus, the sublimated instinct, when it has been repressed, seeks derivatives; tries to undergo conversion into new sublimations; and, if denied this outlet, may give rise to a neurosis. It is possible, indeed, that the sublimated instinct may be unable to resume a crude form, so that there may be nothing but a choice between another sublimation and a neurosis. *Les moines* discloses to us a checked tendency to mysticism which has sought a derivative in literary expression. In like manner, the combative instinct, when checked, may seek a derivative in the perusal or the writing of works of heroic literature.[1]

The monks are emblems of *introversion, regression,* and *repressed mystical sublimation.*

The *introversion* of the monks is obvious. They are "recluses seated on the white mountains." They are "vessels of chastity which never run dry." The poet compares them to the mirror of tranquil waters. One

[1] Cf. Bovet, L'instinct combatif.

LES FLAMANDES AND LES MOINES 91

who looks into this mirror is apt to be fascinated by his own image:

> Miroirs réverbérant comme des lacs lucides
> Des rives de douceur et des vallons de paix.[1]
> [Mirrors shining like limpid lakes,
> Banks of sweetness and valleys of peace.]

We shall have to return to this emblem of the mirror of the waters, for it is one which haunts Verhaeren. In the "collective unconscious" it would seem to be associated with the myth of Narcissus, the beautiful youth, the parent of all introverts.

The *regressive* tendency which accompanies this introversion is likewise expressed by numerous images. The monks turn

> Du côté de l'aurore et de la solitude.[2]
> [Towards the dawn and towards solitude.]

In truth, these are one and the same. He who turns towards "the dawn" (towards his own childhood, and towards the maternal image bending over that childhood), is simultaneously turning towards "solitude" and towards introversion. Various writers have recognised this, and especially Morel, in his *Essai sur l'introversion mystique*. The monks, clad in white, have the guileless candour of children. There are "gentle monks" and "simple monks" for whom this candour has become the only garment of the soul. They are pure types of "infantile regression." They resemble the mystics studied by Morel, those mystics whose persistent longing for the mother leads to a worship of the Virgin Mother and predisposes them to visions like that of the Virgin and Child:

[1] From Les moines (the first poem).
[2] From the same poem.

Ces moines dont l'esprit jette un reflet de cierge,
Sont les amants naïfs de la Très Sainte Vierge ;

Ils sont ses enflammés qui vont La proclamant
Etoile de la mer et feu du firmament.

.   .   .   .   .

Qui La servent enfin dans de telles délices
Qu'ils tremperaient leur foi dans le feu des supplices,

Et qu'Elle, un soir d'amour, pour les récompenser,
Donne aux plus saints d'entre eux son Jésus à baiser.[1]

[These monks, whose mind sheds a light like that of a candle,
Are the simple lovers of the Holy Virgin.

They are enthusiasts who proclaim Her
Star of the sea and fire of the firmament,

.   .   .   .   .

Who serve Her with such rapture
That they would fain steep their faith in the fire of torment,

So that She, one evening of love, to reward them,
Gives to the most holy among them her Jesus to kiss.]

The convent gardener is one of these " simple monks,"
naively devoted to the service of the Virgin Mary :

Au temps de Mai, dans les matins auréolés
Et l'*enfance* des jours vapoureux et perlés,

Qui font songer aux jours mystérieux des *limbes*
Et passent couronnés de la clarté des nimbes,

Il étalait sa joie intime et son bonheur,
A parer de ses mains l'autel pour faire honneur

A la très douce et pure et benoite Marie,
Patronne de son cœur et de sa closerie.

Il ne songeait à rien, sinon à l'adorer,
A lui tendre son âme entière à respirer.[2]

---

[1] From Moine doux, in Les moines.
[2] From Moine simple, in Les moines.

LES FLAMANDES AND LES MOINES

[In the month of May; in the golden mornings
And the *childhood* of the misty and lustrous days,

Which recall the mysterious days of *limbos*,
And pass crowned with the clearness of nimbuses,

He displayed his inward joy and his happiness
At being able with his own hands to deck the altar in honour

Of the sweet and pure and blessed Mary,
Patron of his heart and of his garden;

He dreamed of nothing but of worshipping her,
Of giving her his whole soul to breathe.]

This simple monk has, among his early memories, images recalling those which irradiated the memory of the virginal soul of Verhaeren's little dead friend in *Les tendresses premières*:

> Tout enfant il pleurait aux légendes d'antan,
>
> .   .   .   ‹   .
>
> Où les vierges s'en vont par de roses chemins,
> Avec des grands missels et des palmes aux mains.[1]

[As a child he had wept over the ancient legends,

.   ‹   .   .   .

Which told of virgins, passing along rosy ways,
Bearing great missals and palms in their hands.]

With his eyes fixed on such images, he sees death as "accueillante et bonne et maternelle."[2]

Similar images—arabesques in children's mass books—form the framework of Verhaeren's picture of the "gentle monk":

Il est des moines doux avec des traits si calmes,
Qu'on ornerait leurs mains de roses et de palmes,

[1] From Moine simple, in Les moines.
[2] Welcoming and good and maternal.

Qu'on formerait, pour le porter au dessus d'eux,
Un dais pâlement bleu comme le bleu des cieux.

Et pour leur pas foulant les plaines de la vie,
Une route d'argent d'un chemin d'or suivie.

Et par les lacs, le long des eaux, ils s'en iraient,
Comme un cortège blanc de lys qui marcheraient.[1]

[There are gentle monks whose aspect is so calm
That one likes to picture them with roses and palms in their hands,

And one would provide for them, to be carried over their heads,
A canopy pale blue in colour like the blue of the skies.

For their feet, as they tread the plains of life,
One would fain make a road of silver followed by a road of gold.

By the lakes and beside the waterways they would move
Like a procession of white lilies on the march.]

Thus the same road with its rosy images, its palms, and its lilies, which in the poem of the simple monk led to " motherly death," now leads to landscapes filled with lakes and waterways, which in turn will speedily give place to images of the Virgin. There is, then, good reason for believing that these visions of lakes and waterways are not very different from those of " motherly death," and that they symbolise (as has often been surmised) the fantasy of " narcissism " and of reimmersion in the mother's womb to which the cult of the Virgin Mary seems to be akin.

The poet, however, describes other types of monk, contrasting with those hitherto mentioned. There are the " epic monk," the " wild monk," the " feudal monk," and the " heresiarch." They are strong, virile, tragical, monumental, ardent. These types do not display any infantile characteristics, but nevertheless they likewise give expression to the regressive tendency. They belong to an

[1] From Moine doux, in Les moines.

LES FLAMANDES AND LES MOINES 95

earlier day, to the Middle Ages, being lofty figures from a titanic past.

C'était un homme épris des époques d'épée,
Où l'on jetait sa vie aux vers de l'épopée,

Qui, dans ce siècle flasque et dans ce temps bâtard,
Apôtre épouvantant et noir, venait trop tard,

Qui n'avait pu, suivant l'abaissement, décroître,
Et même était trop grand pour tenir dans un cloître,

Et se noyer le cœur dans ce marais d'ennui
Et la banalité des règles d'aujourd'hui.[1]

[He was a man in love with the days of the sword,
When people threw away their lives to an epic accompaniment,

He was an alarming and sinister apostle, born too late
Into this flaccid century, into this bastard age;

One who had not been able to shrink to the measure of a shrunken epoch.
Who was too big to be kept in a monastery,

And to drown his heart in the swamp of tedium
And the triteness of the rules of to-day.]

The monks represent the glorious childhood of the poor modern world; they represent the past, the days when faith was alive. This past of the world's faith is condensed with the past of Verhaeren's own faith in such a way that the historical evocation becomes, involuntarily, a symbol of the personal drama.[2] We find always in operation the same law, in accordance with which the objective work of art undergoes a spontaneous organisation

---

[1] From Moine épique, in Les moines.
[2] In the poem "Moine épique," the condensation is perhaps even more complex. It may well be that this poem gives expression, in addition, to the fact that Verhaeren's own epic genius feels itself cribbed in the "swamp of tedium" formed by the vague literature of the century then drawing to its close, and in the "triteness of the rules" of prosody. We must not forget that the moment is at hand when Verhaeren's poetry is going to escape from this prison, and rush to the creation of the most lawless free verse.

into an involuntary symbol of a subjective fact in the artist's life. Furthermore, a fondness or a regret for the historical past is in many cases the symbol of a yearning for our own past; and the love of remote and legendary epochs is a sign of a tendency to regression and introversion. The love of the romanticists for the Middle Ages is a typical instance: the dream and the past go hand in hand; flight from the real towards the dream has as its natural accompaniment a flight from the present towards the past. This outlook harmonises extremely well with Morel's [1] striking suggestion that there is a kinship between Pierre Janet's " function of the real " and Bergson's " attention to the present life."

These two functions are closely linked, if they be not indeed identical; and introversion is usually characterised by the enfeeblement of both. In such cases, we may add, a passion for the dream is often associated with a hatred of the real, and a love of the past with a strong dislike of the present. As so often happens with love and hatred, these feelings are apt to be transferred from their objects to the symbols of the objects, from the past and the present of the individual to the past and the present of mankind. There is good reason to believe that the detestation of contemporary life typical of such persons as Rousseau is the outcome of a subconscious reasoning, illogical but profound. We shall see that Verhaeren will be able in time to free himself from this complex, so as to become an impassioned singer of the present. But in the days when he wrote *Les moines*, he was anything but that, for the past impressed him by its grandeur and the present repelled him by its triviality:

Ces temps passaient de fer et de splendeur vêtus
Et le progrès n'avait encor de sa racloire
Rien enlevé de grand, de féroce et de gourd
Au monde où se taillaient les blocs de l'épopée.[2]

[1] Op. cit.
[2] From Les cloîtres, in Les moines.

LES FLAMANDES AND LES MOINES

[These days, clad in iron and splendour, were passing away,
And progress had not as yet, with its strike,
Levelled off from the world where the blocks of epic were being fashioned,
Anything of the grandeur, the ferocity, and the torpor.]

At length a new spirit, the spirit of philosophy, blows across the primitive and Christian world; the monks' grip is tenacious, but they are doomed.

Ils trônèrent pareils, les cloîtres lumineux,
Jusqu'aux jours où les vents de la Grèce fatale
Jetèrent brusquement leurs souffles vénéneux
A travers la candeur de l'âme occidentale.
Le monde émerveillé s'emplit d'esprit nouveau,
Mais les moines soudain grandirent à sa taille. . . .
Ils portèrent ainsi que de puissants faisceaux,
Devant leur Christ nié, devant leur foi chassée,
Qui se penchait déjà du côté de la nuit,
Leurs cœurs brûlant toujours de sa flamme première.[1]

[They reigned thus, the cloisters that were centres of light,
Till the day when the wind from Greece, the land of fate,
Suddenly blew its envenomed breath
Across the candour of the western soul.
The wonderstruck world was filled with a new spirit,
But the monks swiftly grew to its stature. . . .
In front of their Christ denied, their faith driven out,
Their faith which was already being engulfed by the night,
They carried like bright torches
Their hearts that burned ever with the old flame.]

To-day the doom has been fulfilled, and the monks have become mere vestiges of their past selves:

Seuls vous survivez grands, au monde chrétien mort,
Seuls sans ployer le dos vous en portez la charge
Comme un royal cadavre au fond d'un cercueil d'or. . . .
Vous êtes les porteurs de croix et de flambeaux
Autour de l'idéal divin que l'on enterre.[2]

[1] From Les cloîtres, in Les moines.
[2] From Aux moines, in Les moines.

[You alone survive, great, in the dead Christian world;
Alone, without bending your backs, you carry its burden
As if it were the dead body of a king enclosed in a golden coffin. ...
You are the bearers of crosses and of torches
Around the divine ideal which is being buried.]

The fact was that at the very moment when Verhaeren was dedicating these verses to the monks, his own faith had become but a vestige of its former self. One of the poet's intimates tells me that *Les moines* was written " when he had what may be called no more than a memory of faith." It is easy to discern in the historical process which inspires him, a stupendous parallel of his own mental development.

L'hérésiarque makes his appearance, a great figure dating from the past age of the faith which he is ruthlessly destroying within himself. The heresiarch secures expression in images strangely reminiscent of the vision of the burning tower which we have already come to regard as a symbol of perishing faith :

Et là, ce moine noir, que vêt un froc de deuil,
Construit, dans sa pensée, un monument d'orgueil. ...

Et l'œuvre est là, debout, comme une *tour* vivante,
Dardant toujours plus haut sa tranquil épouvante. ...

Les yeux brûlés aux feux rouges des visions. ...

Jusqu'au jour où, poussé par sa haine trop forte,
Il se possède enfin et clame sa foi morte.

Et se carre massif sous l'azur déployé
Avec son large front vermeil de foudroyé. ...

Son ombre, projetée, obscurcira le jour. ...

Tandis qu'à horizon luiront les *incendies.*[1]

[And there, this black monk, clad in a mourning robe,
Builds in his thoughts a monument of pride. ...

[1] From L'hérésiarque, in Les moines.

LES FLAMANDES AND LES MOINES

And the work is there, upright, like a living *tower*
Darting ever higher its silent warning. . . .

His eyes seared with the red fire of visions. . . .

Till the day when, impelled by the excess of his hate,
He becomes himself at length, and proclaims that his faith is dead.

He squares his massive shoulders beneath the canopy of the sky,
With his great forehead scarlet, as of one struck by lightning. . . .

The shadow he casts will block the daylight. . . .

The while, on the horizon, *conflagrations* flare. . . .]

Every one of these images makes more distinct the vision of the tower with fiery eyes. The shadow which blocks the daylight recalls the towers in *La révolte*:

> D'énormes tours obliquement dorées
> Barrent la ville au loin d'ombres démesurées.
>
> [Gigantic towers, gilded aslant,
> Cast huge bars of shadow far across the town.]

But, while faith may perish, there is something that will not perish—the *sublimation* which faith has nurtured. The acquisition of every higher tendency, the religious tendency not excepted, presupposes the derivation of crude instincts towards higher aims. This derivation, which can often be followed step by step, is what we mean by sublimation. Verhaeren, in his poem *Les conversions*, finds pleasure in turning his eyes towards the past of these ardent monks. He sees them as they were before their conversion; creatures with vigorous instincts, untamed desires, and a rugged will:

> Tu montais autrefois au palais de la vie,
> Le cerveau grandiose et les sens embrasés ;
> Les beaux désirs ainsi qu'une table servie
> S'étalaient devant toi sur des terrasses d'or.[1]

[1] From Les conversions, in Les moines.

[In former days you mounted to the palace of life,
Your head filled with grand ideas and your senses inflamed;
Your fine desires, like a table spread,
Were displayed before you on golden terraces.]

They were headstrong, these men of the senses. But " un vent les abat aux pieds d'airain de Dieu," [1] and then all their vehemence is converted (in the strictest sense of the term), is turned against itself, is eager to destroy itself; but so eager that it remains always vehemence and ardour.

In this struggle they wage against themselves, there burns ever the joy of victorious effort:

Ta volonté d'airain superbement maîtresse
A dompté tes désirs, et bridé tes espoirs
Et fait crier ton cœur d'angoisse et de détresse.
Mais ton humilité, c'est encor de l'orgueil. . . .
La règle en sa rigueur grave et préceptorale,
Dont les convers pieux suivent les sentiers d'or,
Tu l'exagères tant que c'est toi qui domines.[2]

[Your iron will, proud of its mastery,
Has tamed your desires, bridled your hope,
And wrung your heart with anguish and distress.
But your humility is still pride. . . .
The rules, in their grave and preceptorial strictness,
Whose golden paths the pious lay-brothers follow,
You overstress so much that you are still the master.]

Verhaeren is emphatically "the poet of energy," of internal energy, of the struggle against oneself. The conversions he loves to limn in his frescoes are fierce struggles in which the will wrings the heart with anguish and distress. When we enquire what are the primary instincts which chiefly manifest themselves, sublimated in such a wrestling of Jacob and the angel, we find, first of all, the combative instinct; next we find the algolagniac

---

[1] A wind casts them down at the brazen feet of God.
[2] From Les conversions, in Les moines.

instinct—that form of algolagnia in which an introvert experiences a voluptuous pleasure in being made to suffer, wishing to be simultaneously victor and victim.[1] Thus we find in Verhaeren a lofty form of sublimation, resembling the *durch Leiden Freude* [2] of Beethoven. To the last, such a sublimation will remain characteristic of Verhaeren, and it is preeminently this which makes of him " the poet of energy." Here are some verses written towards the close of his life, which give expression to the same ardent struggle :

> Mon cœur à moi ne vit dûment que s'il s'efforce ;
> L'humanité totale a besoin d'un *tourment*
> Qui la travaille avec fureur, comme un ferment,
> Pour élargir sa vie et soulever sa force.[3]

> [My own heart is not really alive unless it is striving.
> The whole of mankind needs an *agony*
> Working it fiercely, like a ferment,
> To expand its life and sustain its strength.]

In *Les moines*, the *tree* becomes the symbol of sublimation thus understood. At first for Verhaeren (in *Les flamandes*) the tree was what it usually is according to the psychoanalysts, one of the symbols of crude instinct But now this instinct is struggling against itself. Trees will henceforward have a gnarled and twisted aspect, like the limbs of men in a wrestling bout. They represent sensuality which overcomes itself, in a victory which is still voluptuous. They become identified with the monks who, with the convulsive grip of a fervent will, have " twisted " their own natures.

---

[1] The word "algolagnia" was coined to denote the inner unity of a tendency embracing two instincts, the instinct of suffering and that of making others suffer, the pathological forms of these instincts being known as "masochism" and "sadism" respectively. A profound study of the combative instinct will always disclose in it an algolagniac element. Cf. Bovet, L'instinct combatif, pp. 94 to 99.

[2] Out of suffering, joy.

[3] From La vie ardente, in Les flammes hautes.

Ceux dont les *tourments* noirs ont fait le corps *tordu*.[1]
[Those whose black *agonies* have *twisted* their bodies.]

Tout ce qui fut énorme en ces temps surhumains
Grandit dans le soleil de leur âme féconde
Et fut *tordu* comme un grand chêne entre leurs mains ![2]

[All which was huge in those titanic days
Grew in the sunshine of their fecund soul,
And was *twisted*, like a great oak, by their hands.]

Une allée invaincue et géante de chênes. . . .
Ces arbres vont—ainsi des moines mortuaires.[3]
[An unconquerable avenue of giant oaks. . . .
These trees seem to move, like sepulchral monks.]

Pour en *tordre* le mal, ses mains *tortionnaires*
Ont d'un si noir effort *étreint son corps pâmé*,
Qu'il n'est plus qu'une âme enfin et qu'il vit *sublimé*,
Tout seul, comme un rocher meurtri par les tonnerres.[4]

[To *wring* the evil out of it, with a *twisting* action, his hands
Have with so fierce an effort *wrung his swooning body*,
That it has become only a soul, at length, so that it lives
  sublimated
Alone, like a rock shattered by thunderbolts.]

But sublimation, which used to be religious in quality, can no longer remain religious.

Les poètes, venus trop tard pour être prêtres [5]

---

[1] From Rentrée des moines, in Les moines.
[2] From Les crucifères, in Les moines.
[3] From Soir religieux, the second of the six poems thus named, in Les moines.
[4] From Méditation, in Les moines.
[5] From Aux moines, the second of the two poems thus entitled, in Les moines.

LES FLAMANDES AND LES MOINES

[The poets who have been born too late to become priests] are the successors of the monks. Art is to be conceived as a substitute for faith. Verhaeren shuts himself up in his art as though it were a cloister, thus resembling his contemporary and fellow-countryman Rodenbach, who made an ascetic discipline of art, and imposed on himself the law :

Pour vivre après ta mort sois donc mort dans ta vie.

[That you may live after your death, you must be dead during your life.]

The formula would be Christian in spirit, were it not that the immortality of fame has replaced the immortality of the soul. In like manner, Verhaeren pledges himself thus :

Je vivrai seul aussi, tout seul, avec mon art,
Et le serrant en main, ainsi qu'un étendard,
Je me l'imprimerai si fort sur la poitrine,
Qu'au travers de ma chair il marquera mon cœur.
Car il ne reste rien que l'art sur cette terre
Pour tenter un cerveau puissant et solitaire
Et le griser de rouge et tonique liqueur.[1]

[I, too, shall live alone, quite alone, with my art,
And, grasping it in my hands like a standard,
I shall clasp it so strongly to my breast
That through my flesh it will stamp its imprint on my heart.
For there is nothing left on earth but art
To tempt a powerful and lonely brain
And to intoxicate it with red and tonic liquor.]

The " powerful and lonely " brain is doubtless a reminiscence of de Vigny's *Moïse*, for Verhaeren was a disciple of de Vigny :

[1] From Aux moines, the second of the two poems thus entitled, in Les moines.

O Seigneur j'ai vécu puissant et solitaire.

[O Lord! I have lived powerful and lonely.]

Certainly, the atmosphere is that of *Moïse*. We have the same tone of austere doubt, and of pride that knows nothing of hope. It expresses the introversion of a strong man who in earlier days would have been a priest or a prophet, but who, now that his faith has been wrested from him, feels that his energy and his fervour have become aimless. Paul Bourget, the earlier Paul Bourget of the closing nineteenth century, of the period tortured with sceptical idealism, wrote in like manner of the aimless devotee:

Et ne sait à quel Dieu dévouer tout son sang.

[And does not know to what God he is to offer up his blood.]

If the one who is thus searching for a new god should happen to be a poet, he will try to find his god in his art:

Quand tout s'ébranle et meurt, l'Art est là qui se plante
Nocturnement bâti comme un monument d'or. . . .
Et ce temple toujours pour nous subsistera
Et longtemps et toujours luira dans nos ténèbres,
Quand vous, les moines blancs, les ascètes funèbres
Aurez disparus tous en lugubre apparat,
Dans votre froc de lin et votre aube mystique,
Au pas religieux d'un long cortège errant,
Comme si vous portiez à votre Dieu mourant,
Au fond du monde athée, un dernier viatique.[1]

[When all has been shattered and dies, Art remains,
Built in the night like a golden monument. . . .
We shall always have this temple with us,
For long, for ever, it will lighten our darkness,
When you, white monks, sepulchral ascetics,
Will all have disappeared in mournful pomp,

[1] From Aux moines, the second of the two poems thus entitled, in **Les moines**.

In linen habit and mystic alb,
As you walk solemnly in a long procession,
As if, into the abysses of an atheist world,
You were bearing the last sacrament to your dying God.]

But this new act of faith is a trifle forced; its joy is somewhat lugubrious.

CHAPTER THREE

THE CRISIS

(1887-1890)

WE now reach a tortured and tragical phase. It seems strange, at first, that there should have been so abrupt a transition from the Parnassian art of *Les flamandes* and *Les moines* to the startlingly intimate poems which were a product of extreme mental anguish : *Les soirs*, 1887 ; *Les débâcles*, 1888 ; *Les flambeaux noirs*, 1890. In Albert Mockel's biography, for example, the contrast is disconcerting in its suddenness. No doubt Mockel was too emphatic in his insistence upon the descriptive objectivity of Verhaeren's earliest writings, and upon the religious character of *Les moines*—which was written, as we know, with nothing more than "a memory of faith." In the overwhelmingly sensual health of *Les flamandes* and in the religious and mystical ardours of *Les moines* we have discerned a double menace : on the one hand, a presentiment of the ruin of the flesh which "even in youth is smitten in its very bones"; on the other hand, sadness for the faith which was now no more than the vestige of its former self. This double menace was to be fulfilled, and was to take the form of moral and physical chaos. We have therefore little reason for astonishment at the crisis. Nevertheless, despite these foreshadowings, we cannot but be struck by the suddenness with which the " gold " is transmuted into " blackness."

We have spoken of moral and physical chaos. But

the two interpenetrate one another, and comprise a single entity. The narrow materialism of medical science at that epoch would doubtless have led to the belief that the moral crisis was solely determined by the physical disorder. Neurology has made some progress since then, and is inclined to reverse the order of causation. In doing so, the neurologist does not trouble himself with the question whether he has arrived at ultimate causes. He knows well enough that his descriptions, now that he has discovered this moral or mental element in causation, have become more subtle, more adequate, and more useful. In any case, the close correlation between the physical and the mental is a fact, and it is difficult to separate the two elements.

Concerning the illness from which Verhaeren suffered, I am assured by one of his intimates that the primary cause was his loss of faith; thereafter he led rather a wild life, eating too much, drinking too freely, and also working to excess. All these induced an obstinate neurasthenia complicated with digestive trouble; there was physical depression and there was moral despair. His friend adds: " As regards this epoch of Verhaeren's life, *Les soirs*, *Les débâcles*, and *Les flambeaux noirs* will give you fuller and better information than any words of mine."

The official science of 1890 would have regarded these poignant poems as evil nightmares due to a fit of indigestion. Happily we are no longer satisfied with such facile etiology. Even if the critic should consider the matter from a medical outlook, he will study these creations of the imagination with more sympathy, and will regard them as psychic manifestations presenting far finer and more numerous shades than are presented by the accompanying physical symptoms; he will believe that, for this very reason, a study of the psychic manifestations will enable us to gain a fuller understanding of the patient's inner life, and to ascertain more successfully the cause of his sufferings. Finally, psychoanalytical treatment, representing the extreme left of the psychological trend in medicine, would do what we are proposing to do ourselves. With a medical aim, it would adopt a purely psychological point of view, concentrating attention upon the symbolism of these works of the imagination. The analyst would penetrate through the symbols to discover the hidden conflicts in the patient's affective life, being guided by the principle that in such affective conflicts (conscious or subconscious) will be found the general cause of the nervous disorders on the one hand and of the imaginative creations on the other—in a word, the hidden cause of the crisis considered as a whole.

This way of looking at the matter would appear to be justified in Verhaeren's case Setting out to study the crisis in its psychological aspect, we seem to have elucidated its nature almost completely.

In fact the nervous symptoms from which Verhaeren suffered were unmistakably those which the new psychology regards as symbolical. They were unconscious autosuggestions realising in a masked form a desire whose existence was more or less unknown to the subject. Let us consider what Stefan Zweig writes concerning the poet's break-down in health: " Every noise, every colour, every thought presses in upon him as though with sharp needles; his healthy sensibility becomes hypertrophied; that fineness of hearing, of which one is conscious, say in seasickness, which perceives every noise, even the slightest sound, as though it were the blow of a hammer, undermines his whole organism. . . . The bell on the door had to be removed because it shocked his nerves; those who lived in the house had to wear felt slippers instead of shoes; the windows were closed to the noise of the street." [1]

We read, further, that his stomach rejected food, and this completes the resemblance to sea-sickness. Now it is possible that Verhaeren's digestion had been disordered

---

[1] Zweig, Emile Verhaeren, translated by Jethro Bithell, p. 56.

by excesses; but there is no doubt that he suffered from neurasthenia, as a complication to any other disorder, and determining the course of the symptoms. If we survey these symptoms, we shall note that they exhibit a remarkable unity of "symbolical" meaning. They all indicate a *refusal of what comes from without, be it a sensation or be it a food.* They are a sea-sickness, a nausea against life itself. Perhaps the rejection of food may have represented an autosuggestion of suicide, for this element has been detected in similar cases. At any rate, the "symbolism" of these symptoms is perfectly accordant with that of the poems, except that the symbolism of the poems is much richer and more decisive in its significance. What is disclosed, as we shall see, is (among other things) extreme introversion, a refusal of the outer world, a nausea against life, and an aspiration towards death. It is here, in especial, that we note the sudden clearness of the illumination which the analysis throws upon symbols that at first sight appear involved and extremely obscure.

Without being a sage, one can recognise that Verhaeren's crisis was *a crisis of introversion.* This harmonises with what we already know of the poet, and it also accords with the descriptions of his illness. The latter, we are told, was neurasthenia, and there is a connexion between neurasthenia and introversion. Moreover, the symptoms just described are sufficiently clear. But the indications in the poems are even clearer. They express introversion without any periphrasis:

Se replier toujours sur soi-même, si morne!
Comme un drap lourd, qu'aucun dessin de fleur n'adorne. . . .

Si morne! Et se toujours interdire l'envie
De tailler en drapeau l'étoffe de sa vie.[1]

[To retire perpetually within oneself, so sombre,
Like a heavy cloth unadorned by any design of flowers. . . .

[1] From Si morne, in Les débâcles.

So sombre! And always to refuse oneself the gratification
Of cutting the stuff of one's life into a flag.]

And this retirement into himself is described as being part of the illness:

Déjà sentir la bouche âcre des moisissures
Gluer, et les taches s'étendre en leurs morsures.

Pourrir, immensément emmaillotté d'ennui,
Etre l'ennui qui se replie en de la nuit.

Tandis que lentement, dans les laines ourdies,
De part en part mordent les vers des maladies.[1]

[Already to feel the corrosive mouth of the moulds
Clinging, and the patches spreading under their bites.

To rot, overpoweringly swaddled in tedium,
To be the tedium which becomes the very embodiment of night.

What time the worms of disease are, here and there,
Slowly eating their way into the woven woollen stuffs.]

We find also the sexual images in which some of the Freudian extremists take such delight. As usual in the case of introverts, these images express an introversion of the sexual instinct. The stirrings of that instinct are accompanied by anguish and are followed by remorse. The gratification of the instinct is rejected more or less completely, and it thus becomes pent up; and since the sexual instinct is capable of undergoing all kinds of derivations and sublimations, its introversion may determine the highest development of the spiritual life. Perhaps such an introversion of the sexual instinct is, to some extent, an essential condition of an intense inner life. It follows that the term *autoerotism*, which has been proposed to denote this phenomenon, is unsuitable, for it may give rise to unfortunate misunderstanding.[2] It

---

[1] From Si morne, in Les débâcles.
[2] One might say that the use of this term degrades the inner life into a sort of sexual perversion of a more complex character.

would be better to speak of *autophilia*, to indicate that the instinct undergoes desexualisation in the process of introversion. Nor must we take offence if, from time to time, this autophilia should make use of sexual images, for everyone knows that the purest form of mystical love does the same thing sometimes. Even the skeleton of a Plato retains a vestige of the ancestral tail. This is the sign of evolution, and the evolution of lower instincts into higher mental manifestations need not disturb our self-esteem any more than it is disturbed by the biological evolution from lower animals to man. Whoever accepts the fact of bodily evolution, must accept mental evolution as well. Such writers as Nietzsche and Freud, who have endeavoured to sketch " the genealogy of morals " and of mental life, setting out from the primitive instincts, have merely drawn the psychological inferences of the theory of evolution—though they have often done so in a paradoxical and aggressive fashion. We need not, therefore, veil our faces when we discover in the human imagination, and even in the imagination of a man of genius, that which is the pendant of the caudal vestige in Plato's skeleton. We have merely to recall that the evolution of one thing from another does not mean that the two things are identical—a fact which is forgotten by those who are scandalised at the reasoning of a Nietzsche or a Freud. We do not say that Plato was himself a monkey, or that this or that poetical or religious manifestation is itself sexuality.

Let us have no more prudery than Verhaeren, who did not hesitate to descend into these pullulating depths of the troubled human mind. The vulgar (and there are critics and scientists who must be classed with the vulgar) like to discern in genius something that is morbid and essentially monstrous, simply because the genius, thanks to the sincerity characteristic of genius, dares to see and knows how to see these pullulating depths whose existence within themselves most people refuse to admit. Yet they exist in us all, as the analysis of the subconscious proves beyond dispute. We must recall this sincerity of genius when we are studying Verhaeren, and especially the Verhaeren of the crisis. For never was there a more pitiless sincerity than his, and never did sincerity delve more deeply amid the slimy flora and fauna of our inward recesses. Neither La Rochefoucauld (in whom the roughnesses of cynicism were smoothed over by the polish of the man of the world) nor Nietzsche was more ruthlessly heroic in human vivisection. But there is this difference, that Verhaeren's vivisection was lyrical. Our sensibilities can understand him well enough; but our intelligence can only understand him by means of a translation into its own language. The analysis of the symbols makes such a translation possible.

In view of the preceding argument, we shall not be surprised to find, in the expression of autophilia and introversion, a condensation of the religious image of the cloister with the crudest sexual imagery.

> Et les mauvaises mains tâtillonnes de vice
> Encore et lentement cherchant, sur les coussins,
> Et les toisons de ventre, et des grappes de seins
> Et les tortillements dans le rêve complice ? [1]
>
> [And the evil, busily searching hands of vice
> (Even now slowly seeking on the bed
> The curly hair of the belly and the clusters of breasts),
> And the writhings in the accomplice dream?] [2]
>
> Et, plus intimement encor, mes anciens râles
> Vers des ventres, mufflés de lourdes toisons d'or,
> Et mes vices de doigts et de lèvres claustrales. . . .[3]
>
> [And, still more intimately, my whilom pantings
> Towards bellies muffled in thick tufts of golden hair,
> And the viciousness of my fingers and my claustral lips.]

[1] From Vers le cloître, in Les débâcles.
[2] In subsequent editions these images have been bowdlerised.
[3] From La couronne, in Les débâcles.

THE CRISIS

The first quotation is from a poem entitled Towards the Cloister, and in the second we find the allusion to claustral lips. It would be difficult to discover a better example of the introversion of instinct. In most instances, moreover (as psychoanalysis has proved to be the case in dreams), the cruder images are hidden behind others, the kinship between the cruder and the more subtle being rendered recognisable only by certain indications.

Sometimes, moreover, we have " busily searching hands," things and actions which " grope," " totter," " flutter "—all images of a life that has been disordered and disintegrated as well as thrust back into itself. We rediscover, besides, several of the images we have already noted, as in the poem *Les plaines*, from *Les flamandes*, when autumn has passed by. In the poem entitled The Thatched Roofs, we again meet those roofs which, over there, were " humping their inert backs " :

> A cropetons, ainsi que les pauvres Maries
> Des légendes de l'autrefois,
> Par villages, sous les cieux froids,
> Sont assises les métairies.[1]

> [Squatting, like the poor Maries
> Of the legends of ancient days,
> In village after village beneath the chilly skies
> The farms are placed.]

" Squatting "—this depicts the shrivelled and shrunken life of extreme introversion. The quite unexpected simile of the " poor Maries " recalls what we have already noted, the link between this introversion and the yearning for the mother, or for the Virgin Mary.

Consider, too, the imagery of the following stanza :

> A cropetons, ainsi que les vieilles dolentes,
> Avec leurs cannes aux mentons,
> Et leurs gestes comme *à tâtons*,
> Elles tremblent toutes branlantes.

[1] From Les chaumes, in Les soirs.

[Squatting, like poor old women
With their chins bent over their sticks
And their groping gestures,
They shake totteringly.] [1]

With regard to the sounds of the words used by the poet, note the frequency of the consonantal sounds k, t, and l, whose jostlings suggest the idea of something " disordered," something which " flaps " or " flutters." Verhaeren will frequently make us hear this noise of snapped laths, the noise of castanets; it will always be in connexion with the same images and the same ideas, and the sign will itself betoken similar ideas, so that it cannot be misunderstood. There are several instances in this very sequence of poems, *Les soirs*. For example, in the poem *Le moulin*, one of the most expressive, we have the " très soffreteuses bicoques," [2] with their " carreaux en loques "; [3] and these hovels are exactly like the farms in *Les chaumes*. The latter have " carreaux fendus "; [4] the latter, too, are " très miserablement assises." [5] Elsewhere we listen to the " tic tac débile " [6] of the " tranquille mort des fous," [7] when the poet is haunted with the idea of madness. In another place we have

Un roulement plaintif de chariot quinteux.[8]

[The fretful rolling of a squeaky cart.]

and this image is closely akin to that of the reflections in the water (an unmistakable emblem of autophilia) to which we now come :

---

[1] An alternative version of the last line is " elles s'entrecognent branlantes " (they jostle against one another totteringly).
[2] Suffering hovels.
[3] Shattered window-panes.
[4] Broken window-panes.
[5] Wretchedly situated.
[6] The feeble tic tac.
[7] Quiet death of madmen.
[8] From *Les rues*, in *Les soirs*.

THE CRISIS

Une lune souffrante et pâle s'entrevoit
Et se mire aux égouts, où des clartés pourrissent.[1]

[A suffering and wan moon is glimpsed,
And is mirrored in the foul ditches wherein radiances rot.]

These reflections in mirrors, but especially in water, and preferentially in the water of meres and marshes—in foul and stagnant water—are an obsession throughout Verhaeren's writings, just like the trains and the moons of clock-faces. Their significance is perfectly clear, being that of the myth of Narcissus to which we have already referred. It is natural that the tendency to use such imagery should be fortified by a crisis in which the poet is thrust back into himself. More than once, as in the last quotation, these reflections are associated with images of "foul ditches" or "sewers" and similar repulsive objects. These are the fantasies of autophilia sickened with itself, sickened above all by discovering within itself this pullulation in the abysses. (We may recall that Verhaeren's symptoms reminded us of "sea-sickness.") Sometimes, they are also fantasies of death :

L'égoût charrie une fange velue
Vers la rivière qu'il pollue.[2]

[The sewer bears along a villous sludge
Towards the river which it pollutes.]

Comme d'un panier d'or,
La lune tombe au fond de l'eau,
Et s'éparpille
En ronds qui brillent ;
La lune et tout le grand ciel d'or
Tombent et roulent vers leur mort. . . .
Elle le fausse et le salit,
L'attire à elle au fond du lit
D'algues et de goëmons flasques.[3]

[1] From Les rues, in Les soirs.
[2] From La plaine, in Les villes tentaculaires.
[3] From La baie, in Les vignes de ma muraille

> [As if from a golden basket
> The moon falls to the bottom of the water,
> And scatters itself
> In shining circles;
> The moon and all the great golden firmament
> Fall, and roll towards their death. . . .
> Death violates it and defiles it,
> Drags it to her right down into the bed
> Of algae and of flaccid seaweed.]

La mort enjambe le trottoir
Et l'égoût pâle, où se mirent les bornes.[1]

[Death strides across the pavement
And the pallid gutter in which the curbstones are mirrored.]

Often it is the " moon " which is thus mirrored. Here we have a link between the "reflections" and the "moons" and "clock-faces." If we interpret the clock-face complex as signifying "mortal love," we may in like manner interpret the reflection complex as signifying "mortal love of one's self." In *Les soirs* we find several instances of these lunar reflections:

> Et l'étang plane et clair reflète énormément
> Entre de fins bouleaux, dont le branchage bouge,
> La lune qui se lève épaisse, immense et rouge.

> [And in the level and clear pond is mirrored, enormous
> Amid the tremulous leafage of the slender birches,
> The moon, which is rising, thick, huge, and red.]

These verses are from the poem *Mourir*, and from them there sounds once again the funereal note which attends such tragical reflections in the water—though the idea of death is not so directly expressed as it was in the earlier quotation, where death is described as striding across the pavement. Furthermore, *Mourir*, an autumnal poem, is likewise full of images of the sewer, of putrid decomposition:

[1] From La mort, in Les villes tentaculaires.

THE CRISIS

Un soir plein de pourpres et de fleuves vermeils
Pourrit.[1]

[An evening full of purple lights and crimson rivers
Is decaying.]

Sometimes the reflections are associated with " hounds," the same hounds of fury, love, and death which rage in *La dame en noir*.

Les chiens du désespoir, les chiens du vent d'automne
Mordent de leurs abois les échos noirs des soirs,
Et l'ombre, immensément, dans le vide, tâtonne
Vers la lune, mirée au clair des abreuvoirs.[2]

[The hounds of despair, the hounds of the autumn wind,
Bite with their baying into the black echoes of the evenings,
And the gloom, in its vastness, feels out through the void
Towards the moon, mirrored in the clear water of the drinking-troughs.

The " echoes " are no more than an auditory version of the " reflections." They are closely akin, just as in classical folklore the myth of Echo is closely akin to that of Narcissus. The echoes, like the reflections, are the expression of a fruitless effort to clasp one's own self, an effort which leads only to the void of death. We find these echoes again in *Les débâcles*, once more associated with " hounds " :

Les molosses d'hiver, le gel, le vent, la neige. . . .
Ils hurlent à la mort, écoute ! et leur cortège
S'enfuit, avec des pleurs, vers le néant. Voici,
Qu'ils ululent sinistrement, et qu'on ulule
Vers eux, parmi les lourds échos du crépuscule.[3]

[The Molossian hounds of winter, the frost, the wind, the snow . . .
They raise the view-halloo of death, hark ! and the pack
Flees whimpering towards the void. And now
They howl in sinister fashion, and a howl
Answers them, amid the heavy echoes of the twilight.]

[1] From Mourir, in Les soirs.   [2] From Infiniment, in Les soirs.
[3] From Heures d'hiver, in Les débâcles.

Sometimes the signification of the "mirrors" is more plainly disclosed. It is actually translated for us:

> Ton front comme un tombeau dominera tes rêves,
> Et sera ta frayeur, en des miroirs, la nuit.
> Te fuir !—si tu pouvais ! mais non.[1]

> [Thy forehead like a tomb will dominate thy dreams
> And will affright thee in mirrors at night.
> If thou couldst, thou wouldst flee from thyself! But thou canst not !]

The emblem of the mirror, with a like atmosphere and a kindred meaning, is met with in the poems of Henry Spiess.

Again :

> *Dites, serai-je seul avec mon âme ?*
> Mon âme hélas ! maison d'ébène,
> Où s'est fendu, sans bruit, un soir,
> Le grand mirror de mon espoir.[2]

> [*Say, shall I be alone with my soul ?*
> My soul, alas, is an ebony mansion,
> Where, one evening, was noiselessly broken
> The great mirror of my hopes.]

In the prose fragment, *Le plus précieux des cinq sens*,[3] the mirror reappears in a tragical setting. The hero of this fragment, which is largely autobiographical, looking out of the window sees a blind man who seems to him happy :

Et sans réflechir, sans l'oser, en un extrême tressaut d'exaspération, je saisis mes ciseaux et plus immédiatement encore, éperdu, avec je ne sais quel fierté de moi, je me fis sauter les yeux comme des billes *devant le miroir.*

[Without thinking, without daring, in a terrible access of exasperation, I seized my scissors and, even more directly, at my wits' end, with an indescribable pride in my exploit, *in front of the mirror*, I cut my eyes out as if they had been marbles.]

---

[1] From Le glaive, in Les débâcles.
[2] From Le roc, in Les flambeaux noirs.
[3] Published in the review "La Wallonie," No. 6.

THE CRISIS

This imaginary act puts the crown on the nervous symptoms we have been studying, symptoms characterised by acute suffering on account of any kind of sensation, and by a renunciation of the outer world. In many other cases, psychoanalysts have been led to interpret fantasies of blindness as symbolical of an extreme introversion in which the subject shuts himself away from the world. The extirpation of the eyes in front of the mirror is the expression of the climax of the drama of autophilia, of the moment when the subject, not content with becoming objectified to his own eyes and with loving himself as a reflection, rejects this duality which is the last vestige of the multiplicity of the world. Henceforward, self-enclosed, he will possess himself in the absolute unity of his own being—that unity to which Morel's mystics made their way in the end.

Now that we know the significance of the reflections, we shall not be surprised to find them linked with the "fluttering" visual and auditory images with which we are already familiar:

> Etre l'errant au monde et le pauvre de soi,
> Avec le feu bougeant d'une âme, qui tremblote
> Derrière une main frêle et ballotte son moi;
> Qui tremblote comme un reflet dans l'eau ballotte.[1]

> [To be a vagrant in the world and one's own pauper,
> With the flickering flame of a soul which trembles
> Behind a frail hand, and flutters its ego;
> Which trembles as a reflection in the water flutters.]

Kindred ideas (a failure of the impetus towards the real world, debility, and withdrawal into the self) are expressed by images of "broken" and "flaccid" things:

> Cassés les mâts d'orgueil, flasques les grandes voiles.[2]

> [Broken the masts of pride, flaccid the great sails.]

---

[1] From Inconscience, in Les débâcles.
[2] From Les malades, in Les soirs.

A tout jamais mortes mes fermetés brandies !
Mes poings ? flasques ; mes yeux ? fanés ; mes orgueils ? serfs.[1]

[For ever dead my well-knitted vigour !
My fists ? Flaccid ! My eyes ? Lustreless ! My pride ? Enslaved !]

As for the "green blight" which was corroding in *Les flamandes*, its devouring influence has been extended :

Des crapauds noirs, velus de mousse,
Y dévorent du clair soleil, sur la pelouse.

[Black toads, hairy with moss,
Are there devouring the bright sunshine on the lawn.]

When studying *Les moines*, we noted that this introversion presented itself also as an infantile regression. It is the same here, for one of the poems in *Les débâcles* bears the suggestive title of *Vers l'enfance* :

Ecoute : et les processions—et puis encor
Les ex-votos en Mai dressés sur les estrades,
Et la Vierge Marie, avec son Jésus d'or,
Et les enfants de chant qui sont des camarades.

Ecoute : et du petit village il s'en souvient
Ton cœur ; écoute : et puis, accueille en confiance,
A cette heure d'ennui, ton bon ange gardien,
Le tien, qui te rhabillera de ton enfance.

[Listen : the processions—and then, too,
The ex votos, in the month of May, ranged on the platforms,
And the Virgin Mary with her gilded Jesus,
And the choir children who are comrades.

Listen : your heart recalls the little village,
Listen : and then, in this hour of tedium
Trustfully welcome your good guardian angel,
Yours, who will reinvest you with your childhood.]

Elsewhere, the poet imagines the blessedness of a cloister ; but it is an infantile blessedness. (We may

[1] From *Le roc*, in *Les flambeaux noirs*.

THE CRISIS

interpret this as an introversion which has a regressive character.) He has a longing for the "quite humble ways" of these "cloisters of the simple souls":

> Voici—me rabaisser à des niaiseries :
> Petites croix, petits agneaux, petits Jésus,
> Petite offrande douce aux petites Maries
> En des niches, avec des fleurs peintes dessus.
>
> Prière, à jointes mains, en des recoins d'église ·
> Et se recommencer enfant, avec calcul.[1]

[Look how I descend once more to trifles :
Little crosses, little lambs, little images of Jesus,
Dear little offerings to little statues of Mary
In niches where flowers are painted on the wall.

Prayer, with clasped hands, in a nook of the church,
Deliberately becoming a child once more.]

These verses are like those of the *Moine doux* and the *Moine simple*. Is it again necessary to point out that the images of the Virgin and of the Child symbolise the yearning for the mother ? Sometimes, as in the beginning of the passage next quoted, the fantasy is plainly one of a return to the primitive limbo—or of a return to the mother's womb :

Avant que ne sortît du somme, l'endormi,
Le premier homme, on a vu mes pareils sur terre. . . .

Leurs doigts, qui n'ont jamais touché le mauvais feu,
Dansent des airs lointains, sur des flûtes tremblantes,

Les *puérils* et les vaguants, mais loin du mal :
Et les doux égarés par les bruyères vertes :
Hamlet rirait peut-être, hélas ! mais Parsifal ?
Oh ! Parsifal bénin et clair comprendrait certes ![2]

[*Before there awoke from his slumber the sleeper,*
The first man, those like me were seen on earth. . . .

---

[1] From S'amoindrir, in Les débâcles.
[2] From Inconscience, in Les débâcles.

Their fingers, which have never touched the wicked fire,
Dance as they play airs of long ago on trembling flutes;

They are *infantile*, they are wanderers, but far from evil.
And the gentle ones who are straying on the green moorland:
Alas, Hamlet might laugh! But Parsifal?
Oh, Parsifal, kindly and pure, would certainly understand!]

The reader will probably remember how Parsifal is depicted in Wagner's work. He is a manifestation of the Virginal child, redeeming the world by the " simple purity of his heart." *Parsifal* also represents Wagner's own return to the religious spirit of his early days, a spirit which was linked in his mind with the memory of the mother. Parsifal represents the victory over desire, and over woman the temptress. Preeminently, he symbolises the return to the mother, to childhood, to primitive purity; he symbolises a negation of sexuality—the " wicked fire " which the " infantile " fingers have not yet touched.

Regression is likewise expressed by an image which recalls the effort of the " ferryman " to make his way " up-stream " :

> Sur ce roc carié que détraque la mer,
> Vieillir, triste rêveur de l'escarpé domaine,
> Les chairs mortes, l'espérance en-allée,
> A *rebours* de la vie immense et désolée.[1]

> [Upon this worn rock which is vexed by the sea,
> To grow old, sad dreamer of the scarped domain,
> Flesh dead, hope vanished,
> *Retracing* life which is huge and desolate.]

In another passage, Verhaeren is no longer writing symbolically, but addresses himself directly to the understanding. Here he gives plain expression to autophilia :

[1] From Le roc, in Les flambeaux noirs.

THE CRISIS

Quelqu'un m'avait prédit, qui tenait une épée,
Et qui riait de mon orgueil *stérilisé*;
Tu seras nul et pour ton âme inoccupée
L'avenir ne sera qu'un regret du passée. . . .
Te fuir!—si tu pouvais! mais non.[1]

[Some one holding a sword prophesied to me,
Making mock of me for my *sterilised* pride:
Thou shalt be null. For thy vacant soul
The future shall be nothing but regret for the past. . . .
If thou couldst, thou wouldst flee from thyself! But thou canst not!]

But in this desire " to belittle oneself " (*S'amoindrir* is the title of the poem which contains the reference to " the cloister of the simple souls "), there is an element of rage which is neither implicit nor explicit in the idea of regression. " There is nothing more closely akin to love than hate is," and we witness here a definite transformation of the love of self into the hatred of self. Consider the following passage, in which autophilia and introversion are expressed, at first by the symbols we already know (blind man, echo), and then in a bald and abstract fashion. But soon this vain effort to clasp oneself is, owing to exasperation that the effort is fruitless, transformed into hatred, into a delight in giving pain, into what the Germans call *Schadenfreude*:

Autant que moi malade et veule, as-tu goûté. . . .
Le coupable conseil de l'inutilité?

Et doux soleil qui baise un œil éteint d'aveugle? . . .
Et neutre et vide écho vers la taure qui meugle?

O les rêves de rien, en un cerveau mordu
D'impossible! S'aimer, dans un effort qui leurre!
Se construire, pour la détruire, une demeure!
Et se cueillir, pour le jeter, un fruit tendu![2]

[As ill and listless as myself, have you tasted . . .
The guilty counsel of uselessness?

[1] From Le glaive, in Les débâcles.
[2] From Conseil absurde, in Les débâcles.

And the sweet sunshine which kisses the darkened eye of the
   blind man ? . . .
The neuter and vain echo which answers the mooing heifer ?
Oh, the dreams of nothing in a brain gnawed
By the impossible ! To love oneself, in an ensnaring effort !
To build for oneself a dwelling, simply that one may destroy it !
To pluck a tempting fruit, simply that one may throw it away !] [1]

   This fierce delight in self-injury undergoes exacerbation in the poem *Vers le cloître*—a cloister which has a certain kinship with " the cloisters of the simple souls." But in the latter, everything was childlike and kindly ; here everything is bitter and cruel :

Et se mesquiniser en pratiques futiles
Et se faire petit et n'avoir qu'âpreté,
Pour tout ce qui n'est pas d'une âcre nullité,
Dans le jardin vanné des floraisons hostiles.[2]

[To demean oneself by futile practices,
To become petty, and to feel nothing but asperity
For everything which is not characterised by an acrid nullity,
In the garden which has been winnowed of hostile blossoms.]

   The foregoing passage reminds us of the infantile convent, though the tone has changed. Here is another strophe which expresses, like the one quoted earlier, the desire " to belittle oneself "—but expresses it, now, in all its fury :

Oh ! la constante rage à s'écraser, la hargne
A se tant torturer, à se tant amoindrir,
Que tout l'être n'est plus vivant que pour souffrir
Et se fait de son mal sa joie et son épargne.[3]

[Oh the perpetual rage to crush oneself, the morose desire
To torture oneself so much, to belittle oneself so much,
That one's whole being lives only to suffer,
And of one's ill one makes one's joy and one's treasure-house.]

---

[1] The " neuter " echo is, no doubt, a castration fantasy.
[2] From Vers le cloître, in Les débâcles.
[3] From the same poem.

THE CRISIS

Here, again, are some verses which give frank expression, athwart this desire for asceticism and self-mutilation, to the hatred and the horror of self.

Je rêve une existence en un cloître de fer,
Brûlée au jeûne, et sèche, et râpée aux cilices,
Où l'on abolirait, en de muets supplices,
Par seule ardeur de l'âme enfin, toute la chair.
Sauvage horreur de soi si mornement sentie! . . .
Dites, ces pleurs, ces cris et cette peur du soir!
Dites, ces plombs de maladie en tous les membres,
Et la lourde torpeur des torpides novembres,
Et le dégoût de se toucher et de se voir? [1]

[I dream of an existence in an iron cloister,
Burned with fasting, parched, and scraped with the hair shirt,
Where, in dumb torment, by nothing but the ardour of the soul,
One would at length annihilate the flesh.
Fierce horror of oneself, so gloomily felt! . . .
Say, these tears, these cries, and this fear of night!
Say, this leaden feeling of illness in all the limbs,
And the dull torpor of torpid Novembers,
And disgust at touching and seeing oneself?] [2]

We see that there is a close connexion between autophilia and autophobia, and we feel that they are closely related. This kinship is exactly the same as that between love and hate, and its underlying cause is to be found in the algolagniac instinct to which reference was made on p. 84, in connexion with *Les flamandes* and with the poem *Au carrefour de la mort* in *Les bords de la route*. If love can be so quickly transformed into hate, this is because (however paradoxical it may seem) hate was already present as a component of love. When love undergoes introversion, it is natural that its component

---

[1] From Vers le cloître, in Les débâcles.
[2] After the last verse comes the image noted on an earlier page of the "busily searching hands of vice."

should likewise be introverted, and this brings us back to the ascetic sublimation already met with in *Les moines* —there is a voluptuous delight in suffering, in self-inflicted pain :

Tu n'en peux plus et tu n'espères plus ; qu'importe !
Puisque ta haine immense encore hennit son deuil,
Puisque le sort t'enrage et que tu n'est pas morte
Et que ton mal cinglé se cabre en ton orgueil.

Et que ce soit de la torture encore ! encore !
Et belle et folle et rouge et saoule—et le désir
De se boire de la douleur par chaque pore,
Et du vertige et de l'horreur.[1]

[You are at the end of your tether, you are hopeless ; what matter—
Seeing that your overwhelming hate still whinneys its lament,
Since your fate infuriates you, and since you are not dead,
And your smarting misery rears in your pride.

And let there be torture, more and yet more,
Lovely and mad and red and drunken—and the longing
To imbibe pain by every pore,
And dizziness and horror.]

This strange delight in suffering, in self-inflicted pain, is doubtless one of the primary determinants of the ascetic tendency, which is in fact a pent-up and sublimated cruelty. Nietzsche, who was an expert in this field, wrote of asceticism : " It was the last power invented by antiquity, after it had become bored by the spectacle of the hunting of beasts and of fights between men."[2] But asceticism is more complex than this quotation would imply, and Nietzsche was not one to overlook the element of the will-to-power in the ascetic temperament. That is why he insists upon asceticism, and the formula of his own asceticism is the maxim *amor fati*. He means that we must not put up with necessity, but must love

---
[1] From Eperdument, in Les débâcles.
[2] From Human, All-Too-Human.

it, must *will* it, in such a fashion that in experiencing the thraldom of necessity we are submitting to our own will and are enjoying the delight of feeling that we are our own master. Now, Vehraeren goes even further, if possible. Not only does he wish his wound to be what it is, but he turns the knife in the wound. In effect, he says to fate: " You think you are crushing me. But I will what you are doing, and to prove it I add my own quota." The whole *Dialogue* which opens *Les débâcles* might be quoted :

> La vie, hélas ! ne se supporte et ne s'amende
> Que si la volonté la terrasse d'orgueil. . . .
> —Certes je veux *nouer mes tortures* en moi :
> Comme jadis les grands chrétiens mordus de foi
> S'émaciaient avec une ferveur maligne,
> Je veux boire les souffrances, comme un poison
> Vivant et fou ; Je cinglerai de mon angoisse
> Mes pauvres jours ainsi qu'un tocsin de paroisse
> S'exalte à disperser le deuil sur l'horizon.

> [Alas, life is intolerable and cannot be bettered
> Unless the will quell it with pride. . . .
> —Certainly I wish to *weave my tortures* within myself,
> As in former days the great Christians, bitten by faith,
> Took a malign pleasure in emaciating themselves,
> I want to drink sufferings, like a poison
> Living and mad ; With my anguish I will lash
> My miserable days, just as the tocsin of the parish church
> Delights in spreading woe far and wide.]

This asceticism, as previously in the poem *Vers le cloître*, though now less directly, presents itself once more as the antidote to the " void " of autophilia :

> Cet héroisme intime et bizarre m'attire :
> Se préparer sa peine et provoquer son mal,
> Avec acharnement, et dompter l'animal
> De misère et de peur qui dans le cœur *se mire*
> Toujours ; se redresser cruel et contre soi,
> Vainqueur de quelque chose enfin, et moins languide,
> Et moins banalement en exstase du vide.[1]

[1] From Dialogue, in Les débâcles.

[This intimate and strange heroism allures me :
To prepare one's own pain and induce one's own suffering
With fierce zeal, and to tame the wild beast
Of wretchedness and fear which in the heart *mirrors itself*
Always ; to stand erect once more, cruel to one's self,
Victor at length over something, and less languid,
So that your ecstasy of voidness is no longer utterly trivial.]

The allusions in the former of these last two quotations to the " great Christians bitten by faith " and to the " tocsin of the parish church," and the words " to weave my tortures," confirm us in the belief that this " strange asceticism " is akin to genuinely religious asceticism, that which was acclaimed in *Les moines*. Nevertheless, there is a notable difference. Faith is now dead. Although its reminiscence, asceticism, survives, it is no longer religious, no longer a sacrifice to God, no longer penitential. It functions in the void, and has no aim external to itself :

Si le bonheur régnait dans ce mâle égoisme,
Souffrir pour soi, tout seul, mais par sa volonté.[1]

[If happiness reigned in this virile egoism,
To suffer for oneself, quite alone, but by one's own will.]

This aimless asceticism is especially conspicuous in *Les débâcles*, comprising the main theme of the book, or at least furnishing its atmosphere. The fact is made plain in the opening words :

. . . Sois ton bourreau toi-même ;
N'abandonne l'amour de te martyriser
A personne, jamais. . . .
Les maux de cœur qu'on exaspère, on les commande.[2]

[. . . Be your own executioner ;
Never relinquish to any one the delight of martyrising
Yourself. . . .
Heartaches which we aggravate, we are masters of.]

[1] From Les malades, in Les soirs.
[2] From Dialogue, in Les débâcles.

THE CRISIS

This stanza seems like the translation into lay terms of the passage previously quoted from *Les moines* :

La règle en sa rigueur grave et préceptorale, ...
Tu l'exagères tant que c'est toi qui domines,

[The rules, in their grave and preceptorial strictness, ...
You overstress so much that you are still the master,]

and the translation sums up the change that has been effected.

We thus verify the existence of a true ascetic tendency which, when resolved into its elements, is found to consist mainly of a voluptuous delight in suffering, of the will-to-power, and of the fighting instinct—all being " pent up," introverted, and directed exclusively towards the subject himself. The religious or moral reasons which seem to be the causes of this tendency are, primarily at least, effects rather than causes. They are a rationalisation of the tendency ; they are a canalisation of it and a sublimation ; but they do not constitute it. The tendency may persist after they have disappeared. Thus it comes to pass that in *Les débâcles* the ascetic tendency presents itself in isolation, looking irrational and knowing itself to be so. This phase of instability, of loss of balance, which is disastrous if it be not overcome, will be overcome in the case of Verhaeren, who will resolve it into harmony. He will know, as Nietzsche knew, how to give a fresh meaning to his asceticism. Even during the crisis, we feel that he is reaching out for this. And yet, fundamentally, it always remains the same asceticism.

From first to last, its kinship with religious asceticism is disclosed by the emblems used to express it.

Crosses are among these emblems. We see them in *Les flamandes* as the ominous sign of the death of the flesh, and their significance becomes explicit at the " cross-roads of death." Now the meaning is again made clear, for the cross signifies the way in which the flesh kills itself and martyrises itself :

Une torture en moi qui frappe et me lacère ? . . .
Une torture, à coups de clous et de marteaux ?

Là-bas, ces grandes croix au carrefour des routes,
Ces croix !—Oh ! n'y pouvoir saigner son cœur ; ces croix,
Où s'accrochent des cris d'espace et de déroutes,
Des cris et des haillons du vent dans les grands bois.[1]

[A torture within me which strikes, and tears me ?
A torture with blows of nails and hammers ?

Over there the giant crosses at the cross-roads,
The crosses !—Oh, to be unable to bleed out one's heart there ; the crosses,
Where the cries of space and of defeats are caught up,
The cries and the tatters of the wind in the great woods.]

    Les soirs crucifiés sur les Golgothas noirs
    Exaltent les douleurs et les fers dans les plaies.[2]

    [The evenings crucified on the black Golgothas
    Intensify the sufferings and the nails in the wounds.]

Another image is that of the *trees*, which we have already seen to be an expression of religious asceticism. In the quotation from the opening of *Les débâcles* we underlined the words *nouer mes tortures* (weave my tortures), which brings us in touch with the trees which are *noués et tordus* (gnarled and twisted). The trees that line the roads, which were " monks " in the earlier poem, are " pilgrims " in this one :

    On voit d'un carrefour livide et monotone,
    Partir vers l'infini les arbres pélerins.[3]

    [From the livid-tinted and monotonous cross-roads we see,
    Setting out towards the infinite, the pilgrim trees.]

These trees are always gnarled and twisted in the voluptuousness of a voluntarily imposed and ascetic torture :

---

[1] From Heures mornes, in Les débâcles.
[2] From Humanité, in Les soirs.   [3] From Les arbres, in Les soirs.

THE CRISIS

> L'hiver, les chênes lourds et vieux, les chênes *tors*,
> Geignant sous la tempête et projetant leurs branches
> Comme de grands bras fous qui veulent fuir leurs corps,
> Mais que tragiquement la chair retient aux hanches.[1]

> [In winter, the massive old oaks, the *twisted* oaks,
> Groaning under the buffets of the storm, and stretching forth
>   their branches
> Like huge mad arms trying to escape their bodies,
> But tragically fettered to the trunks by the flesh.]

They "try to escape their bodies." Here we have another symbol of the autophilia which censures itself and becomes an ascetic torment.

> Car l'âme des pays du nord sombre et sauvage
> Habite et clame en eux ses nocturnes douleurs,
> Et *tord* ses désespoirs d'automne en leur branchage....
> Oh! les chênes! oh! les mornes suppliciés.[2]

> [For the soul of the gloomy and wild northern lands
> Dwells in them and wails its nocturnal pains,
> And *twists* its autumnal despair in their leafage....
> Oh, the oaks! Oh, the sad victims.]

At length comes an extraordinarily typical symbol, one closely connected with that of the cross. The final poem in *Les débâcles* tells us of the "crown of thorns," the account of which forms the actual conclusion and "crown" of this Passion:

> Et je voudrais aussi ma couronne d'épines!
> Une épine pour chaque pensée, à travers
> Mon front, jusqu'au cerveau, jusqu'aux frêles racines
> Où se *tordent* les maux et les rêves forgés
> En moi, par moi....
> Et, plus au fond, le *rut même de ma torture.*
> Et tout enfin! O couronne de ma douleur
> Et de ma joie, ô couronne de dictature

---

[1] From Les vieux chênes, in Les soirs.
[2] From the same poem.

Debout sur mes deux yeux, ma bouche et mon cerveau.
O la couronne en rêve à mon front somnambule,
Hallucine-moi donc de ton absurdité ;
Et sacre-moi ton roi souffrant et ridicule.[1]

[I, too, long for my crown of thorns !
A thorn for every thought, piercing
My forehead, to the brain, to the delicate roots
Where *writhe* the ills and the dreams forged
Within me, by myself. . . .
And, deeper still, *the very rut of my torment.*
And, last of all, O crown of my sorrow
And of my joy, O crown of dictatorship,
Erect over my eyes, my mouth, and my brain.
O dream crown on my somnambulist brow,
Hallucinate me with your absurdity,
And consecrate me as your king, suffering and derided.][2]

We infer that this ascetic tendency, this desire to lacerate himself, is one of the chief among the elements that induce Verhaeren to vivisect himself, to undertake the pitiless and sanguinary analysis which intensifies the malady, to the greater delight of the sufferer. There is a certain tragical nobility in such a passion for self-conquest at all hazards, a self-conquest which is aimless when faith is lacking to provide a reason for it. We may say that Verhaeren's malady is, to a large extent, deliberately sought ; and the most pathetic feature in the case is that he knows it. He speaks of " the ills forged within me, by myself." But these self-sought ills are not mere semblances. Thanks to a persistent autosuggestion, they grow day by day more real, thus bringing a fierce delight to the man who has willed them. What is the nature of this interest in suffering ? We may say that *suffering is regarded as a substitute for faith.*

Nor is Verhaeren content with the actual suffering

[1] From La couronne, in Les débâcles.
[2] In the part of this poem which is not quoted, occurs the phrase " Mes vices de doigts et de lèvres claustrales," cited on p. 112.

THE CRISIS

of the moment. He wants his sufferings to be even greater; he wants them to assume an epic character. He dreams of a Passion, and of a crown of thorns. Even this does not suffice him, for he dreams also of madness, as if it were a transfiguration:

> Je veux marcher vers la folie et ses soleils,
> Ses blancs soleils de lune au grand midi, bizarres.[1]
>
> [I would fain walk towards madness and its suns,
> Its strange white moon-suns shining at high noon.]

He dreams of madness as of the supreme return to the Virgin—to the mother:

> Serai-je seul avec mon orgueil noir,
> Assis en un fauteuil de haine?
> Serai-je seul, avec ma pâle hyperdulie
> Pour Notre Dame, la Folie?[2]
>
> [Shall I be alone with my black pride
> Seated on a throne of hatred?
> Shall I be alone with my pale hyperdulia
> For Our Lady, Madness?]

To die a madman's death has become an obsession—to die insane like the clocks in the old watchmaker's tale of the mad lady-gnomes:

> L'inconscience gaie et le tic tac débile
> De la tranquille mort des fous, je l'entends bien.[3]
>
> [The cheerful unwittingness, and the feeble tic-tac
> Of the quiet death of madmen, I hear it well.]

Wandering through this "hallucinatory" London which was to become the prototype of "the tentacular towns," he sees "the corpse of his reason." It has the colour of "green blight":

---

[1] From Fleur fatale, in Les soirs.
[2] From Le roc, in Les flambeaux noirs.
[3] From Fleur fatale, in Les soirs.

> En sa robe couleur de feu et de poison,
> Le cadavre de ma raison
> Traîne sur la Tamise.[1]

> [In a gown which is the colour of flame and of poison,
> The corpse of my reason
> Floats on the Thames.]

Around this corpse, in sepulchral array, flock the tragical images that issue from the poet's early complexes—the clashing of the axles, the red orbs of the clock-towers:

> Des ponts de bronze, où les wagons
> Entrechoquent d'interminables bruits de gonds,
> Et des voiles de bâteaux sombres
> Laissent sur elle, choir leurs ombres.
>
> Sans qu'une aiguille, à son cadran, ne bouge,
> Un grand beffroi masqué de rouge,
> La regarde, comme quelqu'un
> Immensément de triste et de défunt.[2]

> [Bronze bridges where the carts
> Jostle, with the unceasing noise of hinges,
> And the sails of sombre barges
> Cast their shadows upon the river.
>
> With the hands on the clock-face motionless,
> A hugh clock-tower, glowing redly,
> Looks down upon the Thames, like a titan
> Sad and dead.]

We seem to be looking once more at the clock-towers which, in *Le passeur d'eau,* "noted the end of his endeavour." The body floating on the Thames might be that of the ferryman overcome in the effort to work his way up-stream. In the background we have images of the Passion:

---

[1] From La morte, in Les flambeaux noirs.
[2] From the same poem.

THE CRISIS

> Ce sont de grands chantiers d'affolement
> Pleins de barques démantelées
> Et de vergues écartelées
> Sous un ciel de crucifiement.[1]
>
> [They are great ship-yards of dementia
> Full of dismantled vessels
> And broken spars
> Beneath a sky of crucifixion.]

This cruel will-to-power which has formed a habit of turning against itself, sometimes attempts in desperation to leap out of the circle in which it feels itself imprisoned. Then we have the most terrifying fancies of misdeeds and murder:

> Désir d'être, soudain, la bête hiératique,
> D'un éclat noir, sous le portique
> Escarbouclé d'un temple à Bénarès.[2]
>
> [Suddenly comes the wish to be the hieratic beast,
> Black and lustrous, beneath the carbuncled
> Portico of a temple at Benares.]

This vision is linked with the deepest of Verhaeren's complexes:

> Masque divin et criminel,
> Avec de grands yeux vides
> Avec, sous le front d'or, un œil d'or éternel. . . .[3]
>
> [The divine and criminal mask
> With huge, empty eye-sockets,
> With, under the golden brow, an eternal eye of gold.][4]

The whole of suffering humanity comes from the ends of the earth to offer up prayers to the idol. But this terrible and deceitful superman dreams of power only to enjoy the delight of doing harm:

[1] From La morte, in Les flambeaux noirs.
[2] From Là-bas, in Les débâcles.
[3] From the same poem.
[4] A *mask* would seem to be a frequent symbol of introversion.

Et se complaire à se sentir cruel et fourbe : . . .
Et les haïr et regretter son impuissance
Non pour les secourir, mais pour rageusement
Les affoler et se prouver sa malfaisance.[1]

[To take pleasure in feeling that one is cruel and false. . . .
To hate them and to regret one's powerlessness,
Not to aid them, but furiously
To drive them mad and to prove one's maleficence.]

This is the same hatred as that which, a moment before, was turned inward. Now it is seeking extroversion. Always the same image of torture occupies the field of vision :

Et devant ce décor incendié maudire
L'homme niais et nul, qui se gave d'espoir,
Alors qu'un symbolique et quotidien martyre
Saigne la vie en croix, au quatre coins du soir.[2]

[And before this scene devastated with fire, to curse
The simpleton, the man of no account, who gluts himself with hope,
What time a symbolical and daily martyrdom
Bleeds out its life on a cross at the four corners of the evening.]

The cruel and divine beast appears again and again, in various forms. It is a mountain which rises up, " idole énorme et nocturne de pierre " (huge and nocturnal idol of stone) :

> Et sa tête s'en va dans les mares lointaines,
> Mirer de la splendeur et du fulgurement.[3]
>
> [And its head vanishes in distant meres
> To mirror splendour and fulguration.]

Towards this introverted and monstrous god, all the evening life writhes in its suffering, a holocaust:

[1] From Là-bas, in Les débâcles. [2] From the same poem.
[3] From L'idole, in Les soirs.

Et quand montent au loin, des vals et des ramées,
Les feux et les brouillards et les plaintes du soir,
A l'heure ardente et triste, on s'imagine voir
Se tordre un holocauste en de rouges fumées.[1]

[And when there rise far off, from the valleys and the branches,
The fires and the fogs and the plaints of the evening,
At this ardent and sad hour, one seems to see
A holocaust writhing in red smoke-wreaths.]

Elsewhere, this strange god disintegrates himself to form a whole population of gods, but it is only the same image become an obsession:

Et mon désert de cœur est peuplé de Dieux noirs. . . .

Avec des yeux, comme les yeux des loups, la nuit,
Avec des yeux comme la lune, ils me regardent. . . .

Mes dieux! ils sont: le mal gratuit, celui pour soi,
L'unique. . . .

Et les uns des autres insoucieux: seuls—tous.
Chacun pour soi rêvant à sa toute puissance,
Sous les plafonds de fer des firmaments jaloux;
Et la taisant, pour l'aiguiser, sa malfaisance. . . .[2]

[The desert of my heart is peopled with black gods. . . .

Their eyes are like the eyes of wolves at night,
Their eyes are like the moon, they look at me. . . .

My gods! they are: gratuitous evil, self-seeking,
The unique. . . .

One heedless of the other: alone—all of them.
Each one for himself dreaming of supreme power,
Beneath the iron canopy of the jealous firmament;
And concealing his malevolence in order to intensify it.]

---

[1] From L'idole, in Les soirs.
[2] From Les dieux, in Les flambeaux noirs.

They are symbols of introversion filled with hate; but the very effort which this hate makes towards extroversion recoils inwards:

> Ils sont mes éternels et mes tortionnaires. . . .
> Ecrasez-moi, je suis victime.[1]
>
> [They are my eternal companions and my torturers. . . .
> Crush me, I am a victim.]

If this hatred could really extrovert itself, if it could culminate in murder, it would be a triumph, for the being, prisoned within the ego, would then at least secure contact with the real world, would demonstrate the possibility of having an external interest, an outwardly directed passion.

> En ces heures de vice et de crime rigides,
> Se rêve un meurtre ardent, que la nuit grandirait. . . .
> D'autres sens te naîtront, subtils et maladifs,
> Ils renouvelleront ton être, usé de rages,
> Et tu seras celui qui fut sanglant un peu,
> *Qui bondit hors de soi* et creva *les mirages*,
> Et, biffant une vie, a fait œuvre de Dieu.[2]
>
> [In these hours of unbending vice and crime,
> You dream of a passionate murder which the night would magnify. . . .
> Other senses, subtle and morbid, will be born in you.
> They will renew your being, worn with frenzies,
> And you will be the one who was bleeding a little,
> *Who leapt out of himself,* scattered *the mirages,*
> And, wiping out a life, accomplished God's will.]

We find the same wish in *La révolte*:

> Vers une ville au loin d'émeute et de tocsin,
> Où luit le couteau nu des guillotines,
> En tout à coup de fou désir, s'en va mon cœur.[3]

---

[1] From Les dieux, in Les flambeaux noirs.
[2] From Le meurtre, in Les débâcles.
[3] From La révolte, in Les flambeaux noirs.

THE CRISIS

[Towards a distant town of rebellion and tocsin,
Where the naked knife of the guillotine is gleaming,
My heart reaches out in a sudden access of wild desire.] [1]

But this will-to-hate and will-to-murder is under an illusion when it believes that it is "leaping out of itself." Such a one as Verhaeren can torture none but himself, can seek out no other victim than himself. Dreaming himself a murderer, he is still ever the ascetic.

> Tuer—être tué—qu'importe !
>
> [To kill—to be killed—what does it matter!]

is the last line of the poem just quoted. The fantasies of maleficence are accompanied by the same images as the fantasies of asceticism. With the Benares idol goes the fantasy "bleeds out its life on a cross at the four corners of the evening"; here, too, we have the holocaust which "writhes" towards the idol; and we have the gods which have become the poet's "torturers." In *Le meurtre*, there is once more a tragical procession of the pilgrim trees :

> Tous les mêmes, luisants de lierre et tous les mêmes
> D'écorce et de rameaux, comme un effarement,
> Sur double rang, là-bas, jusqu'aux horizons blêmes,
> Muets et seuls, les arbres vont, infiniment. [2]
>
> [All alike shining with ivy, and all alike
> In bark and branches, an alarming spectacle,
> In a double file, over there, towards the pale horizons,
> Mute and lonely the trees move in unending processions.]

Thus the wish to murder is, above all, a wish to murder oneself. This will-to-power (maleficent power) breaks away from the ascetic tendency and yet comes back to it. The same phenomenon occurred in Nietzsche. We

---
[1] This poem is, as it were, the first draft of the poem of the same name in *Les villes tentaculaires*.
[2] From *Le meurtre*, in *Les débâcles*.

cannot fully understand the violence of the clash between love and death in Verhaeren, unless we take into account the ascetic tendency in which self-love turns into deadly self-hate.

It is in these poems of the crisis that the coupling of the images *ebony* (or black) and *gold*, as symbols of the clash, begins to force itself upon the reader's attention. A striking use is made of it in *La dame en noir*. The image reappears in *L'idole* :

> Tandis qu'un horizon d'ébène et de soleil
> Regarde encor.
>
> [While a horizon of ebony and sunshine
> Stands at gaze. . . .]

The hateful god of Benares, the "hieratic beast," is disclosed.

> Avec sous le front d'or un œil d'or éternel,
> Sous un plafond de marbre noir.
>
> [With, under the golden brow, an eternal eye of gold
> Beneath a canopy of black marble.]

The same contrast recurs again and again:

> Les quais étaient électrisés de lunes,
> Et le navire, avec ses mâts pavoisés d'or,
> Et ses mousses d'ébène, ornait gaîment son bord.[1]
>
> [The quays were lighted with great electric moons,
> And the ship, its masts dressed with gold,
> And with its ebony crew, gaily adorned the edge.]

Les chats d'ébène et d'or ont traversé le soir.[2]

[The ebony and golden cats have prowled through the evening.]

---

[1] From Les voyageurs, in Les soirs.
[2] From Les livres, in Les flambeaux noirs.

THE CRISIS

The foregoing images contain definite allusions to "eyes" and to "moons": we have the horizon which stands at gaze, the Cyclopean eye of the Benares idol, the electric moons on the quays, the eyes of the cats (see below pp. 149–150); these are golden, and are projected upon an ebony background. Elsewhere, the details of the imagery are blurred, so that nothing remains but the contrast between ebony and gold:

> Oursons d'ébène, et tigres d'or.[1]
>
> [Ebony bear-cubs, and golden tigers.]

But a juxtaposition of this with the passages previously cited makes the significance of the simplified image equally clear.

The most obstinately persistent references to death—to the death for which an ascetic hatred of self had engendered a craving—are conveyed by the use of *iron* as an emblem:

Et vous aussi, mes doigts, vous deviendrez des vers. . . .
Quand vous serez noués—les dix—sur ma carcasse
Et que s'écrasera sous un cercueil de fer,
Cette âpre carcasse, qui déjà casse ;[2]

[And you likewise, my fingers, will become worms. . . .
When you will have been clasped, all ten of you, on my corpse,
And when there will have been crushed, in an iron coffin,
This rugged corpse, which is already breaking up ;]

Sait-on jamais quels imminents sépulcres sombres,
Scellés de fer, vont éclater ?[3]

[Does one ever know which of the ominous, gloomy tombs,
Sealed with iron, are going to burst open ?]

---

[1] From Les villes, in Les flambeaux noirs.
[2] From Mes doigts, in Les débâcles.
[3] From Un soir, in Les flambeaux noirs.

N'entendre plus se taire, en sa maison *d'ébène*,
Qu'un silence de fer dont auraient peur les morts.[1]

[And all the silence one hears in one's *ebony* mansion
Is an iron silence which strikes terror into the dead.]

These images are frequently associated with those of *porches* (sometimes, iron porches), where one is swallowed up, and which crush one :

Heure morte, là-bas, quelque part, en province,
En une ville éteinte, au fond d'un coin désert ;
Où s'endeuillent des murs et des porches, dont grince
Le gond monumental, ainsi qu'un poing de fer.[2]

[Dead hour, over there, somewhere in the country,
In a decaying town away in a remote corner ;
Where mourn the walls, and the porches whose monumental
Hinge grates like an iron fist.]

Psychoanalysts are prone to interpret images of porches and underground chambers as symbols of an unconscious wish to return to the mother's womb, to the nullity of fœtal life, this being the wish of an introvert, and often merging into a wish for death. Unquestionably it seems hazardous to infer from the use of such imagery that the writer is animated by this desire, but we have already noted (p. 121) a similar fantasy in one of Verhaeren's poems ("avant que sortit du somme l'endormi." . . . 3) Moreover, we know how intense is the poet's yearning for the mother. Finally, there is a poem definitely entitled *Sous les porches*, which affords a remarkable confirmation of this classical interpretation :

L'ombre s'affermissait sur les plaines captives,
Et, de ses murs, barrait les horizons d'hiver,
Comme en un tombeau noir, de vieux astres de fer
Brulaient, trouant le ciel de leurs flammes votives.

[1] From Le roc, in Les flambeaux noirs.
[2] From Les malades, in Les soirs.
[3] Before there awoke from his slumber the sleeper. . . .

THE CRISIS

On se sentait serré dans un monde d'airain
Où quelque part, au-loin, se dresseraient des pierres
Mornes et qui seraient les idoles guerrières,
D'un peuple encore enfant, terrible et souterrain.[1]

[The shadows were deepening upon the prisoned plains,
And with their walls they striped the wintry horizons,
As if, in a black tomb, ancient stars of iron
Were burning, piercing the sky with their votive flames.

One felt cribbed in a brazen world,
In which, somewhere, far off, mournful stones
Were rearing their heads—the warlike idols
Of a race still infantile, terrible, and subterranean.]

Elsewhere, iron is replaced by all kinds of "metals" and "knives." The ascetic *Dialogue* with which *Les flambeaux noirs* begins, closes with the words

Les éclatants couteaux de crime et de soleil.

[Flashing knives of crime and of sunshine.]

The Lady in Black is awaiting "the man with the red knife." But the poem *La tête* is one of the most terrible in this respect:

Sur un échafaud noir, tu porteras ta tête
Et sonneront les tours et luiront les couteaux
Et tes muscles crîront et ce sera la fête,
La fête et la splendeur du sang et des métaux.[2]

[On a black scaffold you will carry your head,
And the towers will peal forth, and the knives will gleam,
And your muscles will cry out, and it will be high festival,
The festival and the splendour of blood and of metals.]

Sometimes iron appears in the form of trains and clashing axles; then the tunnels or the stations where the trains are engulfed take the place of the porches.

[1] From Sous les porches, in Les soirs.
[2] From La tête, in Les débâcles.

Turn back, for instance to the account of the trains in *Les villes*, quoted on p. 52. Consider in conjunction with it the following passage:

> Et ce Londres de fonte et de bronze, mon âme,
> Où des plaques de fer claquent sous des hangars, ...
> Gares de suie et de fumée......
> Et tout à coup la mort parmi ces foules....[1]
>
> [And this London of iron and bronze, O my soul,
> Where steel plates clash beneath the arched roofs, ...
> Stations full of soot and smoke......
> And suddenly death stalks amid these crowds....]

The poem about the Benares idol is one of the most poignant. Therein several of the foregoing images converge. We hear again, and even more clearly, the clashing of the wheels and the axles—the clashings which our analysis of *Les tendresses premières* disclosed as the origin of this whole series of images:

> Et regarder, témoin impassible et tragique,
> Dardés, les yeux de fer, et les naseaux, hagards,
> Droit devant soi, là-bas, le ciel mythologique,
> Où le Siva terrible echevèle ses chars,
> Par des ornières d'or, à travers les nuages:
> Scintillement d'essieux et tonnerres de feux.[2]
>
> [And to contemplate, an impassive and tragical witness,
> Flashing, the iron eyes, and the nostrils, distraught,
> Straight before one, over there, the mythological heaven,
> Where the dread Siva ruffles his chariots,
> Along the golden ruts, athwart the clouds:
> Sparklings of axles and thunders of fires.]

When we study these evocations of trains, iron, and death, how can we fail to be struck by their resemblance with the circumstances actually attendant on Verhaeren's death a quarter of a century later? It will be remembered

---

[1] From Londres, in Les soirs.
[2] From Là-bas, in Les débâcles.

THE CRISIS

that he died from an accident on the evening of November 27, 1916. He had just given a lecture in Rouen, and was to return to Paris by train.

The platforms in the station were packed with people. Verhaeren was impatient, and in an irritable frame of mind. When the train was coming in, he tried to get in before it had stopped, stumbled over a portmanteau, slipped upon the step, and, falling under the train, had both his legs cut off.[1]

In the newspapers at that time there were comments upon the strange and apparently prophetic resemblance between Verhaeren's poems and the manner of his death. He had sung the beautiful and tragical horror of railway trains, and he was killed by a train. Those who were familiar with his writings could not but be impressed by this working out of destiny; and the least mystical among them found it difficult to escape the feeling of a preconceived fatality. I was a member of a small literary circle which, in private, held a commemorative gathering. We read Verhaeren's poems aloud. Among others we read *La tête*. "On a black scaffold you will carry your head." Anyone haunted by thoughts of the recent death of the poet, who listened to the reading of this poem; anyone who heard the lines, " and when there will have been crushed in an iron coffin this rugged corpse, which is already breaking up "—must inevitably have felt that these passages contained elements of a prophetic vision. Even more striking is the nightmare poem about the trains in *Les forces tumultueuses*, the poem entitled *La folie*:

> Rails qui sonnent, signaux qui bougent. . . .
> Appels stridents, ouragans noirs. . . .
> Parce que ceux qui les montaient glissent à terre,
> Soudainement, parmi les morts.

[1] Mockel, Emile Verhaeren, p. 169.

[Resounding rails, moving signals. . . .
Strident clamours, black hurricanes. . . .
For those who were boarding them slip to the ground,
Suddenly numbered among the dead.]

Psychology has to take such emotions into account. There is a reason for them, and as a rule that reason has more significance than any ativistic survival of outworn beliefs. A mystical sentiment may be something very different from what it seems ; it may be, not metaphysical, but psychological. The emotion that affects us may be the expression of the confused recognition of a subconscious reality, and analysis may enable us to bring this subconscious reality to light. In the present instance, how can we help thinking of Freud's views concerning deaths apparently due to accident, which are (he holds) in many cases involuntary suicides determined by subconscious complexes. In an earlier work [1] I have endeavoured to show that such an interpretation is acceptable, however strange it may seem at first sight, for it harmonises with a whole series of facts that have been well established during the study of autosuggestion. In Verhaeren, these emblems of iron and of trains give expression to a deep-rooted, subconscious complex, dating from early childhood, and linked from the first with the idea of a death at once longed for and dreaded. There may well have been a tie between the visions of the poems and the facts of the poet's death, without its being necessary to suppose that the visions of iron and of trains were veiled prophesies of a predetermined event. It was not the predestined accident which determined the visions. The causal sequence was that the visions were the expression of the subconscious complex which would, in due time, determine, or partially determine, the accident. Such a view does not deprive the causal sequence of its tragedy, nor does it invalidate the emotion we feel when we contemplate the tragedy.

[1] Suggestion and Autosuggestion, p. 85.

THE CRISIS

We have thus disclosed several of the psychological elements of the crisis. By simplification they may be reduced to two: the tendency to introversion, and the ascetic tendency. Simplifying yet further, we may say that the tendency to introversion finds expression mainly in *Les soirs*, and that the ascetic tendency makes its appearance and becomes dominant in *Les débâcles*. But these two tendencies do not suffice to explain Verhaeren's crisis, for some ascetic introverts enjoy perfect internal equilibrium. According as our own standpoint is religious, on the one hand, or materialistic, on the other, we shall regard this equilibrium as good or as bad. Incontestably, however, it is an equilibrium; and I know of no objective canon which entitles us to regard extroversion as more normal and more desirable than introversion.[1]

We may recall, however, having noted that, at the outset of his crisis, Verhaeren experienced a loss of faith. In a metaphysical disturbance we may discern the reasonable cause of the crisis. The other causes could not become effective without the superaddition of the third determinant. When Verhaeren's biographers tell us that the poet's troubles were the outcome of this disturbance, they do not see to the heart of the matter, but nevertheless they see accurately up to a certain point. The literary expression of the third factor is especially noticeable in *Les flambeaux noirs*, the last portion of the trilogy.

What overwhelms Verhaeren is the vision of universal determinism, of the rigid laws which shackle the world and crush man:

> Un paysage noir, ligné d'architectures,
> Qui découpent et captivent l'éternité,
> En leur paralèles et fatales structures,
> Impose à mes yeux clos son immobilité.[2]

[1] Morel does so regard it, but I think his opinion is the outcome of feeling rather than of logical deduction. Jung takes a different view.
[2] From Les lois, in Les flambeaux noirs.

[A black landscape, aligned with buildings
Which silhouette and prison eternity
With their parallel and inevitable structures,
Imposes its fixity upon my closed eyes.]

In Victor Hugo, the sight of the starry heavens induced a mood of lyrical and fervent contemplation, but for Verhaeren this was but an additional reason for fear. The stars and their unbending evolutions were a soulless determinism rendered visible :

Là-haut le million épars des diamants
Et les regards, aux firmaments,
Myriadaires des étoiles ;
Et des voiles après des voiles
Autour de l'Isis d'or qui rêve aux firmaments.

Je suis l'halluciné de la forêt des Nombres.

Ils me fixent avec les yeux de leurs problèmes ;
Ils sont, pour éternellement rester : les mêmes.
Primordiaux et définis,
Ils tiennent le monde entre leurs infinis ;
Ils expliquent le fond et l'essence des choses,
Puisqu'à travers les temps, planent leurs causes.[1]

[Up there, the scattered millions of diamonds,
And, in the skies,
The myriad eyes of the stars ;
And veil upon veil
Around the golden Isis who is dreaming in the skies.

I am hallucinated by the forest of Numbers.

They fix me with the eyes of their problems ;
They are, that they may rest for ever, the same,
They are primordial and definite ;
They hold up the world between their infinities ;
They explain the basis and the essence of things
For their causes brood adown the ages.]

This metaphysical anguish is mingled with that of the poet's familiar complexes. For him, the astronomical

[1] From Les nombres, in Les flambeaux noirs.

THE CRISIS

heaven is a vast clockwork mechanism. This recalls to us the watchmaker of *Les tendresses premières*. Here are the closing verses of *L'horloger* :

> Mais jour à jour, de plus en plus, les mouvements
>   Innombrables, indéfinis tentaculaires
>   Attirèrent mes yeux déments
>   En leurs vertiges circulaires
>   Si bien que mon esprit,
>   Avec autant d'ardeur, plus tard, s'éprit
> Des tumultes reglés, par les causes profondes
> Qui font, dans le mystère, évoluer les mondes.

> [But, day by day, more and more, the movements,
>   Innumerable, vague, tentacular,
>   Attracted my maddened eyes
>   Into their circular vortices,
>   So that my mind
>   With all the more ardour later became enamoured
> Of the tumults regulated by the inner causes
> Which bring about the mysterious evolution of worlds.]

He now sees the stars fixing him—like the watch-faces and the clock-faces—" with the eyes of their problems " :

> Regards abstraits, lobes vident et sans paupières.[1]

> [Abstract looks, empty and lidless eye-sockets.]

In the following poem, *Les livres*, Verhaeren gives expression to the distress that arises in a modern mind owing to the secular evolution of philosophic doctrines, and their crazy dance in such a mind. But here, likewise, the metaphysical anguish is clad in images representing the poet's familiar complexes :

> Les chats *d'ébène et d'or* ont traversé le soir,
> Avec des cris de vis et de fermoir,
> Ils ont griffé mon cœur et le *miroir*
> De mes yeux clairs vers les étoiles. . . .

[1] From Les nombres, in Les flambeaux noirs.

Lorsque soudain les noirs chats d'or
Se sont assis sur ma muraille
Et m'ont fixé *de leurs grands yeux,*
Comme des fous silencieux.[1]

[The ebony and golden cats have prowled through the evening
With cries like screws and clasps,
They have torn my heart and scratched the *mirror*
Of my eyes that were directed serenely towards the stars. . . .
When suddenly the black and golden cats
Seated themselves upon the wall
And stared at me *with their great eyes,*
Silently, *like madmen.*]

A reference to the strange title of the collection known as *Les flambeaux noirs* will now be appropriate. Here we have a pithy formula describing the clash of gold with ebony, of fire with blackness. In an earlier poem, these images were simply juxtaposed; when the tower was burned, this " torch " (the old clock-tower that was burning, see p. 60) became " black all at once " as it was falling. On this occasion the images are superposed, and blackness is thrust on our attention when we were expecting the image of fire—which has not even time to make its appearance. The same mechanism is displayed in *La dame en noir*: " The moons of my two eyes showing black " (p. 58). We find it again in certain images in *Les campagnes hallucinées*:

<blockquote>
La mort a mis sur le comptoir
Un écu noir.[2]

[Death has staked
A black crown-piece.] [3]
</blockquote>

[1] From Les livres, in Les flambeaux noirs.
[2] From Le fléau, in Les campagnes hallucinées.
[3] The French usually speak of " un écu d'or," a golden crown-piece, and the use of the words *un écu noir* is an abrupt substitution of the image of black for the image of gold.—TRANSLATORS' NOTE.

THE CRISIS

Le deuil, au fond des cieux, tourne comme des meules
Les soleils noirs.[1]

[Grief in the depths of the heavens turns, like millstones,
The black suns.]

Thus the title "Les flambeaux noirs" (black torches) gives the most intense formulation of the clash between black and gold. What can be the meaning of this intimate association of the metaphysical torment with the complexes, if it be not that the former is inseparable from the latter, so that the metaphysical torment only acquires its hallucinatory force in virtue of the complexes. If we are really to understand the crisis, both elements must be taken into account.

What, then, are the relationships, in the production of the crisis, between the metaphysical torment, on the one hand, and the introversion and asceticism on the other? They are not difficult to discover, and we have already touched on them. Where there is faith, there is a reason for introversion and asceticism, so that a mental balance can be sustained. It is probable that an absolute [self-dependent] introversion, like an absolute extroversion, will necessarily culminate in a crisis. But when the introvert sees God within himself, his introversion is no longer absolute; he loves and feels that he is loved; between God and himself there are relationships analogous to those which other human beings, extroverts, form with their fellows. It matters no whit whether the introvert's god possesses metaphysical reality; the god has a psychological reality, and this guarantees an inner balance. Besides, a religious conversion usually implies that the convert recognises certain human duties as incumbent upon him—the love of his kind, charitable deeds, etc.—and these are extroverted actions. That is why the introvert who has been affected with a crisis can overcome the crisis if he succeeds in attaining a balance

[1] From La bêche, in Les campagnes hallucinées.

in his religious life. To give a recent and well-known instance, this is what happened in Tolstoy's case. In like manner, asceticism practised in the name of faith is rational; it simultaneously satisfies the intelligence and the tendencies, and is thus a state of equilibrium.

But when faith vanishes, the balance is upset. Asceticism has become a mill grinding without grist, so that there is nothing left but a senseless passion for self-injury, self-destruction. Verhaeren describes it as "moral deformation," this being the sub-title of *Les débâcles*. As for the impetus towards introversion, which found a whole world in the inner life, it finds there now nothing but vacancy. Hence Verhaeren's image of a being who retires perpetually within himself, "squatting, like the poor Maries"—a creature who bites his lips, and tears his loathed flesh with his own finger-nails. Rodin's "Thinker," but feverish, and sickened with his thoughts:

> Je voudrais me cracher moi-même,
> La lèvre en sang, la face blême. . . .
> Clos tes volets—c'est bien fini,
> Le mors-aux-dents vers l'infini.[1]

> [I should like to spue myself out of my own mouth,
> Bleeding at the lips, pallid of visage. . . .
> Close your shutters—all is over,
> Bolting towards the infinite.]

The mind then attains to an impassibility akin to that of the oriental ascetic, but an impassibility which knows itself vain and devoid of hope:

Et maintenant plus rien en eux jamais ne bouge;
Ni les désirs, ni les regrets, ni les effrois;
Ils n'ont plus même, hélas! le grand rêve des Croix
Ni le dernier espoir tendu vers la mort rouge.[2]

---

[1] From Un soir, in Les bords de la route.
[2] From Quelques-uns, in Les bords de la route.

THE CRISIS

[In them, now, nothing ever stirs;
No desires, no regrets, no alarms;
They have even lost, alas, the fine dream of the Crosses,
Lost, too, the last hope reaching out towards red death.]

Thus the loss of faith leads to a collapse of equilibrium. It is like the tower splitting from summit to base in the conflagration, or like the mirror which broke noiselessly one evening. At first, Verhaeren tries forcibly to extrovert himself, to give himself up to the fierce pleasures of a carnal life. This is the epoch of *Les flamandes*; but the attempt runs counter to deep-rooted tendencies, and the phase cannot last. Then he tries to transform the old faith into a new one, faith in himself and in his art. This is the period of *Les moines*. But the new faith is unattainable. The inner world is narrow and confined; its depths are distasteful; how can one believe in oneself when one knows oneself to be merely an atom at the mercy of the inevitable laws of matter? The new faith is foredoomed to ruin by the ruin of the old faith. Doubt recurs, and collapse is complete.

J'avais foi en ma tête; elle était ma hantise [1]

[I had faith in my head; it was my obsession]

says the poet, just as elsewhere he has told us " I was proud of my tower." But the head was threatened with the same fate as the tower; the poet's faith in himself crumbled as his faith in God had crumbled:

Ah! comme il fut dolent ce soir d'opacité
Où mon âme minée infiniment de doutes,
S'écroula toute
Et lézarda, craquement noir, ma volonté.[2]

[How agonising was that opaque night
In which my soul, hopelessly undermined by doubt,
Foundered completely,
And my will, a black crevasse, broke up.]

[1] From L'heure mauvaise, in Les bords de la route.
[2] From the same poem.

Thus had the tower broken up. It is this tragical collapse of the former equilibrium which conveys the profound significance of Verhaeren's crisis, which teaches the lesson of that crisis. Our tendencies are unreasoning. Psychoanalysis shows, pitilessly sometimes, that the conscious aims we assign to these tendencies are mere "rationalisations." Nevertheless, this process of rationalisation is essential; it is a true biological function. Gonzague Truc defines "grace" (which he laicises) by saying that it is inner health and inner harmony—a condition of "affective convergence."[1] Excellent, but it would be more accurate to speak of a "convergence of affectivity and intelligence." The inner balance cannot be secured unless reason and tendency, the conscious and the subconscious, are simultaneously satisfied. Conflict between these elements, on the other hand, like every grave conflict, leads towards a crisis, towards neurosis.

Verhaeren's education, and perhaps his heredity, predisposed him to an equilibrium established upon religious faith. Loss of faith was followed by a temporary loss of harmony. But Verhaeren was too resilient to rest content with this ruin, and we shall see that ere long he set out upon the conquest of a new equilibrium and a new faith.

[1] La grâce, 1918, pp. 33 and 99.

CHAPTER FOUR

CONVERSION AND DELIVERANCE

(1890 TO 1900)

VERHAEREN'S crisis was, above all, a crisis of extreme introversion, like that of Faust. Like Faust, he could only find deliverance by getting out of himself, and by opening his eyes and his mind to the " multiple splendour " of the world.

"I said to myself," writes Goethe, "that to deliver my mind from this state of gloom in which it was torturing itself, the essential was to turn my attention towards nature, and to share unreservedly in the life of the outer world."[1]

This continued to be one of the precepts of Goethean wisdom. Victor Hugo, who during the first half of his life had been the typical romanticist, the introvert who dives

> Jusqu'au fond désolé du gouffre intérieur,
>
> [To the desolate depths of the inner abyss,]

was to verify it in his turn. After 1843 he found his deliverance by learning to direct his energies towards his fellows, both in his art and in his public activities. At any rate such is the interpretation of Vodoz,[2] who seems to have admirably understood the inward evolution of this poet.

[1] Goethe, Die Campagne in Frankreich.
[2] Vodoz, Roland, un symbole, 1920, p. 70.

Jung thinks that he is entitled to expand Goethe's precept into a law.[1] Absolute introversion and absolute extroversion seem to him critical states—bouillons for the culture of neuroses. We can only escape from them by completing ourselves. The extrovert must learn to look within himself, and the introvert must learn to look without himself; these are the essentials of the new psychotherapy. Furthermore, Jung considers that we may sum up the position by saying that in the extrovert there is abundant expression of sensibility, but repression of thought; whereas in the introvert it is sensibility which is repressed and which has to be exhumed. Such simple generalisations are risky. But here we are not called upon to examine how far this particular generalisation of Jung's is justified, and we may be content to admit that Verhaeren's case seems to fit very well into such a scheme.[2]

The poet's sensibilities had been pent-up and prisoned; they were now to be set free.

Albert Mockel writes: "Until the triumphant St. George revealed himself, Verhaeren had ignored the heart."[3]

This lapidary formula is substantially true. Verhaeren was to find salvation in the heart: in a noble and exalted love for a woman; and in an impassioned interest directed towards human beings in general, towards modern life, towards all the spectacle of the world. This is "the acceptance of the factory" to which we referred on p. 45. It is a true conversion, one of those sudden changes of front thanks to which a human being, hitherto at war within himself, recovers balance and rediscovers joy. The term "conversion" is not an overstatement. In fact, the phenomena of religious psychology are usually psychological, primarily, rather than religious.

---

[1] Jung, The Psychology of the Unconscious, pp. 416 et seq.
[2] Jung, op. cit., passim, especially p. 201.
[3] Mockel, Emile Verhaeren, p. 60.

In other words, they exhibit a form which is independent of and separable from the content; and although traditional thought confounds the form and the content, it is incumbent upon the psychologist to distinguish between them, and to study the form wherever he encounters it. We cannot therefore approve too highly Gonzague Truc's endeavour to laicise the psychology of grace (supra p. 154); our only criticism being that this writer takes too elastic a view of the significance of the term "grace," and thus loses sight of the real causes of the phenomenon.

From the Roman Catholic point of view, of course, a conversion to Catholicism is the only conversion that counts. Psychology, however, cannot discern any specific difference between a Catholic conversion, a Protestant conversion, and a conversion sui generis such as that of Tolstoy.[1] Though such conversions vary in content, they do not differ in form. We recognise in this connexion the importance of the distinction drawn by James, in the field of religious psychology, between "existential judgments" and "propositions of value" or "spiritual judgments"—a distinction accepted by Théodore Flournoy [2] (who, however, phrases it somewhat differently, speaking of the principles of " biological interpretation" and the "exclusion of transcendence "). James and Flournoy were both religious-minded men, and it would seem, therefore, that this distinction might be accepted by all such persons.

The content of a conversion is the theme for a proposition of value, and this is the concern of philosophy. Psychology, on the other hand, being a science of facts, must restrict itself to an existential judgment; and such a judgment permits of the recognition that there is a kinship in the various forms of religious conversion.

---

[1] In this respect, we share the view expressed by William James in his Varieties of religious Experience.
[2] See the opening pages of Une mystique moderne.

But we have to go further, and to admit that, from the psychological point of view, the essential characteristic of conversion is not its religious element—at any rate in the current sense of the term religion. Verhaeren, like Goethe, is not converted to the Christian God; he is converted to men, or at most to a sort of pantheistic monism which might be just as well denoted a philosophy as a religion. But who can deny that the crisis of a despairing introversion, followed by the sudden revolution, through which Verhaeren regained balance, comprise a drama closely paralleled by the experiences of a Tolstoy? The psychological essential of conversion may be summarised as follows. One who has been the victim of a conflict, recovers balance through a sudden, or comparatively sudden, setting free of the forces that have been prisoned in the subconscious, and through the change of direction which the psychic energy thus undergoes. The outcome is a new conception of life, and perhaps a new conception of the universe.

Georges Buisseret has written a penetrating work upon the psychology of Verhaeren's conversion. He understands that the most essential thing was that the poet should find his way out of himself: "Ailing, a sceptic, almost a misanthrope in *Les soirs* and *Les débâcles*, what he needed above all was to escape from the disastrous subjectivism by which he was held captive. Thus *Les flambeaux noirs*, despite their tragical gleam, were the first symptoms of the desirable reaction."[1]

In actual fact, *Les flambeaux noirs* (the sub-title of the book is "Projection extérieure"), which deals with philosophical and objective problems, was the first expression of a move towards the outer world. But the definite assurance of victory was to be given in subsequent years and in subsequent poems.

Buisseret writes in another passage: "It was, I believe, a victory very similar to the one dreamed of by Nietzsche

[1] Buisseret, L'évolution idéologique d'Emile Verhaeren, 1910, p. 76.

who likewise longed for joy at all cost, and in whom we find sufferings and revolts identical with those of Verhaeren. These two men of genius carried on the same ardent and pitiless struggle, the main difference between their respective tones being that the sarcastic ill-humour of Zarathustra is not found in the author of *Visages* and *Forces*." [1]

Our own analysis has already justified the comparison often made between Verhaeren and Nietzsche.[2] But Verhaeren, for his part, was in due time to "leap out of" his introversion.

Stefan Zweig, who has been greatly struck by this conversion towards things without, has given the apt title of "Flight into the World" to the chapter he devotes to its study. This is how he describes the evolution, or the revolution, Verhaeren underwent: "He had arrived at that last possibility, at that possibility which means destruction or transformation. . . . He who had previously felt everything only subjectively, only in isolation, now objectifies himself; he who had previously shut himself off from reality, now lets his veins pulse in harmony with the breathing organism of life. He relinquishes his attitude of pride; he surrenders himself; lavishes himself joyously on everything; exchanges the pride of being alone for the immense pleasure of being everywhere. He no longer looks at all things in himself, but at himself in all things. . . . Supreme solitude is changed to supreme fellowship. . . . He saved himself by no longer fixing his gaze rigidly on himself and deeply probing every feeling of joy and torment, but by turning to the world of phenomena and flinging himself on its problems." [3]

---

[1] Op. cit., p. 85.
[2] The two writers resemble one another especially in the ascetic tendency, in energy, and in their love of risk. But we must not strain the comparison. It would be quite as easy to depict them as contrasted types.
[3] Zweig, Emile Verhaeren, English translation, pp. 68, 70, 76, and 81.

The change did not merely show itself in the poet's writings,[1] his very life took a turn for the better. Verhaeren wedded Mademoiselle Marthe Massin in the year 1892. " She proved to be an admirable companion to the poet, being simple and straightforward, full of courage, and devoted to the pitch of abnegation."[2]

It was at this period, too, that Verhaeren began to display an interest in the people and in socialism, lending his aid to Vandervelde, and working in the art section of the Maison du Peuple.[3]

During the period of transition, the symbols of introversion are still fairly common in the poet's writings. Indeed, we could hardly expect anything else. Cold, the silent immobility of frost, is one of these symbols:

> Et mon âme connaît le pays clair,
> Où le silence est une joie
> Qui, dans l'argent et la neige, flamboie.
> Elle connaît là-bas, la grotte en diadème,
> Belle de froid et de pendeloques de gel,
> Où le luxe des feux myriadaires est tel
> Qu'elle s'éblouit elle-même
> Et, dans son cœur, se satisfait.[4]

> [And my soul knows the serene land
> Where silence is a delight
> Which scintillates in the silvery snow.
> It knows, over there, the grotto with its lovely diadem
> Of frost and of icicles,
> Where the abundance of the myriad fires is such
> That it is dazzled
> And is inwardly satisfied.]

The poet now feels remorseful for his proud isolation:

---

[1] Les apparus dans mes chemins, 1891; Les campagnes hallucinées, 1893; Les villages illusoires, 1895; Les villes tentaculaires, 1895; Les heures claires, 1896; Les aubes, 1898; Les visages de la vie, 1899; Les vignes de la muraille, 1899.
[2] Mockel, op. cit., p. 79.
[3] Buisseret, op. cit., p. 35; Mockel, op. cit., p. 64.
[4] From Au loin, in Les apparus dans mes chemins

> J'ai été lâche et je me suis enfui
> Du monde, en mon orgueil futile.
> J'ai soulevé, sous des plafonds de nuit,
> Les marbres d'or d'une science hostile.[1]
>
> [I was a coward; I fled
> From the world in my vain pride.
> Beneath the canopy of night I raised
> The golden marbles of a hostile science.]

The characters in *Les villages illusoires* are often introverts. They are "the fishermen," side by side and silent at the edge of the darkling water, each buried in himself and ignoring his companions; "the miller," who lives alone on his hill-top, so that people are only apprized of his death because the mill no longer turns: "the snow" in its perfect stillness; "silence" brooding on the horizon; "the gravedigger" talking to his dead.

There are also poems which seem continually to give expression to the yearning for the mother. In actual fact they must have been fashioned from memories of the aunt who was Verhaeren's real mother, whose personality was enshrined in his memory, and to whom we shall have to refer once more in the next chapter. These poems have a tender and ardent atmosphere. Take, for instance, *Souvenir* in *Les visages de la vie*:

> Ceux d'autrefois à qui l'on a fait tord:
> Les doux, qui se donnèrent, sans envie. . . .
> Hélas comme au delà de l'heure humaine,
> On les aime d'un triste et régressif amour.
>
> [Those who have passed away, whom one wronged:
> The dear ones who gave themselves ungrudgingly. . . .
> Alas how, when they are no more,
> We love them with a sad and retrospective love.]

Consider, again, *L'attendue* in *Les apparus dans mes chemins*:

[1] From Saint Georges, in *Les apparus dans mes chemins*.

Elle est morte, sans bruit, tout doucement. . . .
Depuis—elle m'assiste, ainsi qu'on aide un pauvre enfant. . . .
Je suis l'ardent de sa toute présence ;
Je la voudrais plus morte encor
Pour l'évoquer avec plus de puissance !

[She died, without a sound, peacefully. . . .
Since then she has tended me as one tends a child. . . .
I am fain of her all-pervading presence ;
I would gladly have her yet more dead,
So that I might evoke her even more forcibly !]

There recur, too, the images of stagnant waters, putrefactive decomposition, and ruined fertility, which were prevalent during the crisis :

Je suis celui des pourritures grandioses
Qui s'en revient du pays mou des morts.

. . . . .

Leurs yeux, avec du sang ; leurs mains, avec des ors ;
Leurs livides phallus tordus d'efforts
Cassés—et, par les mares de la plaine,
Les vieux caillots noyés de la semence humaine.[1]

[I am the one who comes back from the land of widespread
    corruption,
The one who comes back from the flaccid realm of the dead.

. . . . .

Their bloodshot eyes ; their hands flecked with gold ;
Their livid phalluses contorted with vain
Efforts—and amid the meres of the plain
The old, drowned clots of the human seed.]

Akin to this last image is the following :

> L'heure est venue où les soirs mous
> Pèsent sur les terres envenimées,
> Où les marais visqueux et blancs,
> Dans leurs remous,

[1] From Celui du rien, in Les apparus dans mes chemins.

A longs bras lents
Brassent les fièvres empoisonnées. . . .
Et la glaise comme un paquet
Tombe dans l'eau de bile et de salive.[1]

[The hour has come when the languorous evenings
Weigh upon the envenomed lands,
Where the marshes, clammy and white,
With long, sluggish arms,
Brew in their backwaters
Poisonous fevers. . . .
And the clay falls heavily
Into the water which is but bile and spittle.]

Associated with such ideas, we are continually coming back to the meres as evil mirrors :

Près d'une mare monotone,
Dont l'eau malade réverbère
Le soir de pluie et de misère.[2]

[Near a monotonous mere,
Whose sickly water reflects
The evening of rain and wretchedness. . . .]

Here we have " the crone," the witch of the countryside :

Ame d'entêtement et de mélancholie,
Qui se penche vers des secrets perdus
Et se mire dans les *miroirs fendus*
Des vieilles choses abolies ![3]

[The very soul of obstinacy and melancholy,
Who reaches out towards lost secrets,
And gazes at her own image in the *broken mirrors*
Of old, forgotten things.]

We find other symbols of debilitated life and frustrate fertility ; beggars and cripples, flapping things, things out of joint :

[1] From Les fièvres, in Les campagnes hallucinées.
[2] From Le donneur de mauvais conseils, in Les campagnes hallucinées.
[3] From La vieille, in Les villages illusoires.

> Les lucarnes rapiécées
> Ballottent leurs loques falotes
> De vitres et de papier.[1]
>
> [The patched dormer-windows
> Flap their crazy rags
> Of glass and paper.]

In the same poem, "The Wind," we encounter a number of the images dating from the period of crisis:

> Le moulin noir fauche, sinistre,
> Le moulin noir fauche le vent. . . .
>
> Les vieux chaumes, à cropetons,
> Autour des vieux clochers d'église,
> Sont ébranlés sur leurs bâtons. . . .
>
> Les croix du cimetière étroit,
> Les bras des morts que sont ces croix
> Tombent. . . .
>
> [The black mill is reaping in sinister fashion,
> The black mill is reaping the wind. . . .
>
> The old thatched cottages, squatting
> Round the old church towers,
> Are shaken to their very beams. . . .
>
> The crosses of the narrow cemetery,
> The crosses which are really the arms of the dead,
> Fall. . . .]

Verhaeren is always fond of writing about the wind. In the poem entitled *Les saints, les morts, les arbres et le vent*, the image of the wind is mingled with that of asceticism:

> Les grand' routes tracent des *croix*
> A l'infini, à travers bois ; . . .
> *Arbres, et vents, pareils aux pélerins,*
> Arbres tristes et fous où l'orage s'accroche,
> Arbres pareils au défilé de tous les saints,

[1] From Le vent, in Les villages illusoires.

Au défilé de tous les morts
Au son des cloches, . . .
Oh ! *vos luttes et vos sanglots et vos remords*
Se débattant et s'engouffrant dans les âmes profondes ! [1]

[The high roads trace *crosses*
Ad infinitum athwart the woods ; . . .
Trees and winds resembling pilgrims,
Trees sad and mad, at grips with the storm,
Trees like the procession of all the saints,
Like the procession of all the dead
To the sound of bells, . . .
Oh ! *your struggles and your sobs and your regrets,*
Wrestling and plunging into the abysses of the souls !]

By one of those remarkable identifications that occur in dreams, the trees are confounded with the names of the saints, with the wind :

Oh ! tous ces noms de saints semés en litanies,
Tous ces arbres, là-bas, . . .
Oh ! tous ces bras invocatoires,
Tous ces rameaux éperdûment tendus
Vers on ne sait quel Christ aux horizons pendu ! . . .
Les saints, les morts, les arbres et le vent,
Dites, comme ils se confondent dans la mémoire,

[Oh, all these names of saints scattered in litanies,
All these trees over there, . . .
Oh, all these beseeching arms,
All these branches passionately stretched out
Towards some Christ gibbeted on the horizon ! . . .
The saints, the dead, the trees, and the wind,
How they are mingled in one's memory.]

In *Les soirs* we have already seen the "old oaks" struggling against the wind. We remember the "arms trying to escape their bodies" (p. 131), but the attempt was aimless, being merely made in a feverish desire to escape from oneself. Here the branches, the beseeching arms, are once more stretched out, but this time it is

[1] From Novembre, in Les vignes de ma muraille.

"towards some Christ on the horizon." We feel that a new faith, still vague, is arising ; that a new rationalisation is going to give meaning to the urges. There has been a change, and doubtless it is this change that is expressed henceforward by the appearance of the image of the *wind*, in place of the earlier images of *trees* or of the *cross*. The great difference is that the former image is animated : the wind is a force which passes by, and sweeps us along with it ; a force which ranges through the world. Later, the poet will write :

Si j'aime, admire et chante avec folie,
Le vent, . . .
C'est qu'il grandit mon être entier et c'est qu'avant
De s'infiltrer, par mes poumons et par mes pores,
Jusques aux sang dont vit mon corps,
Avec sa force rude ou sa douceur profonde,
Immensément, il a étreint le monde.[1]

[If I love, admire, and fervently sing the praises,
Of the wind, . . .
It is because the wind enlarges my whole being, and because,
Before permeating, through my lungs and through my pores,
The very blood, which is the life of my body,
It has with its rugged strength or its consummate tenderness,
Clasped the world in its titanic embrace.]

The wind expresses the deliverance from that gigantic force which was "twisted" and "gnarled" within the body of the trees, those phantom pilgrims, those great motionless marchers. The energy which was being wasted within the fenced precinct of a sterile struggle, has now been extroverted, and has taken the world for its career.[2] The breath of life has passed by. Spiritus fiat.

St. George [3] has made his appearance, serene, "flashing

---

[1] From A la gloire du vent, in La multiple splendeur.

[2] In reality, Verhaeren's struggle was still an inward one, but he provided for it an object which was outside himself. Cf. the close of Chapter Six.

[3] Saint Georges, in Les apparus dans mes chemins.

CONVERSION AND DELIVERANCE

like diamonds," fervent ; he has revealed what Albert Mockel speaks of as " the heart " :

Il vient, en bel ambassadeur
Du pays blanc, illuminé de marbres,
Où, dans le parcs, au bord des mers, sur l'arbre
De la bonté, suavement croît la douceur.

[He comes as a beautiful ambassador
From the white country that shines with marble,
Where in the parks, on the sea strand, and on the tree
Of goodness, gentleness grows peacefully.]

Now we have an unexpected and happy symptom. Whereas hitherto there has so often been an abrupt change from gold to black, St. George miraculously effects the contrary transformation :

Il sait de quels lointains je viens,
Avec quelles brumes, dans le cerveau,
Avec quels signes de couteau,
En croix noires, sur la pensée. . . .

Et lui, s'en est allé m'imposant la vaillance
Et, sur le front, la marque *en croix d'or* de sa lance,
Droit vers son Dieu, avec mon cœur.

[He knows from what distant bournes I have come,
With what fogs in my brain,
With what signs cut with a knife,
In the form of black crosses, on my thought. . . .

Then he went away, bidding me be of good courage,
And on my forehead having signed a *golden cross* with his lance,
He went straight back to his God, bearing my heart with him.]

The cross, the black cross, was the symbol of inward torment and of death. Now the cross has become golden, a symbol of life and love. (This transformation is analogous to the substitution of the wind for the dead, the saints, and the trees.) But the life and the love now to be born will no longer exhibit the fleshly luxuriance of *Les flamandes*.

They have been sublimated. Gold henceforward will take the form of the cross. Love—the poet's love for his life's companion, and his love for his fellows—will henceforward take the form of goodness, tenderness, self-sacrifice. St. George, bringing this, brings healing; he negates the images of the crisis:

> Contre les dents du dragon noir,
> Contre l'armature de lèpre et de pustules,
> Il est le glaive et le miracle.
> La charité, sur sa cuirasse, brûle
> Et son courage est la débâcle
> Bondissante de l'instinct noir. . . .
> L'aube s'ouvre, comme un conseil de confiance,
> Et qui l'écoute est le sauvé
> De son marais, où nul péché ne fut jamais lavé.
>
> [Against the teeth of the black dragon,
> Against the armour of leprosy and pustules,
> He is the sword and the miracle.
> Love glows from his breastplate,
> And his courage is the doom,
> The swift doom, of black instinct. . . .
> Dawn comes like a counsel of hope;
> He who hearkens, is saved
> From the marsh where no sin was ever washed away.]

Nevertheless, this St. George exhibits some of the characteristics of infantile regression. The apparition coming from the skies is modelled upon the image of another celestial ambassador, le comte de la Mi-Carême (The Count of Mid-Lent) who in Brabant plays the part of Father Christmas, or St. Nicholas (Santa Claus):

> Et Saint Georges, fermentant d'ors,
> Avec des plumes et des écumes,
> Au poitrail blanc de son cheval, sans mors,
> Descend.
> L'équipage diamantaire
> Fait de sa chute, un triomphal chemin. . . .
> Il m'a rempli de son essor.

CONVERSION AND DELIVERANCE

[And St. George, sparkling with gold,
And with foam and plumes
On the white breast of his unbitted charger,
Descends.
The diamond-rayed trappings
Make his descent a triumphal progress. . . .
He has filled me with his buoyancy.]

Obvious is the resemblance of this figure with that of the wonder-working dispenser of the playthings from paradise :

Au trot de son lent cheval blanc,
Passe, dans les villes du Brabant,
   Le comte de la Mi-Carême.
   Il va, là-haut, de toit en toit. . . .
Son cheval suit tous les chemins
Qu'il lui suggère, avec la main,
Et quand parfois, au loin, s'essorent
   Ses hauts galops silencieux,
   Sa sueur blanche et son écume
S'entremêlent, comme des plumes,
Aux nuages qui vont aux cieux. . . .
   Mais les enfants, eux tous, l'ont vu. . . .
   Traversant l'air superbement,
     Avec sa bête en diamant.[1]

[Trotting by on his slow white steed,
There passes, through the Brabant towns,
   The Count of Mid-Lent.
   Up there he goes, from roof to roof. . . .
His horse takes all the roads
Which the rider suggests with the hand,
And when sometimes, in the distance, there spring upward
   His soft hoof-treads in the sky,
   His white sweat and his foam
Mingle like feathers (plumes)
With the clouds trailing across the heavens. . . .
   But the children, they have all seen him. . . .
   Passing proudly through the air,
     His horse flashing with diamonds.]

---

[1] From Le comte de la Mi-Carême, in Les tendresses premières.

The perpetual recurrence of the same images and the same words is enough to prove the close kinship of the two evocations. In St. George there is, then, a return to the impressions of childhood. The innovation brings with it a waft of memories:

> Feux criblés d'or, feux rotatoires
> Et tourbillons d'astres, ses gloires,
> Aux galopants sabots de son cheval,
> Eblouissent les yeux de ma mémoire.
>
> [Flames spangled with gold, spinning flames,
> Whirlpools of stars, his glories—
> Fire struck from the galloping hoofs of his charger—
> Dazzle the eyes of my memory.]

The whole atmosphere is matutinal like that of childhood:

> Et tout effort humain n'est clair que dans l'aurore. . . .
> Le Saint Georges rapide et clair
> A traversé, par bonds de flamme,
> Le frais matin, jusqu'à mon âme.
>
> [Only at dawn is human effort serene. . . .
> St. George, swift and serene,
> Has sped with leaps of flame,
> Athwart the fresh morning, to reach my soul.]

Moreover, the image of the Virgin, whose significance we know, rises once more on the mystical horizon:

> Ce royaume, d'où se lève, reine, la Vierge,
> Il en est l'humble joie ardente—et sa flamberge
> Y vibre en ostensoir, dans l'air.
>
> [This kingdom out of which the Virgin rises as a queen,
> He is its humble, ardent joy—and his sword
> Glimmers in the air like a monstrance.]

But we must not let these images lead us astray, for the atmosphere is very different from that of the poems in which we previously encountered them. Then

CONVERSION AND DELIVERANCE

there was a mute, gracious, and gentle adoration; there was an urge towards crouching and slumbering, hands clasped, while retracing life's footsteps. At this later date, if the poet still goes back imaginatively into his childhood, it is no longer with the aim of burying himself there " belittled " (p. 123); he wants to rediscover there the primary impetus of boyhood which the subsequent introversion has arrested; he wishes to renew there his fresh vigour; he wishes to make it his starting-point for a leap towards life. There is no longer any question of gowns of coarse serge; of palms, lilies, roses, held by little fingers. St. George is a fighter. He does not dwell in the land of processions, but in the land of cavalcades. He wears armour that is blinding in its brightness; his "aureolar" sword whirls:

> Le Saint Georges, celui qui luit
> Et vient, parmi les cris de mon désir,
> Saisir
> Mes pauvres bras tendus vers sa vaillance.
>
> [St. George he who shines,
> Who comes amid the cries of my longing
> To seize hold of
> My poor arms stretched out towards his courage.]

It is this same courage which St. George enjoins on his devotee at the close of the poem (p. 167). He is vibration, lightning, "a golden tumult": "He has filled me with his vigour." Let the reader compare these words with those written by Verhaeren during the crisis: "To retire perpetually within oneself, so sombre" (see p. 109), and he will promptly realise how extensive the change has been. The profoundest forces of Verhaeren's nature have been extroverted.

At the same time, the harmony of the new tendencies has been prepared, and this finds expression in the beautiful and simple image of the golden cross. The ascetic trend, and the impetus towards life (the cross of gold), converge in the love sacrifice. This is the unexpected gift which St. George, a new Count of Mid-Lent, brings the poet from heaven; and Verhaeren welcomes this surprise with the naive astonishment of a child.

For Verhaeren, love is a discovery; the love of which he now writes is very different from the sensual passion described in *Les flamandes*. He uses quite another tone in these *Heures claires*, serene hours which bring him the simple, sober, and penetrating revelation of genuine love:

> La brise et les lèvres des feuilles
> Babillent—et effeuillent
> En nous les syllabes de leur clarté.[1]
>
> [The breeze, and the lips of the leaves,
> Murmur—and scatter
> In us the syllables of their brightness.]

Like *Saint Georges*, the poems in which this love blossoms or is presaged are still decked with regressive images:

> Dites? Dites? Serait-ce elle qui veut venir,
> Vers l'agonie en feu de mon désir,
> Non pas la mort, mais elle,
> La trépassée et la sainte que je rêve éternelle?[2]
>
> [Say! Say! Can it be she who is coming
> Towards the burning agony of my desire,
> Not death, but she,
> She who died, the saint whom I dream of as immortal?]

But here, as previously in *Saint Georges*, the regression is no more than apparent. It is an effort to reknit that which "is coming" to that which existed in the days of childhood; to unite, athwart the years when the heart was arid, these two fragments of the love life. The yearning

[1] From Les heures claires, ix.
[2] From Dans ma plaine, in Les apparus dans mes chemins.

CONVERSION AND DELIVERANCE

for the mother is too imperious to allow the heart simply to ignore it. Perhaps when this yearning is intense, deliverance from it can be secured by a man only when, to some extent, he rediscovers the mother in his beloved. Otherwise the urge towards the mother would merely be repressed; and might then, like every repressed tendency, give rise to new conflicts. If, however, the idea of the mother can be moulded on the reality of the wife, the urge towards the mother is no longer repressed but derived. Whereas hitherto this urge has had a paralysing influence, damming up or penning up the energies, it can now find an outlet towards the real:

> Doucement mère, avec ses doigts d'aurore,
> L'amante est là, qui fait éclore
> En des cerveaux de soir, la lumière fragile.[1]

> [Like a gentle mother with her auroral fingers
> The beloved is there, and she kindles
> In darkling brains a delicate light.]

This surrender to maternal arms is one of the persistent images of the new love, in which there is so much candour and simple trust. We shall find it again some years later:

> Très doucement, plus doucement encore,
> Berce ma tête entre tes bras,
> Mon front fiévreux et mes yeux las; . . .
> C'est toi qui m'es la bonne aurore. . . .[2]

> [Very gently, yet more gently,
> Cradle my head in your arms,
> My fevered brow and my weary eyes; . . .
> For me, you are the good dawn.]

Need we be surprised, after this, to find that a fresh, auroral atmosphere bathes these Serene Hours, and that this newly blossoming love resembles a new childhood?

---

[1] From Les saintes, in Les apparus dans mes chemins.
[2] From Les heures d'après-midi, vii.

Et je te sens si bien en paix de toutes choses,
Que rien, pas même un fugitif soupçon de crainte,
  Ne troublera, fût-ce un moment,
  La confiance sainte
Qui dort en nous comme un enfant repose.[1]

[I feel that you are so absolutely at peace with all things,
That nothing, not even a passing breath of fear,
  Will trouble, were it but for an instant,
  The holy confidence
Which slumbers in us as a child slumbers.]

Nor need we be surprised to find that the poet delights in reviving, as the appropriate setting for his love, the garden of the *Les tendresses premières*, with its flowers in their delicate beauty, its limpid ponds :

Voici—pareils à des baisers tombés sur terre
    De la bouche du frêle azur—
  Deux bleus étangs simples et pures,
Bordés naïvement de fleurs involontaires.

O la splendeur de notre joie et de nous-mêmes,
En ce jardin où nous vivons de nos emblêmes ![2]

[Here, like kisses fallen to earth
    From the lips of the delicate azure,
  Are two ponds, blue, simple, and pure,
Bordered artlessly with flowers unaware.

Oh the splendour of our joy and of ourselves
In this garden where we are nourished by our emblems !]

The peacock and the insects of the garden of childhood's days, the garden of paradise (pp. 42, 43), are likewise recognisable :

Au clos de notre amour, l'été se continue :
Un paon d'or, là-bas, traverse une avenue . . .
Un insecte de prisme irrite une cour de fleurs. . . .[3]

[1] From Les heures claires, iv.   [2] From Les heures claires, i.
        [3] From Les heures claires, xviii.

CONVERSION AND DELIVERANCE

[In the precinct of our love it is still summer:
A golden peacock over there is strutting down an avenue . . .
A prismatically-tinted insect teases a bevy of flowers.]

> Nos bleus et merveilleux étangs
> Tremblent et s'animent d'or miroitant ;
> Des vols émeraudés, sous les arbres, circulent.[1]

[Our blue and wondrous ponds
Are a-tremble, and quicken with gleaming gold ;
There is a flash of emerald wings among the trees.]

No longer is this a childhood desired with a morbid craving ; it is the past which has been revivified, reincorporated into the present. All the keen sensations of childhood—rivulets which have long been lost from sight in their underground channels, so that their flow could only be detected in tones muffled by distance—have found their way to the surface once more, to burst forth with renewed strength from a fresh spring. The poet, his whole being filled with joy at this deliverance, feels that love is opening the world to him :

> Et notre âme, comme agrandie, en cet éveil,
>   S'est mise à célébrer tout ce qui aime,
> Magnifiant l'amour pour l'amour même,
>   Et à chérir, divinement, d'un désir fou,
> Le monde entier qui se résume en nous.[2]

[Our soul, exalted, as it were, in this awakening,
    Devotes itself to celebrating all that loves,
Magnifying love for love's own sake,
    And to cherishing divinely, with a mad longing,
The whole world that is summed up in us.]

The need for *action* is another characteristic of one who is undergoing extroversion. Now it is natural that action should be acted rather than sung. It is in his life, above all, that Verhaeren exhibits the impulse to action —in the social activity which is human love grown active.

[1] From Les heures claires, xvii.
[2] From Les heures claires, xxviii.

The drama *Les aubes* reflects the social aspirations of the Verhaeren of that date (1898), his ardour for the idea of internationalism, his movement towards the humanist paradise of democracy, towards the city of justice. But his writings now convey, in addition, an imperious longing for action.

As for *Les saintes*, although this poem still contains vestiges of the idea of the mother, and although we might anticipate that it would be an invitation to some mystical nirvana, it is really a call to action:

> Chacune, au long de sa personnelle avenue,
> Sans rien me dire est advenue,
> Avec, en main, la fleur-merveille
> Cueillie à l'aube et qui conseille
> Des actions plus belles que tout rêve.[1]

> [Each one along her special avenue
> Without saying anything to me has come
> Bearing in her hand the wonder-flower
> Plucked at dawn, the flower which whispers of
> Actions more beautiful than any dream.]

A little later will come a poem definitely consecrated to Action:

> Lassé des mots, lassé des livres,
> Qui tiédissent la volonté,
> Je cherche, au fond de ma fierté,
> L'acte qui sauve et qui délivre.[2]

> [Weary of words, weary of books,
> Which enfeeble the will,
> I seek in the depths of my pride
> The deed which saves and sets free.]

"I seek," says the poet. In truth, action is still a wish rather than a realisation. Verhaeren admires it from afar, and would fain throw himself into the fray:

---

[1] From Les saintes, in Les apparus dans mes chemins.
[2] From L'action, in Les visages de la vie.

CONVERSION AND DELIVERANCE

La vie, elle est là-bas violente et féconde,
Qui mord, à galops fous, les grands chemins du monde.
Dans le tumulte et la poussière,
Les forts se sont pendus à sa crinière.[1]

[Life, she is over there, passionate and fecund.
Galloping madly, she eats up the great highways of the world;
Amid the tumult and the dust,
The strong cling to her mane.]

But this tumult and dust are not wholly congenial to one who is emerging from a phase of intense introversion. Action is multiform; it may be

La vie en cris ou en silence,[2]

[Life in clamour or in silence,]

and it is rather where there is silence that Verhaeren seeks the deed which will be unmistakably his own:

Et je le veux puissant et entêté,
Lucide et pur, comme un beau bloc de glace;
Sans crainte et sans fallace,
Digne de ceux
Qui n'arborent l'orgueil silencieux
Loin du monde, que pour eux-mêmes.[3]

[And I want it to be mighty and steadfast,
Lucid and pure like a beautiful block of ice;
Fearless and flawless,
Worthy of those
Who raise the flag of silent pride
Far from the world, and for themselves alone.]

This rescues the tendency to introversion; and the rescue is necessary, for the tendency must not be repressed. It is, no longer, exclusive; it is balanced by the reverse tendency, the loving tendency, outwardly directed towards fellow human beings.

[1] From L'action in Les visages de la vie.   [2] From the same poem.
[3] From the same poem.

> Et je le veux trempé, dans un baptême
> De nette et large humanité,
> Montrant à tous sa totale sincérité
> Et reculant, en un geste suprême,
> Les frontières de la bonté.
>
> [And I want it to be steeped in a baptism
> Of frank and broad humanism,
> Displaying to all its absolute sincerity,
> And, with a superb gesture, enlarging
> The frontiers of goodness.]

Social activity will be no more than an episode in Verhaeren's life. His true sphere of action will be his writings. Of course, these writings are themselves action—an action which does not lose sight of living humanity; which aspires to be counsel, precept, comfort; which, too, is social. Almost always, the poet seems to be addressing an interlocutor, or rather a crowd whose tribune or prophet he is. The abrupt imperative "Say!" with which his poems are so often and so strikingly interspersed, are a sign of this spontaneous need and fixed desire to address his fellow men, to convince them, to act on them. When we encounter this word, we feel that we have been waylaid by somebody who has an urgent message for us.

What, then, is his message? It is the message of his new *faith* in the world, in life, in human energy and human fervour; a faith which at that period was still nothing more than a stammering amazement:

> Oh! vivre et vivre et se sentir meilleur
> A mesure que bout plus fervemment le cœur;
> Vivre plus clair, dès qu'on marche en conquête;
> Vivre plus haut encor, dès que le sort s'entête
> A déssècher la sève et la force des bras;
> Rêver, les yeux hardis, à tout ce qu'on fera
> De pur, de grand, de juste, en ces Chanaans d'or,
> Qui surgiront, quand même, au bout du saint effort.[1]

---

[1] From *L'action*, in *Les visages de la vie*.

[Oh, to live and to live, and to feel oneself better
In proportion as the heart boils more fervently;
To live more serenely when one marches to victory;
To live yet more intensely when fate obstinately endeavours
To dry up the sap and the strength of one's arms;
To dream, with bold eyes, of all that one will do
That is pure, is great, is just, in these golden Canaans
Which will appear, whatever happens, at the close of the blessèd struggle.]

The poet is intoxicated by the *crowd*, whose fever works like a ferment in the towns. He loves to feel himself lifted by this surging wave, sustained by this stormy clamour. The fervour which he now experiences is the joy of extroversion:

> Et tout à coup je m'apparais celui
> Qui s'est, hors de soi-même, enfui
> Vers le sauvage appel des forces unanimes.[1]
>
> [And all at once I seem to myself one
> Who has fled out of himself
> Towards the fierce call of unanimous forces.]

Henceforward, the *crowd*, the *town*, become for Verhaeren symbols of the extroversion which is still ebullient, disordered, "tumultuous"; but in which, through the chaos, he feels the elaboration of a new equilibrium. And when, in the modern town and its fever, he sees that there is being forged for humanity, too, a new equilibrium and a new faith, he subconsciously identifies this turning-point in the history of mankind with the turning-point in his own life. He uses one to express the other, and this is what gives so much intensity to his poem, *The Crowd*:

> Oh! dis, sens-tu qu'elle est belle et profonde,
> Mon cœur,
> Cette heure
> Qui chante et crie au cœur du monde?[2]

[1] From La foule, in Les visages de la vie.
[2] From the same poem.

[Oh, say, do you feel how beautiful and profound,
O my heart,
Is this hour
Which is singing and crying in the heart of the world ?]

Perhaps it is. But what is above all beautiful and profound is the hour which has struck and is singing in the heart of the poet, the decisive hour of his life, the hour pregnant with the future. The town materialises around him all the ferment of his life. In an anguished intoxication, he discerns there the image of his former complexes, which are resurging from the depths of his being :

Des gens hagards courent avec des torches,
Une rumeur de mer s'engouffre, au fond des porches,
Murs, enseignes, maisons, palais, gares,
Dans le soir fou, devant mes yeux, s'effarent. . . .
Un cadran luit, couleur de sang, au front des tours.[1]

[Haggard folks are running with torches ;
A noise as of the sea is swallowed into the depths of the porches ;
Walls, sign-boards, houses, palaces, and railway stations,
In the mad evening, before my eyes, are affrighted. . . .
Red as blood, a clock-face shines from the front of the towers.]

But he sees also in the town the image of to-morrow's faith, which is being elaborated within him, and which is filling the void left by the loss of the old faith.

Que t'importent et les vieilles sagesses
Et les soleils couchants des dogmes sur la mer ;
Voici l'heure qui bout de sang et de jeunesse,
Voici la violente et merveilleuse ivresse
D'un vin si fort que rien n'y semble amer.
Un vaste espoir, venu de l'inconnu, déplace
L'équilibre ancien dont les âmes sont lasses ;
La nature paraît sculpter
Un visage nouveau à son éternité. . . .

[1] From La foule, in Les visages de la vie.

Le temps est là des débâcles et des miracles
Et des gestes d'éclair et d'or
Là-bas, au loin, sur les Thabors.[1]

[What matter to you the old wisdoms,
The setting suns of the dogmas as they sink into the sea?
This is the hour that boils with blood and with youth;
This is the fierce and wondrous frenzy
Of a wine so strong that nothing seems bitter in it.
A giant hope, hailing from the unknown, replaces
The old balance of which our souls are weary;
Nature seems to be fashioning
A new countenance for its eternity. . . .

Come has the time of crashes and of miracles,
Of manifestations of lightning and of gold,
Over there in the distance, on the Tabors.]

These images of Mount Tabor and (a moment ago) of Canaan are instructive. The search for a faith is going on, a faith which can satisfy Verhaeren's strongly religious temperament, and also the faith of a prophet who is to be a lawgiver to mankind. In a lovely carol abounding in the familiar Catholic symbols, the poet describes the mysterious dawning of this new faith, which is to be knitted to the old faith of his childhood's days just as the new love was knitted to the early affections, the wife to the mother, St. George to the Count of Mid-Lent. In this case, doubtless, as in the others, it is thus that the new can be born without giving rise to conflicts, inasmuch as it assimilates the old instead of repressing it:

> Oh! vous, les gens, les vieilles gens,
> Qui regardez passer dans vos villages
> Les empereurs et les bergers et les rois mages
> Et leurs bêtes dont le troupeau les suit,
> Allumez d'or vos cœurs et vos fenêtres,
> Pour voir, enfin, par travers la nuit,
> Ce qui, depuis mille et mille ans,
> S'efforce à naître.[2]

[1] From La foule, in Les visages de la vie.
[2] From Décembre, in Les vignes de ma muraille.

[Oh you people, you old people,
Who see passing through your villages
The emperors and the shepherds and the magian kings
And their beasts of burden which follow them,
Light up with gold your hearts and your windows
To see at length athwart the night
That which, for thousands and thousands of years,
Has been pressing to be born.]

But this faith is merely "pressing to be born"; it is "some Christ on the horizon." We are in an epoch of vague preparation; in an hour that is still critical, and palpitating like a drama:

On sent qu'un même instant est maître
D'épanouir ou d'écraser ce qui va naître.[1]

[One feels that the hour is ripe
Either for the blossoming or for the crushing of that which is about to be born.]

These words apply equally to humanity-at-large and to the poet—to the stage which both have reached. The condensation explains how it is that at this period of his life Verhaeren was enabled to give so magnificent a poetic expression to the anguish of the modern mind. We have one more example of the way in which an objective drama can only be organised into a work of art when its roots draw nourishment from the life of a kindred subjective drama.

Although the new ideal is still in the throes of birth, Verhaeren himself has definitely regained contact with life, and he is filled with wonder at the fact. He already feels the impetus which may be termed faith in life; joy in recovered health, and renewed confidence.

At the date when *Les flamandes* was written, life was a succulent and fleshy fruit. In addition to the symbolism

[1] From La foule, in Les visages de la vie.

of gold, Verhaeren was fond of using for it the emblem of a laden espalier:

Les forts montent la vie ainsi qu'un escalier,
Sans voir d'abord que les femmes sur leur passage
Tendent vers eux leurs seins, leurs fronts et leurs visages,
Et leurs bras élargis en branches d'espalier.[1]

[The strong mount life as we mount a stairway,
Without seeing at first that the women whom they pass
Are stretching out towards them their breasts, their foreheads, and their faces,
And their arms that spread like the branches of an espalier.]

To-day the espalier has become a *trellised vine*. Life is less greedy, but more intoxicating than before. The image of the vine is Verhaeren's favourite during the continuance of the frenzied desire to rediscover life. The idea of the trellis is even incorporated into the title of one of the collections, *Les vignes de ma muraille* (the vines on my wall). But the poem *L'ivresse* in *Les visages de la vie* is doubtless the most exalted of all:

J'étais entré dans ce caveau, l'âme légère,
Uniquement séduit, par la beauté des verres
Et la folie et son levain,
Qui sommeillent, au fond du vin,
Quand l'ivresse puissante et débordée,
Fondant le monde, au feu qu'était mon cœur,
Grandit soudain jusques à l'infini, l'idée
Que pauvre et nul je m'étais faite du bonheur.

[I had gone into this wine cellar, light of heart,
Attracted merely by the beauty of the glasses,
And by the madness and its yeast
Which slumber in the depths of the wine,
When the mighty and surging intoxication,
Melting the world, at the furnace which my heart was,
Magnified of a sudden to an infinite degree
The paltry notion I had formed of happiness.]

[1] From Hommage, in Les bords de la route.

In the same poem we find a transition to other images, those of ships setting out on a voyage, and those of the sea :

> Toute la vie éclose, en ces pays du Rhin,
> Tenait et s'éclairait, dans le raisin :
> C'était pour lui que les monts étaient verts
> L'été brûlant, les gars joyeux, le fleuve ouvert
> Aux navires passant, joufflus de voiles,
> Et s'éloignant, la nuit, sous des grappes d'étoiles.

> [All the life that burgeons in these Rhenish lands
> Was retained in and shone forth from the grape :
> It was for the grape that the hills were green,
> The summer ardent, the young folk gay, the river open
> To the passage of ships with bellying sails
> And setting out at night beneath the clusters of stars.]

The last image revives a memory of childhood, for we read at the beginning of *Liminaire* in *Les tendresses premières* :

> Je me souviens du village près de l'Escaut,
>   D'où l'on voyait les grands bateaux
> Passer, ainsi qu'un rêve empanaché de vent
>   Et merveilleux de voiles,
>   Le soir, en cortège, sous les étoiles.

> [I recall the village on the banks of the Scheldt,
>   From which one could see the great ships
> Passing by, like dreams plumed with wind,
>   Wondrous with sails,
>   In the evening, a procession beneath the stars.]

In the foregoing reminiscence, the garden is framed in this vision and that of the factory, both of which contrast with its old-fashioned and secluded peace. For the child, the ships, like the factory, represented the outer world. The ships were starting on their way to the great world ; it was natural that their image should be revived (like that of the factory) at the moment when the poet was undergoing extroversion, and when he too was setting out for the conquest of the world. *Les visages de la vie* (Aspects of Life) ends with the poem *Vers la mer*, a poem which seems to give the signal for departure. Intoxication still reigns over this sea, for it is sparkling with " grappes de joyaux " (clusters of jewels). Soon, in his Tumultuous Forces, the poet will not close with " Towards the Sea," but with " At Sea " ; and still later, his Sovran Rhythms will close with the poem The Ship. He who is to-day about to sail, will then have gained the open sea, and will voyage in a victorious calm :

Nous avancions, tranquillement, sous les étoiles ;
La lune oblique errait autour du vaisseau clair. . . .
Il tanguait sur l'effroi, la mort et les abîmes,
D'accord avec chaque astre et chaque volonté,
Et maîtrisant ainsi les forces unanimes,
Semblait dompter et s'asservir l'éternité.

[We moved forward quietly beneath the stars ;
The slanting moonbeams shone around the bright ship. . . .
Which pitched and sended over terror, death, and the abysses,
Which was in harmony with every star and every will,
And which, thus mastering the blended forces,
Seemed to tame and subjugate eternity.]

We have not yet reached this stage, but the ship has weighed anchor ; she is making for the offing, life is opening up, life is God.

L'Eternelle, qui est la vie.[1]

[The Eternal, who is life.]

The word " vie " seems at this date to be a magic syllable for Verhaeren. He is intoxicated by it ; positively haunted. It is not improbable that this is why the syllable *vi* recurs with such strange insistence in the titles of the

[1] From L'attente, in *Les visages de la vie*.

poems of this period: V*i*llages illusoires, V*i*lles tentaculaires, V*i*sages de la v*i*e, V*i*gnes de ma muraille.[1]
Owing to the operation of the tendency with which we are familiar, pain, the voluptuousness of suffering, is an invariable element of the joy of life:

> Et je t'aime d'autant que je te fais du mal
> Et que je souffre aussi, ma tant martyrisée,
> Par tes regards et tes pensées.[2]
>
> [And I love you in proportion as I hurt you,
> And as I am hurt too, my tortured one,
> By your looks and your thoughts.]
>
> Au fond de la torture, on voit des yeux sourire:
> Nous sommes tous des Christs qui embrassons nos croix.[3]
>
> [In the deeps of torture, we see smiling eyes;
> We are all of us Christs embracing the cross.]

This is why the "vine" is "twisted" like the ascetic trees; "torture" or "torment" always arouse in Verhaeren the frenzy of intoxication. He pictures a ship laden with Sirens. Here we have an image which condenses all the foregoing, and summarises what has just been said concerning this hour of intoxication.

---

[1] Verhaeren is an artist in words, and a special study of auditory symbolism might be devoted to his writings. I fear, however, that psychology, in its present stage of development, would not take us very far along this path. We have already noted (Chapter III, p. 114) the frequent recurrence of the consonants c (k), t, and l. In the titles of his poems, Verhaeren has a fondness for a group formed by the liquid l and another consonant, preferably c; or for l with the vowel u: Les débâc*l*es, Les campagnes ha*ll*ucinées, Les forc*e*s tumu*l*tueuses, La mu*l*tiple sp*l*endeur. Note also the recurrence of the syllable *flam* from the first collection, Les *flam*andes, by way of Les *flam*beaux noires to Les *flam*mes hautes. There must be something more than coincidence here, but it would be hazardous to rush headlong into an interpretation.

[2] From L'amour, in Les visages de la vie.

[3] From La joie, in Les visages de la vie.

CONVERSION AND DELIVERANCE

>Les Sirènes, couvertes d'or,
>Tordaient, comme des vignes,
>Les lignes
>Sinueuses de leurs corps.[1]
>
>[The Sirens, covered with gold,
>Twisted like vines
>The sinuous lines
>Of the bodies.]

Let us pause awhile to consider this poem about the Sirens, and we shall learn more from it. It represents the first appearance in Verhaeren's writings of the figures of classical mythology, and therefore marks a turning-point in his art. It is the herald of Pegasus and Venus in *Les forces tumultueuses*; of Hercules and Perseus in *Les rythmes souverains*.

>Deux vieux marins des mers du nord
>S'en revenaient, un soir d'automne,
>De la Sicile et de ses îles mensongères,
>Avec un peuple de Sirènes
>A bord.
>
>[Two old sailors, men of the northern main,
>Came back home again, one autumn evening,
>From Sicily and its delusive isles,
>With a company of Sirens
>On board.]

The Sirens are creatures of sunlit and delusive Sicily—creatures of Mediterranean mythology. That is why they seem strangers at first "sous un vent morne et monotone" (under a mournful and monotonous wind) and amid the spindrift of the northern seas. The moody dwellers on the coast do not even hear their song:

>Ils ne comprirent rien à ce grand songe
>Qui enchantait la mer de ses voyages,
>Puisqu'il n'était pas le même mensonge
>Qu'on enseignait, dans leur village.

[1] From Au nord, in Les vignes de ma muraille.

[They understood nothing of this great dream
Which delights the sea with its journeyings,
For it was not the same fable
That was taught in their village.]

Verhaeren seems here to be astonished at his own failure to realise sooner how an ever-young poetry is breathed by these ancient myths. For his part, he has wanted to create other " fables," other myths, with the types of " his village " (think of the Illusory Villages). It would be a pity for him to renounce this highly individual art, this art racy of the soil. Consequently he does not renounce it; but he glimpes another art, more objective, and bearing a more universal stamp. It is towards such an art that he is now evolving. Such is the art in which he wishes to renew his being—" se retremper " (to resteep himself), as he writes elsewhere :

Sur des récifs cabrés en cavales qui fument, . . .
Le corps baigné dans l'or, les Sirènes s'appellent. . . .
Dites, les voix des soirs légendaires en mer !
Et comme on les entend
Là-bas, au Nord, le cœur battant !
Et comme on va, vers leur folie,
Avec la joie ou la melancholie
De retremper son être en ces brassins de vie
Qui fermentent encor aux confins de la mer.[1]

[From the reefs, rearing like steaming mares, . . .
Their bodies bathed in gold, the Sirens are calling one to another. . . .
Think of the voices of the fabled evenings at sea !
How one hears them,
Over there in the north, with beating heart !
And how one goes towards their madness
With joy or with sadness,
To resteep one's being in these vats of life
Which are still fermenting at the sea's farthest bounds.]

Between one poem and the other, a long road had been traversed. In the former, the northerners did not

[1] From L'eau, in Les visages de la vie.

hear the Sirens. Now, not only do they hear the nymphs, but they answer to the call. The resurrection of the myths is at hand.

It is interesting to note that the use of the symbols of the North and of the South as representing barbaric art and classical art respectively has been stressed by Vodoz [1] in his critique of Victor Hugo's *Le mariage de Roland*, a poem expressing that which in Hugo, too, may be termed the acceptance of the classical. Nothing can be more natural than the use of such symbolism, especially in view of the fact that the romanticists have themselves set up "northern poesy" in opposition to "southern poesy." This has been common form since the days of Chateaubriand and Madame de Staël. Moreover, was it not the Italian sunshine which opened Goethe's eyes to the fresh youth of classical beauty.

Very natural, too, was it that the moral evolution of Verhaeren, like that of Hugo, should have brought an aesthetic evolution in its train, should have led the poet to search for a more objective art, for an art that was less exclusively internal. From this point of view the series of *Les villages illusoires*, for instance, already marks a notable transformation. These poems have been termed the master work of the symbolist school. Unquestionably, they are among the most richly symbolic of Verhaeren's poems. Preeminently they fulfil Mallarmé's definition of the symbol, as something that simultaneously conveys images, sentiments, and superposed ideas. We have already seen how rich a field for analysis is offered by *Le sonneur* and *Le passeur d'eau*. The reader will perhaps have been surprised that we did not say more about this collection. But de Smet,[2] who has a special admiration for *Les villages illusoires*, and who holds that in these poems we can find the germs of all the subsequent works, has made a detailed analysis of them, to which little

[1] Vide supra, pp. 33 and 155.
[2] Emile Verhaeren, sa vie et ses œuvres, vol. ii, passim.

need be added here. He has shown how the Illusory Villages issued from real villages, and above all from Verhaeren's native village; and how these images, transmuted by a seer's emotions, served for the expression of a moral or a social idea. What we have to point out here is the evolution which this collection obviously marks in the poet's art. It manifests itself by the appearance of the moral and social idea, and by the convergence of the symbols in the direction of this idea. In the days of *Les flamandes* and *Les moines*, Verhaeren inclined towards a plastic and objective art, which could only serve to symbolise internal dramas involuntarily and almost unconsciously. During the crisis, on the other hand, the poems were nothing but symbols of what was going on within, images arising in many cases out of the ostensible incoherence of dreams and nightmares, in accordance with the imperious laws of the emotional life and of the unconscious, and guided solely by the logic of feeling. The illusory villages are symbols of the inner life, and the poet is well aware that in them he is giving expression to himself by means of these evocations of childhood. At the same time, however, they are intended to symbolise an objective idea: that of a desperate persistence in The Bellringer; and that of a stubborn hope in The Ferryman, who, despite all, continues to hold the green reed between his teeth; that of destiny thricefold great, past, present, and future, in The Ropemakers [1] (brethren of the Parcae of classical mythology) who are twisting a rope of strands coming from the far horizon; the idea of menacing patience and of the approaching social revolution in The Blacksmith.[2] These are symbols with two faces, one turned inwards and the other outwards. They are complete symbols, endowed with all the richness of the dream, but superadding the richness of thought. This more objective art is already dawning in some of the poems of the collection entitled *Les flambeaux noirs*

[1] **Les cordiers.** [2] Le forgeron.

(The Books, The Numbers), and in some of those in the collection entitled *Les campagnes hallucinées*. But it is above all in *Les villages illusoires* that this duplex symbolism comes to fruition. The poems in that collection form, as it were, the pivot of Verhaeren's art. In his subsequent writings, the elements of objectivity and of thought will gain ground, as the poet turns towards a more classical ideal. At the same time, the visions will lose much of their hallucinatory force, their dreamlike aspect, their "dusky and ruddy fog"[1]—all that has hitherto been so characteristic of Verhaeren. We are entitled to regret what we are losing, even while we rejoice at what we are gaining. But we are passing from the North to the South, and we must not expect to do so without experiencing a change of climate.

The poems which, in my opinion, most potently reflect the period of "conversion and deliverance" are those contained in the two collections entitled *Les campagnes hallucinées* and *Les villes tentaculaires*. To these may be added *Les aubes*, a drama which portrays the same conflicts, and shows a blazing countryside (as in *Les meules qui brûlent* in *Les villages illusoires*) from which the wretched villagers have to seek refuge in the towns. It is well to note that this drama concludes with an unexpected reconciliation at the very moment when a similar reconciliation between opposing forces was taking place in Verhaeren's soul.

Let us linger for a while among these Countrysides and these Towns. We have here a fine example of a symbol with two faces: on the surface it is the exodus of the people from the country into the industrial towns; within, it is Verhaeren's "conversion," the poet's sublime vision of a new life and a new art.

Les campagnes hallucinées conjure up from beginning to end the images of the crisis. But these images are

[1] Brume fuligineuse et rouge.

now made so objective as to express the crisis taking place in the countryside where poverty and depopulation were increasing to an alarming extent. Though this objectivation is important, in that it is a happy sign of Verhaeren's psychic evolution, we should be grossly misled were we to see athwart the poetic vision nothing more than the problems of the agrarian crisis and of industrial civilisation.

"Verhaeren is a poet, not an economist. If, when describing the depopulation of the Belgian countryside, he has failed to mention the successful efforts of those engaged in ameliorating agricultural conditions, we are not entitled to surmise that he has ignored this betterment. The truth is that, on emerging from his crisis of profound pessimism, Verhaeren was still allured by gloomy ideas; he wished, at that time, to depict great sorrows, and great sorrows only. One who fails to recognise the fact is incapable of passing a just opinion on Verhaeren."[1]

Excellent! But Smet has not said all there is to say on the matter. We have to show how far the images of *Les campagnes hallucinées* still express Verhaeren's own crisis, how they renew and perfect the images of *Les débâcles* or of *Les soirs*.

First there are the symbols of sterility familiar to us as early as *Les plaines mornes* in *Les flamandes*.

> De pauvres clos, ourlés de haies
> Ecartèlent leur sol couvert de plaies ;
> De pauvres clos, de pauvres fermes,
> Les portes lâches. . . .
> Ni lin, ni blé, ni frondaisons, ni germes. . . .[2]
>
> [Sorry enclosures, hemmed in by hedges,
> Their soil quartered, and covered with wounds ;
> Sorry enclosures, sorry farmsteads,
> The doors hanging loose. . . .
> No flax, no corn, no leaves, no seeds. . . .]

[1] Smet, op. cit., vol. ii. p. 67, note.
[2] From *Les plaines*, in *Les campagnes hallucinées*.

CONVERSION AND DELIVERANCE

Le sol et les germes sont condamnées.[1]

[The soil and the seeds are doomed.]

These seeds fated to be poisoned or doomed recall the cross on the cow's forehead (p. 86), and many other images of ruined fecundity.

Quelqu'un a dû frapper l'été
De mauvaise fécondité,
Le blé, très dru, ne fut que paille. . . .
Le semeur d'or des mauvais germes,
Aux jour d'avril dorant les fermes,
Les vieux l'ont tous senti passer.[2]

[Some one must have struck the summer
With an evil fecundity,
For though the corn grew thickly it was nothing but straw. . . .
The golden sower of bad seed,
During the April days gilding the farms,
All the old folk felt him passing by.]

In these symbols of seeds which have brought forth no fruit there are condensed the havoc wrought by rank fleshliness, and the introversion of instinct. It is interesting to find the same symbols in one of the classical myths relating to introversion, the myth of Proserpina carried off by Pluto:

Ruricolasque boves leto dedit arvaque jussit
Fallere depositum vitiataque semina fecit,[3]

we read in Ovid. The oxen die, the fields bring forth no crops, the seeds are blighted.

As we have seen, this "introversion of instinct" is a deviation of part of the sexual energy towards the inner life (consequently it is a process of desexualisation). The deviation is sometimes expressed by "inverted actions,"

---

[1] From Chanson de fou, in Les campagnes hallucinées.
[2] From Pèlerinage, in Les campagnes hallucinées.
[3] Ovid, Metamorphoses, v. 479-480.

and occasionally, as we saw during the crisis, by directly sexual symbols.

> Le Satan d'or des champs brûlés
> Et des fermiers ensorcelés
> Qui font des croix de la main gauche.[1]

> [The golden Satan of the parched fields
> And of the bewitched farmers
> Who make the sign of the cross with the left hand.]

The symbol of "inverted actions" is here closely associated with the "sterile seeds" in the poem entitled *Pèlerinage*. In the following extract the symbol approximates to the directly sexual. All these symbols are intimately akin.

> Sur sa butte que le vent gifle,
> Il tourne et fauche et ronfle et siffle,
> Le vieux moulin des péchés vieux. . . .
> Tous passèrent par le moulin. . . .
> Les conjureurs de sort et les sorcières
> Que vont trouver les filles-mères ; . . .
> Ceux qui n'aiment la chair que si le sang
> Gicle aux yeux, frais et luisant ; . . .
> Les vagabonds qui habitent des fosses
> Avec leurs filles qu'ils engrossent ; . . .
> Les fous qui choisissent des bêtes
> Pour assouvir leur rut et ses tempêtes. . . .
> Ceux qui projettent leurs prières
> Croix à rebours et paroles contraires, . . .
> Tous passèrent par le moulin.[2]

> [On a hillock buffeted by the wind,
> The mill turns and sickles and snorts and whistles,
> The old mill of the old sins. . . .
> All of them have gone through the mill. . . .
> The fortune-tellers, and the witches
> Whom the unmarried mothers seek out ; . . .
> Those who love the flesh only when the blood
> Gushes visibly forth, fresh and lustrous ; . . .
> The vagabonds who live in the ditches
> With their girls whom they make with child ; . . .

---

[1] From Pèlerinage, in Les campagnes hallucinées.
[2] From Le Péché, in Les campagnes hallucinées.

CONVERSION AND DELIVERANCE

> The madmen who choose the beasts
> To appease the rut of their passions. ...
> Those who offer up their prayers
> With inverted crosses and words said backwards, ...
> All of them have gone through the mill.]

These images are but variations on the theme of "sterile" or "poisonous" seeds. We read in the same poem :

> Ils sont montés—et quand ils sont redescendus. ...
> Chargés de farine et de grain
> Par groupes noirs de pélerins,
> Les grand' routes chariaient toutes,
> Infiniment comme des veines,
> Le sang du mal parmi les plaines.
> Et le moulin tournait au fond des soirs,
> La grande croix de ses bras noirs.

> [They went up, and when they came down again. ...
> Carrying flour and grain
> In black groups of pilgrims,
> All the highways bore along
> Like arteries, unceasingly,
> The evil blood athwart the plains.
> And the mill turned in the depth of the evenings
> The great cross of its black arms.]

The last image recalls The Mill in *Les soirs*, which is now further elucidated. The mill, which was the symbol of sensual health in *Les flamandes* (with the "miller" and the "flour"), has ever since those days expressed ruined health, the introversion of instinct, and, possibly, introversion in its general sense. To this is added the "cross" of its black arms wherein is expressed the whole drama of the crisis, which finds so tragical a portrayal in the beautiful poem in *Les soirs*.

Le péché should be compared with *Le donneur de mauvais conseils*. But we do not wish to make any further analysis of the crisis, and this we should be constrained to do were we to pursue this line of investigation.

We see, however, that *Les campagnes hallucinées* is flesh and bone of *Les soirs*, and the poems in the former collection can be fully comprehended only when brought into relation with the latter. Then such songs as the *Chansons de fou,* incoherent and inexplicable at a first reading, can be interpreted word by word, and offer us a content of surprisingly full meaning. The first of these songs, for instance, to our great surprise, is a remodelling of the episodes of the Clockmaker in Early Affections— from the huge, haunting eye

> Avec des yeux plus grands que n'est grande sa tête.
>
> [With eyes bigger than its head.]

down to the three lady-gnomes

> Nous, les trois fous,
> Qui épousons, au clair de lune,
> Trois folles dames sur la dune.
>
> [We, the three madmen,
> Who wedded, in the moonlight,
> Three mad ladies on the dunes.]

Nor is the episode of the gnomes asleep in the clock-cases forgotten:

> J'ai su qu'il habitait un bouge
> Avec des morts dans ses armoires.
>
> [I knew he dwelt in a hovel
> With dead people in his cupboards.]

All this is interlaced with images of "flour," of "mills," and of "sterile seeds":

> Car nous avons pour génitoires
> Deux cailloux.
>
> [For we have as testicles
> Two pebbles.]

CONVERSION AND DELIVERANCE

The last of the Songs of Madmen condenses the ruin of the flesh with the loss of faith. We have already made acquaintance with " rodents " as symbols of a gnawing and threatening evil. In *Les flamandes*, for instance, " all the little mice were as still as could be " (p. 87). Here the rats " reverberate in the bell " and " eat the host," and we are reminded of the bell in *Le sonneur*, and the sacred wafer trampled under foot in *La révolte*.

We need not prolong the game of guessing riddles. These examples will suffice to show how *Les campagnes hallucinées* may be interpreted, and how the countrysides are still " personal landscapes."

Other " personal landscapes " are constituted by the Tentacular Towns which henceforward take Verhaeren in thrall. They are the symbol of his extroversion, of his social activities, of his growing faith in human effort, of the labours of to-day " pointed " toward the future. Here we encounter the symbolical acceptance of the factory. The poem entitled *Les usines* (Factories) has earned well-merited celebrity ; it is in fact the focal point of the *Villes tentaculaires* ; the great industrial town is the limitless enlargement of the small factory of the poet's childhood. This acceptance is fraught with anguish, it does not occur without an inward struggle, without a secret reserve. There is, in these hymns to the real, an indescribable desolation :

Et des files, toujours les mêmes, de lanternes
Menant l'égoût des abattoirs vers les casernes.[1]

[And always the same rows of street lamps,
Guiding the effluent of the slaughterhouses towards the barracks.]

But there is also an effort to overcome this disgust, a constant will towards enthusiasm. A resigned acceptance of the inevitable does not suit Verhaeren's tempera-

[1] From Les usines, in Les villes tentaculaires.

ment; he wishes for, and he will through his own effort achieve, the joyful acceptance of the new life against which the old Adam within the poet is still in revolt. Verhaeren will come to love the trains which were once so like death to him:

> L'esprit des campagnes était l'esprit de Dieu;
> Il eut la peur de la recherche et des révoltes,
> Il chut; et le voici qui meurt, sous les essieux
> Et sous les chars en feu des nouvelles récoltes.[1]

> [The spirit of the countryside was the spirit of God;
> It was alarmed by research and by revolts,
> It has fallen; and now it is dying beneath the axles
> And beneath the fiery chariots of new harvests.]

The promise which the future holds for him will prevent Verhaeren from regretting the past:

> Le rêve ancien est mort et le nouveau se forge. . . .
> Et qu'importe les maux et les heures démentes,
> Et les cuves de vice où la cité fermente,
> Si quelque jour, du fond des brouillards et des voiles,
> Surgit un nouveau Christ, en lumière sculpté,
> Qui soulève vers lui l'humanité
> Et la baptise au feu de nouvelles étoiles?[2]

> [The old dream is dead and a new dream is being forged. . . .
> What matter, then, the ills and the frenzied hours,
> And the vats of vice wherein the towns ferment,
> If one day, surging up from the depths of the fogs and the mists,
> A new Christ arises, sculptured in light,
> Who will lift humanity towards him
> And will baptise it in the fire of new stars.]

Les campagnes hallucinées marks a period when *pity* makes its appearance in Verhaeren's work. Though this collection of poems is inspired by the poet's personal sufferings, he makes use of these sufferings to express those endured by his fellow mortals; thus he comes to

---

[1] From Vers le futur, in Les villes tentaculaires.
[2] From L'âme de la ville, in Les villes tentaculaires.

CONVERSION AND DELIVERANCE 199

understand the anguish of his neighbour. Condensation, which is characteristic of symbolisation, here acts as a sympathetic agent; by mingling the suffering of mankind with the suffering of the poet, condensation reaches a point where it is impossible to differentiate the individual from the general. The understanding of this essential unity in suffering has created pity—and Verhaeren's commiseration embraces the wretchedness of poverty-stricken people and unhappy beasts :

> Et leurs troupeaux rêches et maigres
> Par les chemins râpés et par les sablons aigres,
> Egalement sont les chassés
> Aux coups de fouet inépuisés
> Des famines qui exterminent :
> Moutons dont la fatigue à tout caillou ricoche,
> Bœufs qui meuglent vers la mort proche,
> Vaches hydropiques et lourdes
> Aux pis vides commes des gourdes
> Et les ânes, avec la mort crucifiée
> Sur leurs côtes sacrifiées.[1]

> [And the flocks, rough-coated and thin,
> Along the worn roads and over the harsh sands,
> Are likewise driven
> By the unceasing lash
> Of exterminating famine :
> Sheep whose weariness rebounds from every stone,
> Oxen lowing towards imminent death,
> Heavy, dropsical cows
> With udders empty as gourds,
> And donkeys, with death crucified
> On their tortured flanks.]

Such lines show Verhaeren's kinship to other French poets of pity, to Michelet, to Hugo. This "universal pity" (to which de Smet devotes an admirable chapter in his book on the Belgian poet [2]) is henceforward to be Verhaeren's inseparable companion. It is, indeed, a

---

[1] From Le départ, in Les campagnes hallucinées.
[2] Smet, op. cit., vol. ii. pp. 286 et seq.

"resurrection of the heart." The moment of realisation is, however, likewise a moment of expectation. We may quote in this connexion the poem depicting the vision of the silent women who are weaving patient goodness in the depths of their secret isle:

> Très doucement, avec la douce patience,
> En leurs rêves d'obédience,
> Dès l'aube, elles tressent pieusement
> Les tapis blancs que le silence
> Met sous les pieds du dévouement. . . .
> Elles tissent avec la laine
> L'imperméable vêtement
> Qui fait le tour de la misère humaine.[1]

> [Very gently, with gentle patience,
> In their dreams of obedience,
> As soon as day dawns, they piously weave
> The white carpets which silence
> Spreads under the feet of devotion. . . .
> They weave with wool
> The impermeable garment
> Which goes the round of human wretchedness.]

But there is no landing place as yet on the island; it lies in the sea like a promise:

> J'ai navigué autour de l'île,
> En ma barque, depuis quels jours,
> Vers l'une d'elles qui toujours
> Sans regarder s'attarde et file.

> [I sailed round the island
> In my boat for many a day,
> Heading towards one of them who always,
> Without looking up, lingered behind and span.]

But strength must be found to rescue the spinner who is enchained on the island by fate, and who is herself, as it were, a goddess of fate. It is Andromeda, who on a day to come will be rescued by Perseus.[2] We

---

[1] From Celle de l'île, in Les vignes de ma muraille.
[2] Rythmes souverains. Vide infra pp. 283-4.

may see in this the symbol of the soul, which is even now, and in its own despite, enchained by early loves and a yearning for the mother. In order to complete the rescue we must delve into the profoundest depths of the subconscious. Verhaeren was greatly assisted in the task by working at his three dramas, *Le cloître*, *Philippe II*, and *Hélène de Sparte*. In his poems we have witnessed his struggle to hitch his soul and his passion on to new objects. This constitutes the positive side of the work of deliverance. There is also, however, the negative side, and that is to detach the soul from the internal objects, the personal objects, which still hold it captive. In order to do this it is necessary to reveal even more clearly that which slumbers in the subconscious. This is the part—an involuntary one—played by the dramas.

CHAPTER FIVE

AN OEDIPUS TRILOGY

IN the past, critics have been unjust in their condemnation of Verhaeren's dramas, and it may be that this injustice will continue. There is a very simple reason for the unfairness: Verhaeren is a poet, a lyrical artist; therefore it is concluded, or at least implied, that he cannot be a playwright. Such a method of reasoning, by no means uncommon, arises out of the essentially prosaic conception of the drama which it is the fashion nowadays to adopt. Lyricism on the stage is looked upon at best as no more than the hors d'œuvre. In spite of Hugo's *Les burgraves* (which by the way had to await the poet's centenary celebration before it came into its own), and in spite of Wagner's stupendous efforts, the eyes of the critics have not yet been opened. They speak to us of " the classical drama " in connexion with the most prosaic of plays, so long as the muscles of the work in question appear to be strenuously directed towards action. But if we go deeper into matters, we have to ask ourselves whether this is in reality their criterion of the classical. Of course it is not. Having decided that the romantic drama is poetry, they conclude, by a singularly illogical method of reasoning, that classical drama cannot be poetry. Lack of lyricism, or rather, lack of poesy, is their true criterion of "classical drama." A more delicious piece of incongruity could hardly be imagined. How can they have forgotten that classical drama in the highest sense of the term, i.e. Greek drama, arose and took birth from music? Nay, more. No plays are more lacking in "action," in the modern sense of the word, than such tragedies of Æschylus as the *Choephori*, the *Suppliants*, the *Seven against Thebes*, and the *Prometheus*. These dramas are certainly not lacking in action of a kind ; but the action is intellectual and lyrical ; it is not material and episodic. Such action is the ebb and the flow of emotions, an ebb and a flow rendered palpable by the chorus. To-day action is material, and almost cinematographic. Strange, indeed, that Wagner's ideas should find no enthusiasts among us! But when our critics have become imbued with those ideas, they will perhaps be more generous towards Verhaeren's dramas.

Though these plays are lyrical, they are real dramas ; for Verhaeren's lyricism is essentially dynamic, and full of movement. Such lyricism always contains within itself the essence of drama. Jean Bard, a highly original young artist and an enthusiastic admirer of Verhaeren, who once mischievously observed to me "I do not care for action in drama," has had the daring idea of staging, not Verhaeren's plays, but some of his poems. While these are being recited, they are simultaneously acted, and thus demonstrate before our very eyes all the hidden dynamic which is potential within them. The success of the experiment seems conclusive in favour of lyrical drama. In especial does it reveal the dramatic genius of our poet ; for if the poems alone are so dramatic, how should his plays not likewise be full of the same spirit ? We shall soon be able to show that they are preeminently so.

Drama and lyricism are often taken as the objective and subjective aspects of the same entity. But, indeed, when one speaks of art, these two aspects cannot be considered as contrasted entities. Objective art is always to a certain extent subjective ; in truth it is often more subjective than is usually suspected. In the course of the present study this has been proved time and again. We need but recall the symbolic part played by imaginative creations; or, again, how the imagination makes use of images from the outer world to express the feelings, whether conscious or unconscious, of the subject; how the outward symbols are used to express these inward emotions far more than to describe the outer world. Lyrical drama will, therefore, probably be subjective. It will utilize situations in the exterior life to symbolise the internal conflicts of the poet; and this symbolisation may be accomplished with or without the knowledge of the author himself.

Here my readers will demur. The three psychological dramas written by Verhaeren confront us with situations which, at the least, may be described as strange, but which some will certainly regard as monstrous. The situations are pressed on our notice with insistence, one might even say paroxysmally. *Le cloître* deals with a son who has killed his father; in *Philippe II*, the father kills the son; in *Hélène de Sparte*, murder is flavoured with incestuous and inverted passions. Fine company, forsooth! When we insist that these dramas are subjective, do we mean to imply that the poet has committed parricide and incest, or that he is endowed with a perverted and amoral nature? Certainly not; any more than Sophocles was a parricide and an incestmonger because he wrote the *Œdipus* trilogy (a work surcharged with lyricism). The poet needs only to be spontaneous, or unusually sincere in his lyricism, in order to indue with life those "monsters" which modern psychology has shown to be slumbering in the depths of our subconscious; just as paleolithic monsters are revealed to those who delve deeply enough into geologic strata as relics of the creatures that dwelt in our ancient world. Verhaeren has met these monsters; he has described them so faithfully that one is amazed at finding how closely the prophetic vision of the poet confirms the scientific researches of the psychologist.

Freud was the originator of the idea of the "Oedipus complex." By this complex we have to understand a subconscious trend in two directions: incestuous love of the mother; and mortal hatred for the father. Freud has been reproached, not without good reason, for the use of the terms "incestuous love" and "mortal hatred." As a matter of fact, the Oedipus complex has revealed itself to be of very frequent occurrence. And yet it would be false to maintain that the majority of men are in fact or by desire either incestuous or parricidal. The affair is much more simple. These impulses must be classed among the paleolithic monsters we were speaking of a moment ago; they are vestiges of very early childhood, dating from a period of life when the child is absolutely amoral; vestiges which have been subsequently thrust down into the subconscious at the first onset of the "moral age." To such an extent is this the case that an Oedipian (and who can say positively that he has no Oedipus complex?), far from being a parricide, may love his father sincerely. Now in those early years of amorality the words "incestuous love" and "moral hatred" have no meaning, for the child is completely ignorant of what incest is, and for him "absence" is synonymous with "death." We can well understand that a little child may have an exclusive love for its mother, a love which may go hand in hand with moments of jealousy of the father, hand in hand with a desire to get rid of the father as an obstacle and a rival.[1] It is also easy to understand how the adult imagination, wishing to express in actual words these violent passions of a little child, should find no better terms than "incestuous love" and "mortal hatred." This explains the frequency with which parricidal and incestuous phantasies (usually disguised under the cloak of symbols)

[1] Cf. Paulhan, Les transformations sociales des sentiments.

occur in the dreams and the imaginative creations of adult men.

We may agree with Adler [1] that the Oedipus complex is itself above all symbolical. We know with what sort of ideas the concepts of the father and the mother are often condensed. In Verhaeren, as we have seen, the idea of the mother is condensed with that of the dream, with introversion; the idea of the father, with that of the real, with extroversion. Thus the Oedipus complex may, in Verhaeren, be represented by the conflict with which we have already made acquaintance.

I may remind the reader that in the following pages the words "father" and "mother" would be understood by many commentators in a symbolical sense: the "idea of the father" and the "idea of the mother" with all their respective connotations. If the Freudian explanation appears to be too paradoxical, some readers may prefer such an interpretation.

However much tastes may differ on this point, there is no gainsaying the fact that the "Oedipus complex," when it is intense, seems to have a preponderating influence upon the whole psychic development of the human being. If we trace its origin to a very early and very violent love for the mother,[2] it is possible that this complex is the attribute of every normal boy endowed with sensitive feelings. Should it be intense, it would be the sign of exceptionally refined sensibilities. Verhaeren's dramas reveal in the most striking manner a very powerful Oedipus complex, and they reveal this complex with a clarity by no means inferior to the revelation in the trilogy whence the name of the complex has been derived.

The hero of *Le cloître*, Dom Balthazar, is a gloomy and vehement monk, who has come to the cloister in order to bury his remorse for his crime and to hide

---

[1] Adler, Ueber den nervösen Charakter, 1919, p. 5.
[2] Or the person who "mothers" the child.

it in God. But his secret weighs him down, and the remorse will out. He confesses his misdeed, and publicly announces that murder led him to the cloister:

> Mon père est mort, je l'ai assassiné,
> La tête folle et sauvage de vin.[1]
>
> [My father died, I murdered him
> When my mind was frenzied and made wild with wine.]

He tells his auditors where his father was sleeping, and goes on:

> Mon père ouvrit les yeux et tout à coup surgit
> Muet et soupçonneux devant ma haine. . . .
>   Ma rage
> Se ralluma, rien qu'à sentir ses doigts brutaux
> Et secs, serrer ma chair en leur étau. . . .
> Il paraissait, lui seul, être tous mes aïeux
> Si grande était sa taille et si dure sa force.
>
> [My father opened his eyes, and suddenly rose up
> Mute and suspicious, confronted by my hate. . . .
>   My fury
> Rekindled, merely at the feel of his brutal
> And withered fingers squeezing my flesh as in a vice. . . .
> He seemed to be the embodiment of all my forefathers,
> So huge was his stature and so obdurate his strength.]

This last detail is very significant. We shall meet with it again in *Hélène de Sparte*. Analysts have recognised that the gigantic and archaic "father," is the father as pictured by the tiny child. The dreams and phantasies (not to mention popular tales of giants) which conjure up the image of the father are, as a rule, akin to these impressions of very early childhood.

In *Le cloître* the motive of hatred for the father is not perfectly clear. The murder takes place "one evening when I was drunk." It is therefore a blind hate, welling up from the depths of the being who himself does not

[1] Act Two.

understand it. The one thing that is clear to Balthazar is that his hatred of his father constitutes a revolt against an authority which ruthlessly oppresses him, against those "brutal and withered fingers squeezing my flesh as in a vice."—"My father was stern, and I was a wild fellow. He seemed like an obstacle in my path: my vices coveted his wealth."

In considering *Le cloître* we find but one aspect of the Oedipus complex exposed, for the love of the mother does not at any time enter into the picture. We find only the negative component of the complex (hatred for the father), not the positive component (love of the mother). Such being the case, we may make use of an interpretation of this phenomenon furnished by Adler,[1] and need not have recourse to Freud. Adler would probably say that *Le cloître* is for the subconscious the drama of the son who, feeling his powers waxing, revolts against paternal authority. This interpretation would be, in large part, accurate. We have already mentioned the actual conflict which took place between Verhaeren and his father at the outset of the poet's career; nor did we overlook the significance of the "factory" in this connexion. Now the stresses arising out of a conflict where the vocation of a lifetime is in the balance, cannot fail to leave upon the subconscious an impression which in later life may revive in the form of fantasies. Verhaeren is, as has been rightly observed by Albert Mockel, a "poet of energy." He has been compared with Nietzsche, the philosopher of the will-to-power. The heroes of Verhaeren's plays, and Dom Balthazar with the rest, are, like Hernani, "forces which speed along"; even more than Hernani, they are conquering forces, powers which seek dominion. The whole of the action in *Le cloître* is concerned with ascertaining which monk shall succeed to the prior when he dies; who shall be the force capable of curbing the other inmates' wills;

[1] Op. cit.

who shall be strong enough to grasp the crosier. It is essentially a drama of the will-to-power.

But here we must point out that, excellent as this interpretation may be, it does not exclude the other. For in the two subsequent dramas, *Philippe II* and *Hélène de Sparte*, we are confronted with the same primary theme, which is, however, completed by the secondary theme; we shall find these plays imbued with the will-to-power and the will-to-love.

Knowing this, we can the better understand what sort of a " crime " has brought Balthazar to the " cloister." The cloister is for Verhaeren a familiar symbol of introversion. The " monks " in their " cloister " are for the poet the obverse of the " Flemish women," " the carnal ideal."[1] *Les flamandes* represents extroversion and sensuality; *Les moines* represents introversion and mysticism. The " crime which leads to the cloister " may therefore be explained (in a somewhat schematic terminology it is true, but a terminology which is both concise and easy to understand) as : " the Oedipus complex which leads to introversion."

> J'ai tué mon père ! j'ai tué mon père !
> Et l'on m'enferme ici
> Comme une bête en une cage
> Pour étouffer les cris
> Et les remords de mon âme sauvage.[2]
>
> [I killed my father, I killed my father,
> And they have locked me up here
> Like a beast in a cage
> So as to stifle the cries
> And the remorse of my tempestuous heart.]

Various authors have drawn attention to this link between the Oedipus complex and introversion.[3] While studying *Les tendresses premières* we had occasion to

---
[1] Cf. Les flamandes, the last verse of the concluding poem.
[2] Act Four.
[3] Cf. in particular, Morel, op. cit.

point out that the tendency to introversion, in a boy, is often linked with the idea of the mother; whilst the tendency to extroversion is linked with the idea of the father. In the specific case of Verhaeren, the struggle, during the twentieth year of his age, against paternal authority, was at the same time a protest of his inner being against the realism of the factory.

Le cloître, therefore, may well symbolise the intense crisis of introversion through which Verhaeren passed —just as, in the *Oedipus at Colonus*, the blindness which afflicts Oedipus, causing him to turn his gaze within, must symbolise the same introversion which follows in the footsteps of the same "crime."[1] There is now nothing to be surprised at if we find Balthazar describing his crimes in terms of *Les débâcles* and *Les flambeaux noirs*:

> Mon crime est un orage en flamme
> Qui mord et brûle et saccage mon âme. . . .
> Je suis comme un buisson de péchés noirs :
> Toutes les épines du sacrilège
> Se recourbent sur moi, comme des ongles noirs;
> Le manteau saint qui me protège
> Ment sur mes épaules ; j'en suis couvert ;
> Mais la lèpre pourrit ma chair.[2]

> [My crime is a flaming storm
> Which bites and burns and ravages my soul. . . .
> I am like a thicket of black sins :
> All the thorns of sacrilege
> Are turned against me like black nails ;
> The holy mantle which protects me
> Rests a living lie upon my shoulders; I am covered by it ;
> But leprosy gnaws my flesh.]

In especial does the "lying mantle" recall the days of *Les moines*. That was the period when Verhaeren, at the very time when he was wrapping himself in the sumptuous folds of his religious poems, knew full well that

---

[1] This is perhaps the symbolic content of all the myths which deal with blindness.
[2] Act Four.

AN OEDIPUS TRILOGY

his faith was dead; and he was confusedly preparing for the crisis. "Leprosy gnaws my flesh"; but in those days St. George was to come, the messenger of a new faith who was to exorcise "the leprosy and pustules" (p. 168).

The theme of the drama *Philippe II* is the struggle unto death between father and son. The young and ebullient, feeble and morbid Don Carlos can no longer submit to his father's authority:

> Oh! nos haines, oh! nos rages inassouvies. . . .
> Je suis resté, comme un enfant, sujet du roi.[1]
>
> [Oh, our hatred, oh, our unappeased fury. . . .
> I have remained, like a child, subject to the king.]

Don Carlos wishes to command in his turn. Aided by his love, the Comtesse de Clermont, he intends to escape to Flanders. In that country he will reign; they will love one another far removed from the cold, suspicious king, who spies on them at every turn. His impatience is passionate:

> D'ailleurs ce que le roi pense ou dit:
> Que nous importe, à l'heure où c'est moi seul qui monte,
> Où mon impatience, avec fièvre, décompte
> Les trop nombreux instants qui retardent encor
> Mon arrivée en Flandre, avec mes clairons d'or?[2]
>
> [Besides, what matters what the king says or thinks:
> At the hour when it is I alone who climb
> Whither my impatience, feverishly, ticks off
> The all too numerous minutes which still delay
> My arrival in Flanders with my golden trumpets?]

And he allows himself to be lulled with the idea that:

> Un cri
> De délivrance acclamera notre cortège
> En leur cités dont renaîtront les privilèges.[3]

[1] Act One. [2] Act Three, Scene One.
[3] Act Three, Scene One.

[A cry
Of deliverance will acclaim our progress
Through their cities whose privileges we shall restore.]

It is necessary, therefore, that he shall tear himself away and shall liberate Flanders from the tyranny of his father. Once more we are faced with a dramatisation of the will-to-power; but there is something besides. "Flanders!"—at the very word, one who is accustomed to analyse symbols will prick up his ears, will be on the scent, for he will remember that our native land, in our fantasies and our dreams, is often the symbol of that other homeland, the maternal bosom, the mother.[1] We may well ask ourselves whether the act of wresting Flanders from the hands of the king does not subconsciously represent the act of the little boy who appropriates to himself the mother, and wrests her from the father. This interpretation is confirmed in the most remarkable manner when we come to study the character of the Comtesse de Clermont. She is no ordinary lover; we are forced to see in her a reincarnation of the idea of the mother. It is left to Fray Bernardo, the king's confessor, to tell the king of this, and thus to reveal it to ourselves:

Don Carlos l'aime. Elle ressemble à la reine votre compagne. Toutes deux viennent de France; on les croirait sœurs.[2]

[Don Carlos loves her. She is like the queen, your spouse. Both come from France; they might well be sisters.]

In connexion with this *foreign* king who is to make himself master of Flanders, the foreign king who symbolises the father, and in connexion with the princess *hailing from France*, who plays the part of the mother, it is interesting to recall a passage already quoted from Bazalgette's book where he is writing about Verhaeren's

[1] Cf. Vodoz, op. cit., apropos of the Song of Roland.
[2] Act Two.

family on the maternal side: "The Debocks belonged to this countryside, and were proud of the fact. Their mother came from Herenthals; her name had been Lepaige, which suggests a *French origin*. The Debocks gave a friendly reception to the '*foreigner*' Gustave Verhaeren, Emile's father, who was from Brussels. . . . It is probable . . . that the Verhaerens were of Dutch origin." It would likewise not be a difficult matter to find among Verhaeren's infantile impressions the source of the peculiar duality of the maternal symbol in this play. Why, we ask, should there be a simultaneous love for Flanders and for the beloved? Why is the beloved as it were the "sister" of the mother? We may conjecture that we have here a reminiscence of two maternal figures: the mother, and the aunt, both of whom had their place in Verhaeren's childhood; indeed, we have already learned that the aunt was like a mother to the boy. But we need not venture farther along the path of possibilities; let it suffice that the maternal role of the beloved is proved beyond question.

After having been shown that we have in the mother and the countess the figures of two "sisters," we are presented with a scene which cannot fail to appear somewhat strange. King Philip and the countess are talking about Don Carlos, just as a father and a mother might talk of their child, of the education of their son!

La comtesse:

Sire, j'ai pour *l'infant* une tendresse ardent.
Que m'importent l'excès de ses haines *mordantes*
Et ses abattements et ses fureurs *d'enfant!*
Je l'aime tel qu'il est et suis fière qu'il m'aime.
Je ne raisonne point combien cet amour même
Touche parfois à la pitié, combien. . . .

Philippe II (tout à coup sévère):

C'est outrager mon fils que de l'aimer ainsi. . . .

LA COMTESSE :
> ... Si je donne à
> Don Carlos ma tendresse attentive et soumise,
> Je lui montre le courage qu'il faut aux rois.
> Je le grandis et je le gagne
> Au bel orgueil de se sentir infant d'Espagne. ...

PHILIPPE II :

> Moi seul et des hommes choisis par moi forment le cœur et l'esprit d'un futur roi d'Espagne. ... Vos conseils, votre adresse, votre amour, tout est nuisible.[1]

[THE COUNTESS :

> Sire, I have an ardent tenderness for the *Infante*.
> What do I care for his biting hatreds
> And his fits of despondency and his *childish* tantrums!
> I love him as he is, and I am proud of his love for me.
> I do not pause to think how near this love
> Sometimes is to pity, how ...

PHILIPPE II (suddenly severe) :

> It is an insult to my son to love him thus. ...

THE COUNTESS :

> ... If I give to
> Don Carlos my attentive and submissive love,
> I show him the courage which all kings should have.
> I enhance his own worth, and I win him
> To the splendid pride of feeling he is Infante of Spain. ...

PHILIPPE II :

> I alone, and men chosen by myself, shall shape the heart and the mind of Spain's future king. ... Your counsel, your cleverness, your love—all are harmful.]

Such a conversation is perhaps not very appropriate, taking place as it does between Philip II and his son's beloved. But though we may have objective grounds for criticism, the characters play their symbolical and unconscious part in a most admirable fashion. The father and the mother are here fighting for the son. The

[1] Act Two.

scene records one of those commonplace talks wherein the father is all severity and good sense, and the mother all feeling and affection; it is a scene whereat the child is often present, powerless and mute, where he feels that his fate is being decided, and where, in his imagination he magnifies into cruelty the severity of the father.

The countess is frequently assigned the part of mother in her relations with Don Carlos. Sometimes the actual word is used:

Don Carlos:
Oh! tu me fus, et sœur et mère, autant qu'amante.[1]

[Oh, you have been both sister and mother, as well as love to me.]

Don Carlos:
Je sens qu'elle m'est sûre et bonne et nécessaire. . . .
Elle m'est la santé rendue.[2] *Elle accompagne,*
Sur des chemins nouveaux, mes pas encor tremblants.[3]

[I feel that she is trusty, that she is good and necessary to me. . . .
She is my health restored. *She accompanies me*
As I take my first trembling steps upon new roads.]

La comtesse:
Ce n'est plus moi qu'ils punissent et tuent, c'est lui,
Le pauvre enfant en qui je réveillais la vie.[4]

[The countess:
It is no longer I whom they are punishing and killing; it is he,
The unhappy child whom I was awaking to life.]

---

[1] Act Three, Scene Two.
[2] Here seems to be a condensation of the *aunt* (Verhaeren's true mother, whose figure appears in Les tendresses premières in connexion with convalescence) with the *wife* whose love, when the poet was emerging from the crisis, was likewise " la santé rendue."
[3] Act Two.   [4] Act Three, Scene Two.

La comtesse (maternelle) :
> Berce en mes bras ta fièvre et ton triomphe, ô roi !
> Espère et sois heureux de ta belle folie,
> Goûte la volupté de tes désirs ; oublie
> Ton passé morne et prends ton rêve merveilleux
> Pour un monde réel que t'aurait fait un dieu.[1]

[The countess (maternally) :
> Lull your fever and your triumph in my arms, O king !
> Hope, and be happy in your fine frenzy,
> Taste the voluptuousness of your desires ; forget
> Your gloomy past, and take your wondrous dream
> For a real world which a god would have made for you.]

Truly it is the essential mother who speaks these words ; it is the mother spirit which, in the depths of the being, gives the rhythm to this captivating lullaby whose concluding words constitute so open an invitation to introversion. One of the characteristics of introversion is wilfully to renounce the real in order to dwell in the realm of dreams, to make for oneself out of the dream an equivalent of the real, to see in the world of dreams a better and finer realm. In extreme cases this flight into the land of dreams brings about a " loss of the function of the real,"[2] a " disadaptation " to life.

Don Carlos, like Balthazar, is, from beginning to end of the drama, an introvert. In the very first scene he is a prisoner in the Escurial, " rigid and black," another cloister. We hear him exclaim :

> Oh mon rêve fermé, que j'ai peur d'entr'ouvrir.[3]

> [Oh my closed dream, which I dread even to half-open.]

Towards the end, where he allows himself to be lulled to rest by the countess ("maternally "), he beholds in her the image of the " Virgin " and he dreams of " withdrawing from the world," just like a monk, while folded in her mystical arms :

---

[1] Act Two.   [2] Cf. Morel, op. cit., pp. 24-25.
[3] Act One.

Don Carlos (comme s'il priait) :
Ce n'est plus que ta voix que je voudrais entendre
Pendant l'éternité ;
Ce n'est plus qu'entre tes yeux et leurs regards
Que mes désirs hagards
Voudraient descendre,
Pendant l'éternité ;
Et ce n'est plus, qu'en ton âme profonde,
Que je voudrais me retirer du monde
Pendant l'éternité.

. . . . .

Tu m'es la Vierge
Tromphante parmi les forêts d'or des cierges.[1]

[Don Carlos (as if in prayer) :
Your voice alone do I wish to hear
For all eternity ;
It is only in your eyes and their glances
That my wan desires
Wish to descend
For all eternity ;
It is only into your deep soul
That I wish to retire far from the world
For all eternity.

. . . . .

You are for me the Virgin,
Triumphant amid the golden forest of candles.]

If we recall the fact that monks are in Verhaeren's writings the symbol of introversion, we shall understand somewhat better the meaning of the strange nocturnal vision, in the first act, when the father, mute as a shadow, spies upon the lovers, and when the " black monk " follows the father at a distance, spying upon the latter in his turn :

Tu vois, là-bas, ce moine noir qui, par mégarde, semble gagner le coin où disparut le roi. Eh bien ! ce moine-là, c'est l'espion du Saint-Office. Philippe II surveille, mais il est surveillé. Chaque pas qu'il fait vers nous, quelqu'un le fait vers lui. Regarde, il rentre et le moine disparaît.[2]

[1] Act Three, Scene Two. [2] Act One.

[Do you see, over there, that black monk who, as if by accident, seems to make for the very spot where the king disappeared? Well, that monk is the spy of the Holy Office. Philip II may keep watch; but he, too, is watched. Each step he takes towards us is dogged by one taken towards him. Look, he is going in, and the monk has disappeared.]

Somewhat earlier in the scene Don Carlos had said:

Ce n'était point mon père qu'il fallait craindre, c'était les moines, eux seules sont redoutables.

[My father need not be feared; we need fear only the monks; they alone are to be dreaded.]

Is it not obvious that, just as in *Le cloître*, the Oedipus complex seems to lead inevitably to introversion? The menace of a too intense introversion, of a "monkish" dominion, brings the man to the realisation of the real danger, the true enemy. This fact is only hinted at in *Philippe II*. From the beginning to the end of this play, the enemy is the father, and the revolt against him grows and grows until it becomes a mortal hatred.

DON CARLOS:
Le mal atteint en vous je ne sais quel excès.
Lorsque je songe à lui, je songe à vous mon père.
Que je gouverne un jour, j'oublierai tout, hormis
L'horreur que j'ai de vous, et la sourde colère
D'être quelqu'un de votre sang.

. . . . .

Je sens un projet sombre en mon âme germer;
Le chrême est effacé dont vos tempes sont ointes,
Et vous pouvez remercier à deux mains jointes
Le Ciel, qu'en cet instant, je me sois désarmé.[1]

[DON CARLOS:
Evil in you seems to exceed all bounds.
When I think of evil, I think of you, my father.
If ever I come to govern, I shall forget all, save
The horror I have of you, and the speechless rage I feel
At being one of your blood.

. . . . .

[1] Act Two.

I feel a sombre purpose germinating in my soul;
The chrism which annointed your brow is wiped off,
And, with your two hands joined, you may thank
Heaven that at this moment I have laid my arms aside.]

Now Don Carlos is weak and at the mercy of his father. It is the father who kills the son; this act will be a kind of revenge on the son for having wished to kill his father. We might almost call it a posthumous revenge if we admit that Philip II (who makes his first appearance in the play as a nocturnal vision, and passes off the stage without saying a word) possesses certain characteristics of a shadow and of a remorse.[1] However this may be, the theme of the drama is closely akin to that of *Le cloître*, in which play the burden of his parricide leads the hero to his doom. Don Carlos and Dom Balthazar are both of them victims of the Oedipus complex.

We will leave the dramas for a while in order to reconsider *Liminaire*, the opening poem in *Les tendresses premières*, for the analysis of *Philippe II* has brought to light certain novel aspects of that poem.

In *Liminaire* Verhaeren devotes the following lines to the memory of his parents:

> Mes simples vieux parents, ma bonne tante!
> Oh! les herbes de leur tombeau
> Que je voudrais mordre et manger. . . .
>
> [My simple, old parents, and my good aunt!
> Oh, the grass on their grave,
> Which I would fain bite and eat. . . .]

In *Ardeurs naïves* there is a yet shorter reference, as we saw on pages 48, 49: " How many people have died, her parents and mine." This is not much of a funeral oration! The paucity of the reference may of course be due to the fact that Verhaeren was more with his

---

[1] Concerning the significance of mutes, cf. Régis and Hesnard, op. cit., p. 174.

aunt than with his parents. For his aunt alone does he feel real filial affection. He tells us this himself in a moving prose poem, *Ce soir*, which has hitherto remained unpublished.[1] His sorrow at the loss of his aunt finds pathetic and simple expression: " O you the best loved among my dead, the only one I ever really loved ! " And it is doubtless the aunt's image which has served as model, from an early age, for the maternal imago,[2] and the forms of the Virgin and Child. " My whole childhood seemed to hang on your heart. . . . Are you the beneficent Diana whom the legends of old depict for us, not the mother but the aunt, the virgin sitting by the cradle, patient, tender, and self-sacrificing, as though she were the sister of a happier sister ? "

But can this be the only reason for the almost complete silence concerning the parents ? The extraordinary intensity of the Oedipus complex which the dramas have revealed leads us to seek in this complex a deeper meaning, the outcome of infantile experiences. Indeed, this is no case of indifference but, on the contrary, a drama of the Oedipus complex within the sensitive young soul of the poet. The tragical desire had no sooner been born than it was repressed, as was meet. The fact that his mother did not belong to him but was wrested from him by his father and by business affairs, far from allaying the tragedy (as it does in many children) only intensified matters, stimulating the child's hatred for business and the "factory," exacerbating his revolt against paternal authority, and increasing his yearning for the mother. For the aunt, be she never so good, cannot completely take the place of the "happier sister,"

[1] See Appendix, pp. 310 et seq.
[2] The word " imago " is taken from the title of a novel by Carl Spitteler. It is used by German psychoanalysts and has been adopted by Théodore Flournoy. It is now current likewise among psychoanalysts in Great Britain and the United States. The term denotes an interior type, a type moulded upon real persons (in especial upon the father or the mother), and which, from the depths of our subconscious, continues to guide our actions, and to stimulate our sympathies and our antipathies.

and there seems to be a veil of melancholy over his love for the mother-substitute. In the poem *Ce soir* there occurs a passage which is fraught with deep meaning: " Silently, and as though absent from the existence of others, you loved me with a *repressed maternity*, with the dream of a solitary woman, sad, apart, and alone. Have you ever loved otherwise ? " Perfect reciprocity of love breathes through every word—even to its sadness ! The words *repressed maternity* are specially significant : for if the instinct for motherhood has been repressed in the aunt, the instinct towards the mother has likewise been repressed in the child. He is in search of a mother-substitute, just as she is in search of a child-substitute. Both feel lonely and aloof from other mortals, and this makes their mutual affection so perfectly harmonious. In the passage just quoted, and, in fact, in almost everything which the imagination creates for us in relation to those we love, we must scrutinise each detail (especially in the present instance the expression *repressed maternity*) —must look for a double and reciprocal meaning.

It is therefore this circumstance (the mother wrested from the child's affection by the father and by business affairs), combined with the child's precocious and sensitive emotional character, which must account for the special intensity of the Oedipus complex in Verhaeren. We shall have to grasp the fact fully if we are really to understand his dramas.

With this guiding idea in mind let us reconsider some of the verses in *Liminaire* :

> Oh, the grass on their grave,
> Which I would fain bite and eat !

The violence of the inward drama exhales from the words, to be instantly repressed. What is the meaning of the desire to bite and to eat the grass ? We meet with the same desire in another poem of Verhaeren's ; but here the desire is filled with overflowing and fierce voluptuousness:

Et pendant qu'il la chauffe, ils vont par les saulaies,
Par les sentiers moussus, faits pour s'en aller deux,
Ils vont toujours, tirant les feuilles hors des haies,
Les mordant avec fièvre et les jetant loin d'eux.[1]

[And while he is ardently wooing her, they stroll along the willow walks,
By mossy paths just wide enough for two,
They stroll along, and ever as they go they pluck the leaves from off the hedges,
Feverishly biting them and throwing them away.]

Vois-tu, j'ai si souvent songé avec envie
A cette heure affolée où j'entrerais en toi
Comme un vainqueur soudain avec toute ma vie,
Où mes yeux te verraient, après l'instant d'effroi,
Haleter de bonheur et crier de tendresse
Et mordre le feuillage en ne le sachant pas.[2]

[You see, I have always dreamed with longing
Of the mad hour when I would go in unto you
Suddenly, like a conqueror, giving my whole life,
When my eyes would see you, after the first moment of fright,
Breathless with happiness and crying with tenderness
And biting the leafage not knowing what you did.]

But the act of biting comes also to Don Carlos hurling his hatred at his father:

Il agit par détours, je n'agis que par bonds.
Comprends-tu ma fureur et mon désir de mordre?[3]

[His ways are devious, but I leap to my goal.
Can you understand my fury and my desire to bite?]

---

[1] From Amours rouges, in Les flamandes.
[2] From Dialogue rustique, in Les blés mouvants.
[3] From Philippe II, Act One.

AN OEDIPUS TRILOGY

> Ah ! mon frère Don Juan, lorsqu'on est moi,
> Comprends-tu que l'on crie et que l'on morde ? [1]

> [Ah ! my brother Don Juan, since I am I,
> Can you understand that I cry out and that I bite ?]

> N'ayez crainte ; le roi ne court aucun danger.
> Avant de m'en venir, j'ai *muselé* ma haine.[2]
> [Fear nothing, the king runs no risk.
> Ere coming here, I *muzzled* my hate.]

In *Le cloître*, Dom Balthazar the parricide exclaims from the pulpit to the crowd :

> Moi Balthazar duc de Rispaire,
> J'assassinai, avec ces deux mains sanguinaires ;
> Regardez-les, ce sont des mains
> Plus féroce que des *mâchoires*.[3]

> [I, Balthazar, Duke of Rispaire,
> I slew, with these two bloody hands ;
> Look at them, they are hands
> More fierce than *jaws*.]

We see now that the subconscious did well to use the symbol of biting the grass on the grave to express, at one and the same time, the monopolist and passionate love of the child for the mother, and the jealous revolt against the father—in fact, to voice in a single phrase the whole of the Oedipus complex. Unawares, of course ; for we must never forget that this complex is repressed from early childhood, and only exists in the subconscious ; it is a " paleolithic monster," but is an active monster for all that !

Repression of this complex is so great in Verhaeren's case that no sooner does he utter the cry than it is instantly stifled, as though he feared he had said too much. Without any transition, quite abruptly, other and apparently

---

[1] From Philippe II, Act Two. [2] Ibid., Act Two.
[3] From Le cloître, Act Four.

unconnected ideas surge up. But these ideas are only superficially unconnected ; the abruptness of the transition signifies, as we know, that the emergence of new images masks a subconscious reasoning :

> J'appris alors quel pays fier était la Flandre ! . . .
> Je sus le nom des vieux martyrs farouches ;
> Et maintes fois, ivre, fervent, pleurant et fou,
> En cachette, le soir, j'ai embrassé leur bouche
>   Orde et rouge sur l'image à deux sous.
> J'aurais voulu souffrir l'excès de leur torture,
>   Crier ma rage aussi et sangloter vers eux,
>   Les clairs, les exaltés, les dompteurs d'aventure,
> Les arracheurs de foudre aux mains de Philippe Deux.[1]

> [Then I learned what a proud country was Flanders ! . . .
>   I learned the names of the fierce martyrs of old,
> And many a night, frenzied, fervent, weeping, and mad,
> Secretly, at eventide, I kissed their mouth,
>   Dirty and red on the penny picture.
> I should have liked to suffer the excess of their torture,
>   Cry forth my wrath and sob out my heart to them,
>   The bright ones, the exalted ones, the doughty adventurers,
> Who wrested the thunderbolts from the hands of Philip the Second.

Philip II ! There we have it. We are thus brought in contact with the drama bearing that name, in the analysis of which we have unearthed the tragedy of the son in revolt against the father. We see that those who " wrested the thunderbolts from the hands of Philip II " are playing the same part as Don Carlos. *Philip II* is the father ; *they* are the son who rises against the father. They wrest Flanders, symbolising the mother, from the tyranny of the king ; and they become masters in their own country. The sudden change of subject in *Liminaire* was apparent merely, seeing that the new images are no more than a fresh symbolisation of the same Oedipus complex. A few verses farther on the revolters perform the same act of " biting " which we had previously in

[1] From Liminaire, in Les tendresses premières.

the lines about the grave. This time, however, as in *Philippe II*, the biting is an outcome of anger:

> C'étaient les tisserands et les foulons sordides,
> Mordant les rois comme des chiens ardents,
> Et leur laissant aux mains la trace de leurs dents.
>
> [They were weavers and sordid fullers
> Biting the kings as though they were mad dogs,
> And leaving the marks of their teeth in the royal hands.][1]

The intimate condensation of the mother with Flanders leads us to surmise that Verhaeren's deep affection for his homeland is one with his original love for his mother, a love which, as we have seen, was in large part transferred to his aunt. The last book of the series *Toute la Flandre*, which is entitled *Les plaines*, opens with a poem (likewise named *Liminaire*) wherein the Flemish lad's affection for his native Flanders is expressed by a symbol pregnant with meaning for us. The condensation of the mother with Flanders gives rise in this poem to a most curious result which illustrates the theory in the happiest way:

> Soudain son corps s'affale aux pentes d'un fossé,
> Le sang lui bat et les tempes et les narines.
> Alors *mettant à nu sa farouche poitrine*
> Et l'appuyant sur le sol dur et crevassé
> *Longuement, sourdement,* dans ce coin solitaire,
> Les *poings serrés,* il sanglote contra la terre.
>
> [All at once his body falls on the sides of a ditch,
> The blood beats in his temples, in his nostrils.
> Then, *baring his distraught breast,*
> And pressing it against the hard and crannied earth,
> *For a long while, secretly,* in this solitary place,
> With *clenched fists,* he sobs upon the ground.]

These lines are akin to those concerning the bitten grass on the grave. In addition, we can hardly fail to be

---

[1] The Oedipus complex is accountable for the strange nightmare visions of L'aventurier in Les villages illusoires. The rival of the employer is, symbolically, "the rival of the father."

reminded of the action of a little child pressing passionately against the mother who suckles it. The lad bares his chest, eagerly, just as the baby in its impatience uncovers the maternal breast ; a reversal of roles which is consonant in every respect with the mechanism of spontaneous symbols, and a reciprocity which is to be witnessed in dreams. The "repressed maternity" referred to in connexion with another poem is an example of the same order.

As to the "hard and crannied earth" which has no logical reason for appearing here, either we must attribute the reference to the exigencies of rhyme (a rare fault in Verhaeren), or else we must recognise that the detail has special significance in the construction of this symbol. Our interpretation of the foregoing lines is absolutely in keeping with the second conjecture. We have the continuation of the reversal of roles. The earth is "dry," the earth is thirsty, at the moment when the child presses his breast to it for comfort. This is followed by the words "for a long time, secretly . . . he sobbed," which is symbolic of the infant imbibing the mother's milk. The detail about the "clenched fists" completes the picture.

The condensation of the mother with the native land is of frequent occurrence. Somtimes this condensation is conscious ; in such a case it is a stock metaphor, a mere comparison of the native land to a mother. The common link has been utilised by Verhaeren in a dedication, and though Verhaeren, like other poets, makes use in these lines of the trite image, we know that for him it is a truth, a thing both vital and unconscious :

> C'est là qu'est le foyer
> Où mon amour profond ose te bégayer
> Ce qu'un mot net et trop précis ne peut dire.
> Tu m'y rejoins, ô Flandre, avec ton lent sourire,
> Tu prends mes mains entre tes mains
> Et doucement tu les poses, et sur ton sein,

Et sur tes yeux sacrés d'où coulèrent les larmes.
Oh ! le tremblant respect qui m'envahit alors,
Tandis que tu m'étreins en tes larges bras forts
Contre ton flanc, revêtu d'armes.

[There is the hearth
Whither my deep love dares come to stammer forth
That which precise and definite words could never say.
Thither you come, O Flanders, with your slow smile ;
You take my hands betwixt your hands
And tenderly you lay them upon your breast
And upon your holy eyes whence gushed forth tears.
Oh, the trembling respect which invades my being then,
The while you press me, with your great, strong arms,
Against your weaponed side.]

Flanders is here again the mother; and though the actual mother is not once mentioned in *Les tendresses premières*, the poet makes up for the omission when he devotes a collection of poems to *Toute la Flandre*, to the land which was a second mother to him.

The analysis which started tentatively in *Le cloître*, and which developed yet further in *Philippe II*, is to receive a deeper significance still when we consider *Hélène de Sparte*. This drama, which has lightheartedly been stigmatised as "queer," and wherein the critics could only see exceptional and paradoxical situations, is in reality obeying in the strictest manner the laws of a subconscious logic. It is Verhaeren's supreme merit that, in spite of his conscious rational faculties, he was able to remain true to this subconscious process of reasoning, no matter how baffling it might appear.

Helen is a fateful person whose path through life is strewn with loves, with murders, and with frenzy. Electra speaks of Helen as an ἀνάγκη, an inner doom which, weighing upon her [Electra's] life, makes of that life, like that of Dom Balthazar, a "flaming storm." Now we have a recrudescence of the tortures and frenzies occurring in *Les débâcles* and in *Les flambeaux noirs*;

but in *Hélène de Sparte* they appear in a more controlled and classical guise :

Mais ignorez-vous donc qu'elle seule est la cause
De cette ardente mort que je nourris en moi ?
C'est elle ma fureur, ma fièvre et mon effroi ;
Elle qui me fait peur, ainsi qu'un incendie
Qui m'entoure la nuit, de ses flammes brandies.
Si Ménélas, vers elle, un jour n'était allé
Certes, jamais, nul orage n'aurait brûlé
De sa foudre mon cœur tranquil et solitaire.
J'écouterais encore et mon père et ma mère
Me parler doucement, près du foyer, le soir.
Le sol ne serait point couvert de leur sang noir,
Clytemnestre jamais, n'aurait connu Egiste.
La vision d'horreur qui dans mes yeux persiste
Ne me poursuivrait point, avec des gestes fous,
Et je ne craindrais pas d'aller vers n'importe où,
Hagarde et torturée et démente et funeste,
Comme erre au loin et crie et se déchire Oreste.[1]

[But do you not know that she alone is the cause
Of this consuming death which I harbour within me ?
She is my fury, and my fever, and my fright ;
She fills me with alarm, as would a conflagration
Encircling me at night with its leaping flames.
Had Menelaus not approached her upon a certain day,
No storm would have seared
With its lightning my quiet and lonely heart.
I should still be listening to my father and mother
Talking quietly to me by the fireside at nightfall ;
The ground would not be stained with their black blood,
Clytemnaestra would never have known Aegistheus.
The ghastly vision which is never absent from my sight
Would not pursue me thus with its wild gestures,
And I should not fear to go, no matter whither,
Wan and tortured and mad and baleful,
Like Orestes, who wanders afar, wailing, and rending himself.]

The " leaping flames " and the " storm " which " sears " bring us back to the " flaming storm " which ravaged Balthazar's heart. The evocation of the parents at the

[1] Act One, Scene Two.

AN OEDIPUS TRILOGY

hearthside, an evocation which is immediately followed by the picture of their blood drenching the earth, helps to steep us further in the same atmosphere. But there is no mistaking the significance of Castor's incestuous love for his sister Helen :

Hélène est à mes yeux, non ma sœur, mais la femme
Dont l'Europe et l'Asie ont respiré la chair. ...
Celle que j'aime avec démence et avec rage
Et d'un amour si brusque, et si rouge, et si fort
Que j'exulte à sentir le feu qui me ravage
Jusqu'en ses os et ses moëlles, brûler mon corps.[1]

[Helen, in my eyes, is not my sister, but the woman
Whose flesh has been longed for by Europe and by Asia. ...
She whom I love madly and ferociously
With a love so sudden, so red, and so strong,
That I exult in the feeling of the fires which consume me
To my very bones and their marrow, burning my body.]

Here we are once more confronted with the Oedipus complex. The substitution of the sister for the mother is by no means rare in such fantasies (" Oh, you have been both sister and mother, as well as love to me," exclaims Don Carlos). It requires no great penetration to understand that Helen and Menelaus subconsciously represent the mother and the father. Their entry upon the scene is superb :

Regardez tous : voici le char de *pourpre* et *d'or*
Qui traverse la plaine
Et Ménélas qui tient les rênes
Et les *chevaux plus noirs que l'ébène,*
Et la foule qui suit
Avec les bras levés et les rameaux brandis
Et qui acclame, au cœur de son pays,
Hélène !
Ils sont si grands tous deux que l'on dirait des Dieux.[2]

[1] Act One, Scene Four.   [2] Act One, Scene Three.

[All of you, look! here comes the chariot of *purple* and *gold*
Across the plains,
And Menelaus who holds the reins,
And the *horses blacker than ebony*,
And the crowd following after,
Raising arms and brandishing branches,
Acclaiming to the heart of the country
Helen!
Both are so great, one would think they were gods.]

This last verse is very significant. We have seen when analysing *Le cloître* that Balthazar's father took on vast proportions. This growth of stature in the fantasy is a reminiscence of the size of the parents as viewed from the standpoint of a little child. Let us also notice the contrast, gold against black, between the "chariot of purple and gold" in which Helen comes, and the "horses blacker than ebony" driven by Menelaus. The mother is surrounded by the symbol of love, whereas the father is placed near the symbol of death. Castor's love for Helen is one with his deadly hatred for Menelaus:

CASTOR:
Vraiment, que n'est-il mort dans l'horreur de la nuit,
Quand le carnage ameutait l'air de ses vertiges
Et qu'Ilion brûlait.

POLLUX:
Il vit, te dis-je, il vit.

CASTOR:
Ah! quel rouge dessein hante soudain mon âme!
Et qu'importe la vie ou la mort d'un vieillard.[1]

[CASTOR:
Oh why did he not die in the night of horror
When carnage filled the air with its frenzy,
And when Ilion flamed?

POLLUX:
He lives, I tell you, he lives.

[1] Act One, Scene Four.

CASTOR:

> Ah! what red purpose suddenly invades my soul!
> And what matters the life or the death of an old man.]

The whole action and the words remind us of Don Carlos when he exclaimed : " I feel a sombre purpose germinating in my soul." Throughout the three plays, the fantasy of parricide is identical, except that in Helen of Sparta the father, the real object of the deed, is less obvious. Hatred is no longer felt for the father as such, but for the possessor of Helen (or of the mother). This, however, is not a repression. On the contrary, the analysis is leading us to detect the positive and primitive side of the Oedipus complex, love for the mother, which was completely hidden in *Le cloître*. In that play only the negative aspect, the revolt against the father, was manifested. In *Philippe II*, the mother put in an appearance, but tentatively, almost unrecognisable under the twofold symbolisation of Flanders and the beloved. In *Hélène de Sparte* the fantasy comes openly into line with the incest fantasies. No longer does the beloved replace the mother; here we have the sister acting as mother-substitute. The symbol approximates to the thing it really represents, and the latter becomes more clear. We may observe that if the mother image is altered and rejuvenated under the features of the sister, this is compensated by the fact that Menelaus, the father, is presented as an " old man."

But in the second act we encounter an unexpected incident, an incident which has no equivalent in the two earlier dramas. The Oedipus complex becomes transformed into the Sappho complex; that is to say, we pass from incest fantasies in the first act to fantasies of homosexuality in the second. Early in the play, Helen receives the declaration of her brother Castor's love, which seems to sear her like a flame.

Je te désire
Sans hesiter, violemment et tout à coup ;
Je ne suis pas celui qui feint et qui sait dire
Ce qu'il ne pense pas quand son cœur est jaloux ;
J'aime, je hais, avec fureur, avec rancune,
Et je passe en criant vers ton cœur effaré
Qu'il sera libre un jour et suivra ma fortune.[1]

[I desire you
Unfalteringly, violently, and precipitately ;
I am not one to feign, nor one who knows how to say
That which he does not think, when his heart burns with jealousy ;
I love, I hate, passionately, resentfully,
And I go, crying towards your affrighted heart,
That one day it will be free and will follow my fortunes.]

In the next scene, Castor's place is taken by Electra, and Helen has to hearken to a second declaration of love even more passionate and mad, this time from a woman:

Tu es toute ma vie. . . .
C'est mon destin, à moi, de ne sentir mon cœur
Que comme un feu qui brûle et mord et dont j'ai peur.
Oh ! ce pas saccadé des nocturnes Furies
Qui retentit jusqu'en ma chair pâle et meurtrie
Et me foule, et m'entraîne et m'affole toujours !
Et voici que je sens rugir en moi l'amour
Et que je pleure et crie et que je meurs et t'aime.[2]

[You are the whole of life for me. . . .
I have been fated to feel my heart
Burning like a fire, devouring me and filling me with fear.
Oh, the tramp of the nocturnal Furies
Which reverberates in my very flesh, so pale and bruised,
Which tramples upon me, and allures me, and drives me mad !
I feel love raging within me,
I weep and cry, I die, and I love you.]

The transformation in the second act is presented to us under the guise of words, lyrically : but in the third act it is dramatised. Castor's hate increases, as previously hate grew in Don Carlos :

[1] Act Two, Scene Two.   [2] Act Two, Scene Three.

Je vous hais tous. Mais lui, le roi, possède et garde
Impunément, ici, dans son lit, sous son toit,
Celle dont la splendeur fait mon âme hagarde.
Je ne puis plus attendre et ma tête est en feu ;
Je me vois emporté par ma fièvre et ma rage,
Par les bonds de mon cœur, par les cris de mes vœux,
Comme par un terrible et despotique orage.
Je suis hanté. Hélène est là, ici, partout,
Je dévore sa chair en mes rêves voraces,
J'assiège ses flancs nus avec mes désirs fous.
Et Ménélas me raille, et m'a volé ma place.
J'ai mes desseins. Je sais qu'il est là-haut. J'y vais.[1]

[I hate you all. But he, the king, possesses and keeps,
Unpunished, here, in his bed, beneath his roof,
Her whose beauty ravages my soul.
No longer can I wait, my brain is afire ;
I see myself swept along by my fever and my frenzy,
By the leaps of my heart, by the cries of my longing,
As though by a terrible and despotic tempest.
I am haunted. Helen is there, she is here, is everywhere ;
I devour her flesh in my voracious dreams,
I assail her naked flanks with my mad desires.
Menelaus mocks me, he has stolen my place.
My plans are ripe. I know he is up there. I go thither.]

Happier than Don Carlos—if one may speak of happiness in such a connexion—Castor is able to go the full length of his hate ; he kills Menelaus (the image of the father) on the mountain side.[2] But vengeance follows swiftly in the steps of murder. In the following scene, Electra slays Castor. She is impelled by a love frenzy similar to that which drove him to his deed of blood In psycho-analytical language, this signifies that Sappho replaces Oedipus, the fantasy of homosexuality takes the place of the incest fantasy. We have the same situation as that in the previous act when Electra replaced Castor ; but what was then passion, has now become action, and the interior conflict has been exteriorised.

[1] Act Three, Scene Two.   [2] Act Three, Scene Three.

In the fourth act, Electra, in her turn, vanishes. The drama concludes in the heart of Helen herself, and takes the form of a beautiful sapphic ode in which all nature joins, which pursues the distraught Helen's beauty like an obsession:

UNE NAÏADE :
>Hélène, ô toi qui vis et respires sur terre
>Dans un corps plus brillant que le ciel étoilé,
>Nos grottes de lumière et nos flots translucides
>Te feront un palais bougeant de joyaux clairs.
>L'amour est souple et doux entre nos bras liquides
>Et de longs baisers d'or glisseront sur ta chair. . . .

UNE BACCHANTE :
>   Nous sommes les Thyades
>Et nos corps sont de flamme, Hélène, et nous t'aimons ;
>L'ombre comme un vin noir nous enivre et nous brûle
>Et nos danses, la nuit, font trembler les forêts.[1]

[A NAIAD :
>Helen ! O you who live and breathe on the earth
>In a body more lovely than the starry skies,
>Our grottoes of light and our translucent waters
>Will make for you a palace of glowing jewels.
>Love is supple and sweet in our liquid arms,
>And long, golden kisses will glide over your limbs. . . .

A BACCHANTE :
>   We are the Thyades,
>And our bodies are of flame, Helen, and we love you.
>Darkness, like a black wine, intoxicates and burns us,
>And our nightly dances make the forests tremble.]

But Helen does not hearken to the love words of these dream creatures; she has fled the living in order to escape from incest and from homosexuality. She has taken refuge in a dream, which is still haunted by the memory of these monstrous loves.[2] In the invitation

---

[1] Act Four, Scene Four.

[2] These "monstrous loves" illumine the images in Le péché, the poem we discussed as part of the collection entitled Les campagnes hallucinées—and all the like images.

of the naiads and in the translucent waters of their grottoes we have the suggestion of a fantasy of autophilia, of narcissism. Helen has become an introvert. She is now no more than a spirit confronted by the creatures of her dream. These creatures take shape ever more definitely; the world of men, of the real, recedes into the background and vanishes.

Narcissus succeeds Sappho, just as the latter succeeded Oedipus. First came incest, then homosexuality, and finally narcissism, profound introversion: such are the three stages of the drama. "All the same," the reader may protest, "it is very queer. The analysis discloses nothing more than a pathological condition, an exceptional case, which in no way reveals that secret logical process of which you spoke." We are coming to that. Psychoanalysts have described these three stages (fantasies of incest, of homosexuality, and of narcissism) as those through which the subject usually passes during the course of a properly conducted analysis. They maintain that this evolution represents the precise progress of an instinct which is undergoing introversion. Many different theories could be adduced, but this is not the place for such an examination, any more than for a discussion of the various interpretations of the Oedipus complex—the comparatively literal interpretations of Freud, and the comparatively symbolical interpretations of Adler.[1] We must note that such fantasies, far from being exceptional, pathological, or paradoxical, seem to represent the natural progress of an imagination guided by a tendency to introversion. These fantasies are as natural as introversion, as natural as the inner life itself. This is what

[1] Freud holds that it is part of the polymorphous concept of regression, and represents a regression of the sexual instinct which during the course of its prepuberal development (a phase investigators are apt to overlook) might go through a similar process in an inverse direction. (Cf. Freud, Three Contributions to the Theory of Sex.) Adler, on the other hand, maintains that these fantasies make use of sexual images merely as symbols to represent an evolution which may not be fundamentally sexual.

it behoved us to show. It is true, they usually so offend our conscious thought by their apparent illogicality and immorality, that for the most part they are repressed, and at best are only allowed to come to life in the realm of dreams and under cover of the night. But a great poet, as Schopenhauer has said, is one who in the waking state is able to do that which ordinary mortals are only able to do in dreams.

There is, however, an important difference, to which we drew attention in the Introduction. In the waking state, the rational faculty works upon the raw material furnished by the imagination, corrects apparent absurdities, in a word, rationalises them. The three phases of this drama of introversion should take place within one and the same soul, and in a dream that would probably be the course of development. The logic of the conscious rejects such a sequence and demands that the phenomena shall be presented in terms more harmonious to that logic. This is why each phase is symbolised by a different person. The Oedipus drama is the one which is playing itself out in Castor's heart; and, when he leaves Helen in the second act, the natural course of events would be for the drama to continue within him, and he should now be possessed by the homosexual fantasy. Instead of this, Electra is assigned the part. But note how admirably well chosen she is to replace Castor, the Oedipian. Electra, in the classical drama, is the female counterpart of Oedipus. So much is this the case, that psychoanalysts speak of the Electra complex as the obverse of the Oedipus complex (love of a little girl for the father, and jealousy towards the mother). The characters of Castor and Electra fit into one another even more completely, and Electra is aptly chosen to succeed Oedipus. For whereas the mythological sense relates Electra to the Oedipus complex, the myth of Castor and Pollux is a homosexual fantasy. In Verhaeren's drama, Castor is the first to take the stage. He is an Oedipian, but the connotations of the myth we associate with his name give us a premonition of homosexuality. Now Electra appears. Similar memories of the myth in which she figures lead our thoughts back to her past life, and here we find the counterpart of the Oedipus complex. She, herself, voices this in the speech we have already quoted : " Had Menelaus not approached her upon a certain day. . . ." When the drama enters the third phase, Electra yields place to Helen.

These various substitutions bring a reversal of roles into play, a reversal similar to that which we noted earlier between Flanders and the mother, on the one hand, and the child, on the other. Thus, when in Act Two Castor and Helen separate, the reversal is mathematically precise and perfect ; properly speaking it is Helen who should disappear and Castor who should remain and love a man ; whereas in the play it is Castor who disappears and Helen who remains and is loved by a woman. In order to satisfy the logic of the subconscious, the role should form a unity ; it should be played from beginning to end of the drama by one person only, the beloved, who should be a man ; there would then be a multiplicity in the objects of this man's love. But the logic of the conscious has, like Molière's doctors, " changed all that " ; the unity is made to exist in one person only—but it is in the loved object, and that object is a woman, Helen. In the third phase, when narcissism prevails, the subject and the object are fused.

It is well that this should be so ; and these successive complications are not without significance. At the moment when Castor has to merge his personality into a homosexual fantasy, it is natural that he should become identified with a feminine character ; it is also natural that an Oedipian should identify himself with the " maternal imago," for he carries this imago within himself ; this is precisely what the Flemish lad in the poem did when he condensed the mother with his motherland (supra,

p. 225). It is also quite right that Helen, the symbol of the mother, should remain, throughout the tragedy, the central figure, for she is the very fountain-head of the whole internal drama: " Do you not know that she alone is the cause of this consuming death which I harbour within me ? "

She alone : the mother, or the longing for the mother. No figure could have been better chosen to express this longing than Helen of Sparta, who was stolen by a foreign prince (as Flanders was by Philip II)—who, for ten years, was longed for by an entire people. She is the preeminent and classical figure of the unattainable beloved.

We can now realise how profoundly subjective and lyrical are Verhaeren's dramas, and yet they remain true dramas all the while. Even the "yet" seems to imply too much ; but the prejudice against lyrical drama is so great that one is obliged to take up the cudgels in order to defend the dramatic nature of these works. The inner and subconscious tragedy which they exhale is one of the most poignant it is possible to imagine.

Now it is precisely because of this subjectivity and lyricism that Verhaeren has been able to plumb such tragical depths. We must never forget that his dramas were born as simple poems. The primary inspiration of each was a lyrical nucleus around which the action of the drama was subsequently to gather. The work was slow, and underwent a period of patient incubation. This is why Verhaeren's plays delve so deeply into the subconscious : they are excavations, as it were, around the original poem, which had gushed forth like a spring. Whereas Verhaeren's other works were given to the world almost as soon as he wrote them (a fact which permits of our noting the periods of his life by means of the dates at which his works were published), the dramas were written concurrently with other works, and were begun many years before they were published.

AN OEDIPUS TRILOGY 239

The lyrical nucleus of *Les aubes* is Hérénien's speech to the people in the fourth act, an outburst against war and the army, and in favour of an understanding between the peoples; in *Le cloître*, the lyrical nucleus is the confession made by Dom Balthazar in order to cleanse himself, to reinstate himself through truth and humility; in *Philippe II*, it is a monologue spoken by Don Carlos when he is simultaneously broken with weariness and fevered with enthusiasm; finally, in *Hélène de Sparte*, the most significant of all the dramas, the lyrical nucleus is hidden away at the very close of the tragedy in the sapphic ode which follows every step of Helen's inner dream and which forms the whole of scene four in the fourth act. On the back of the manuscript page containing the passages quoted above, we find the following note in Verhaeren's handwriting: " This was the first page I wrote for my drama about Helen, February 1901." The drama was not published until 1912; a considerable lapse of years! The whole action of the play converges towards this point, and towards this beautiful vision of Helen, who is the leading personage throughout the drama.

Such work is in itself a veritable analysis of the subconscious. The analysis is similar to those conducted by psychoanalysts, only in this case it is spontaneous. It seems to play that "cathartic" role which such psychologists as Breuer, Franck, and Auguste Forel attribute to these analyses. By delving into the recesses of the subconscious, by revivifying the emotions which have been repressed, the patient is able to "exteriorise" them and to deliver himself of their burden. He decondenses whilom condensations. He liberates that part of his vital energy which had been monopolised by the subconscious, and which had acted like a brake upon all his movements towards life. This "descent into hell" which is the object of therapeutic analysis may also be accomplished spontaneously. The myth of Orpheus who descends into the realm of the shades in order to rescue Eurydice, the legend of the Greeks warring for Helen, the old tales about hidden treasure, Dante's Inferno—all these may be interpreted as the expression of a spontaneous analysis. Verhaeren's Oedipian dramas are a similar "descent into hell." Henceforth his vital impulse will no longer be enchained, but it will be able freely to march towards mankind and towards the universe of the "multiple splendour."

The descent into "the desolate depths of the inner pit" becomes, by dint of subjectivity, a revelation of universal truths. Can we imagine anything more universally human than Sophocles' dramas or Dante's Divine Comedy? These poems reveal the "collective unconscious," and because of this they share the characteristics of myth. We do not exactly know why we are profoundly moved by the strange situations or the fantastic visions they contain. The fact is that the situations and visions are fantastic in appearance merely; they express the human subconscious, our own subconscious, in symbolical language by the mouth of those whose vision is turned towards the inner life. *Verhaeren's drama is akin to myth.* This is the very essence of all truly lyrical drama. The myth is the objective, the universal, form, which belongs to this kind of drama, to the Greek drama; there is none more dramatic, none more universal.

Les aubes lies outside the Oedipus trilogy. In this play Verhaeren is concerned with social questions; he is "exteriorising" himself. And yet he is doing so less than at a first glance one might suppose. The struggle of Hérénien, the tribune, against the Regency of Oppidomagne is closely akin to the theme we have just been dealing with—the rebellion against Philip II, against the tyrant, against the father. Hérénien resembles Artevelde, and there comes a time when the ungrateful people " assault his threshold," where he, too, " stands " expectant. But there is more than this ; the very first scene takes us to the heart of the conflicts with which we have now grown familiar. First we have the symbol of conflagrations, in which towers collapse. The flames " bite " the heavens, and the crowd of ragged insurgents sees in these flames the symbol of its hate :

> Les flammes qui mangent,
> A cette heure, leurs granges,
> Me paraissent être nos dents. . . .
> [The flames which, at this hour,
> Eat their barns,
> Seem to me as though they were our teeth.]

In this scene of fire and flame, Hérénien senior, the father of the tribune, dies. A man of the old faith, which has been rejected by his son, he dies attended by the village priest and the men of the plough, he dies in the midst of the dying countryside. The same struggle is present; but Hérénien—and Verhaeren—are finding deliverance through social work, by means of the " tribune's " role into which they throw themselves with enthusiasm. Hérénien is to die, but his death takes place in the triumph of the new faith ; he will continue to live in the living work he has created, and in his son (another symbol of a living work), who is acclaimed by the populace. And this work will make towards peace.

CHAPTER SIX

LIFE IN ALL ITS ARDOUR

" HE has filled me with his buoyancy " cries the poet, speaking of St. George. Henceforth " all life is buoyancy," as Verhaeren writes in *Les forces tumultueuses* (1902), the words being the last verse of an exergue near the beginning of the collection. In this same exergue we read :

Dites, se plonger à s'y perdre dans la vie contradictoire—mais enivrante !

Vivre, c'est prendre et donner avec liesse.

Mais les plus exaltés se dirent dans leur cœur :
" Partons quand même, avec notre âme inassouvie,
Puisque la force et que la vie
Sont au-delà des vérités et des erreurs."

[What if one plunges into life until one is lost, into life so contradictory and so intoxicating !

To live, is to take and to give joyfully.

But the most exalted ones have said in their heart :
" Let us go, natheless, with our insatiate souls,
Since strength and life
Are beyond truth and error."]

Such are the inaugural words of Verhaeren's new gospel. Henceforward (we are on the threshold of the twentieth century) the poet is master of his thought, and his poetry assumes the form of heroic prediction.

What are we to understand by " strength and life are

beyond truth and error" (as Nietzsche said: "beyond good and evil")? We are to understand that though the intelligence be incapable of giving us a satisfactory conviction, a faith, a reason for action, we must nevertheless throw ourselves heart and soul into life and action, we must love life passionately as though it were a huge wave bearing us along, and not fret because life may seem irrational and contradictory. Perhaps there is no common measure between intelligence and life. Faith is transferred from the intelligence to action and to instinct; faith is, above all, impetus, buoyancy, intoxication at being alive:

L'instinct me rive au front assez de certitude. . . .
Homme, tout affronter vaut mieux que tout comprendre.[1]

[Instinct rivets enough confidence on my brow. . . .
Man, to dare everything is far better than to understand everything.]

Such a doctrine taking possession of a philosopher could not fail to induce further philosophising, were it only to reconcile this intelligence and this life between which no preestablished harmony exists. But when the same doctrine takes possession of a lyrical writer, it will inevitably turn him away from pure speculation. Verhaeren can certainly not be accounted a philosopher. In this connexion, Jean de Smet has spoken of Haeckel's monism. We may likewise refer to the kinship of his convictions with those of Nietzsche, and with those of the pragmatists; his "buoyancy" may be compared with Bergson's "vital impetus," and with the heroic lyricism of *Jean Christophe*. Thus, ideas which were in the air at the opening of the twentieth century are condensed into Verhaeren's writings—but we must not expect a philosophical synthesis from our poet. He moulds these ideas; hammers them to his liking;

[1] From Les rêves, in La multiple splendeur.

endows them with a commanding aspect; gives them the appearance of a bronze.

What direction will this buoyant energy of life pursue? Two roads are closed to it: that of crude instinct (a stage Verhaeren has passed through never to return); and that of sublimated religion. A third road remains, that of human and social fervour, a keen participation in the sufferings and aspirations of modern times. In *L'amour*, a poem which forms part of the collection *Les forces tumultueuses*, Verhaeren expresses this participation by happily chosen symbols. A return to primitive instinct, to the pandemian Venus, is out of the question, though certain images may recall Kato in *Les bords de la route*:

Vénus,
La joie est morte au jardin de ton corps,
Et les grands lys des bras et les glaïeuls des lèvres
Et les raisins de fièvre et d'or,
Sur l'espalier géant que fut ton corps,
Sont morts.[1]

[Venus,
Joy is dead in the garden of your body;
And the great lilies of your arms, and the gladioluses of your lips,
And the grapes of fever and of gold
Hanging from the giant trellis that was your body,
Are dead.]

Later, Venus becomes Magdalen: and then love is introverted into an ascetic cloister wherein intoxication is wedded to suffering, wherein the soul is turned toward death:

Habille toi de lin, Vénus, voici le Christ,
Voici ses longues mains impératives,
Voici les crins, les clous, les pierres,
Pour y meurtrir et y rouler ta chair;
Voici l'ivresse et la souffrance alternatives;
Voici les couvents blancs et leurs linceuls de murs
Immensément dressés par la mort allouvie.[2]

---

[1] From Vénus, in the sequence L'amour, in Les forces tumultueuses.
[2] From Madeleine, in the sequence L'amour, in Les forces tumultueuses.

LIFE IN ALL ITS ARDOUR

[Clothe yourself in linen, Venus, here is the Christ,
Here are his long, commanding hands,
Here are the thorns, the nails, and the stones
Wherewith to bruise your flesh, wherein to roll your body,
Here is alternate rapture and suffering;
Here are the white convents and their walls like winding sheets
Spread wide by insatiable death.]

But even the day of Magdalen passes beyond recall. By a new metamorphosis, the everlasting Venus is to become the heroine of the revolution, Théroigne de Mérincourt :

Vêts-toi de sang, Vénus, voici quatre-vingt-treize. . . .
Deviens la Théroigne âpre et tragique,
Comme tu fus la sainte et l'amoureuse. . . .
On ne sait quel tonnerre autour des peuples gronde. . . .
Aime l'humanité qui est l'âme meilleure
En tourmente et en vertige vers le bonheur,
Livre et prodigue-toi à tous ceux qui t'appellent.[1]

[Clothe yourself with blood, Venus, here is, eighty-three. . . .
Become the stern and tragical Théroigne,
Just as you have been the saint and the passionate woman. . . .
A strange thunder mutters around the peoples. . . .
Love humanity for it is the better soul
In torment, and ascending the dizzy heights towards happiness;
Give yourself, be lavish of your gifts to all who invoke you.]

This is a beautiful poem, and all the more so because it is profoundly true, because in it the poet gives proof of penetrating and intuitive understanding of the laws of the evolution of the instincts. For from beginning to end we witness the same impulse of love, which is gradually sublimated into religious ecstasy and into social fervour. The sequence is an admirable illustration of the psychology of sublimation.

The first poem in the collection, *Sur la mer*, expresses

[1] From Théroigne de Mérincourt, in the sequence L'amour, in Les forces tumultueuses.

the same evolution in another form. Here we have the crisis with whose imagery we are already familiar :

> Le navire rentra comme un jardin fané,
> Drapeaux éteints, espoirs minés,
> Avec l'effroi de n'oser dire à ceux du port
> Qu'il avait entendu, là-bas, de plage en plage,
> Les flots crier sur les rivages
> Que Pan et que Jésus, tous deux, étaient des morts.

> [The vessel came to port like a faded garden,
> Flags adroop, hopes undermined,
> With the terror of not daring to tell those in the harbour
> That it had heard, over there, from strand to strand,
> The waves crying out along the shore
> That Pan and Jesus, both of them, were dead.]

Pan and Jesus: primitive nature and Christian sublimation; new names for Venus and Magdalen, for Flemish women and monks. But the sailors on the symbolic vessel do not give up hope. Stubborn, as are most of Verhaeren's heroes, they sail away to the conquest of other ecstasies :

> Mais ses mousses dont l'âme était restée
> Aussi fervente et indomptée
> Que leur navire à son départ,
> L'amarrèrent près du rempart ;
> Et dès la nuit venue, avec des cris de fête,
> Ils s'en furent dans la tempête,
> Tout en sachant que l'orage géant
> Les pousserait vers d'autres océans. . . .

> [But the crew, whose soul had remained
> As fervent and indomitable
> As the vessel when it first set sail,
> Moored her near the rampart ;
> No sooner had night come, than with jubilant cries
> They sped away into the tempest,
> Well knowing that a giant storm
> Would drive them forward to other seas. . . .]

LIFE IN ALL ITS ARDOUR

Need we repeat that here once more, while describing human evolution, Verhaeren is describing his own evolution?

The victory of the new ideal is not yet quite secure, and suddenly the old evil delivers an assault. One must ever be on the alert, ever ready to fight. The Amazon will fight. She is the successor to St. George. She, like him, rides along miraculous paths. The whole poem recalls *Saint Georges*; even the dragon is there, the dragon of ancient sin, all scaly with symbols of the crisis:

Et la guerrière se souvient
Du reptile qu'il faut tuer sans cesse
Et qui renaît et qui revient
Et dont les têtes d'or et les gueules redressent,
Comme une vigne en sang, la floraison
Violente de leurs *poisons*.
Elle arrive. Sitôt il *érige* sa force,
Tel un *arbre* dont la râpeuse écorce—
Dartres, langues, suçoirs et dents—
Empeste, au loin, les soirs ardents. . . .
Un remuement d'anneaux *glauques et verts*
Bande son corps dont la lèpre paraît vivante.[1]

[And the amazon remembers
The reptile which must be killed ever and again,
Which is ever reborn and which comes back,
Whose golden heads and mouths raise up,
Like a vine in the season of vintage, the violent flowers
Of their *poisons*.
She comes. Immediately it *rears* its strength
Like a *tree* whose rough bark—
Tetters, tongues, suckers, and teeth—
Poisons, afar, the passionate *evenings*. . . .
A movement of *glaucous and green* rings
Encircles its body whose leprous scales seem to glow with life.]

The Amazon wishes to liberate suffering mankind from the dragon, and at the same time she wishes to free the

---

[1] From L'amazone, in the sequence Les femmes, in Les forces tumultueuses.

soul of the poet. But she is powerless, and allows her weapons to fall from her hands:

> L'humanité restait rivée au bagne. . . .
> Alors que le dragon que saccagea Persée
> Et qu'il dompta, par la pensée
> Et le regard,
> Sortait, après mille ans, de son sommeil hagard,
> Et la mâchoire inassouvie
> Se redressait contre la vie.
>
> [Mankind was still chained to the galley. . . .
> Then the dragon, which had been overthrown by Perseus
> And quelled by his thought
> And his look,
> Awoke after a thousand years from its haggard sleep,
> And with insatiate jaws
> Reared itself up against life.]

Happily Perseus himself will reappear a few years hence, when Verhaeren will write *Les rythmes souverains*. Then he is to be a conqueror once more. But now the Amazon cannot overcome the dragon. This strange heroine is a distant relation of Théroigne de Méricourt, near of kin to St. George, a kind of new Venus who has subdued her primitive instincts:

> Pour se sentir plus à l'aise dans la victoire
> Elle a brûlé l'un de ses seins.
>
> [In order that she may feel more at ease in the fight
> She has burned off one of her breasts.]

The complexes of youth (such as the clock-faces and the trains) are still very tenacious. In the following lines these two images coalesce into the *eyes* of the *train*. The result is an intensification of feeling:

> Rails qui sonnent, signaux qui bougent,
> Et tout à coup le passage des yeux
> Crus et sanglants d'un convoi rouge.
> Appels stridents, ouragans noirs,

Pays de brasiers roux et d'usines tragiques. . . .
C'est parmi vous. . . .
Que s'en viennent chercher asile
Les cerveaux éclatés des déments et des fous.[1]

[Resounding rails, moving signals,
And suddenly the passage of the eyes,
Raw and bleeding, of a red train.
Strident shrieks, black tempests,
A land of glowing brasiers and of tragical workshops. . . .
It is towards you
That come, as if to a refuge,
All the cracked brains of the demented and the mad.]

But these complexes no longer impede the poet's "buoyancy"; they are carried along in its wake. They accompany the buoyancy with their thrill and their anguish:

Le corps ployé sur ma fenêtre,
Les nerfs vibrants et sonores de bruit,
J'écoute avec ma fièvre et j'absorbe, en mon être,
Les tonnerres des trains qui traversent la nuit. . . .
Oh ! les rythmes fougueux de la nature entière
Et les sentir et les darder à travers soi ! [2]

[With my body bent forward at the window,
My nerves aquiver and sonorous with noise,
I listen feverishly, and I absorb into my being
The thunder of the trains which pass in the night. . . .
Oh the vehement rhythms of the whole of nature!
Oh the joy of feeling them as they flash athwart one's body !]

Thus the trains hitherto fraught with symbols of deadly anguish, now become, just as the town and the factory have become, images of the " Forward, march ! " of the new faith in life. Nevertheless, anguish is inherent in them still; through the image of the trains this anguish invades the realms of buoyancy and of joy:

[1] From La folie, in Les forces tumultueuses.
[2] From L'en-avant, in the sequence Les cris de ma vie, in Les forces tumultueuses.

Et mes muscles bandés où tout se répercute. . . .
Communiquent, minute par minute,
Ce vol sonore et trépidant à mon esprit.
Il le remplit d'angoisse et le charme d'ivresse
Etrange et d'ample et furieuse volupté.

[And my taut muscles, wherein everything is repercussed, . . .
Communicate, from minute to minute,
This sonorous and quivering flight to my mind.
This flight fills me with anguish and beguiles me with
A strange rapture and with a plenitude of frenzied voluptuousness.]

The alliance between rapture and anguish, between life and death, does not surprise us : it is the same contrast that we have already seen, the clash between black and gold. The amazing thing is that a complex dating from earliest childhood should have come to symbolise the idea of a march forward. The symbolisation had already begun in *La foule*, a poem belonging to the collection entitled *Les visages de la vie*.[1] The transfer is a perfectly natural one. Such complexes of anguish more or less intense are normally formed in the child during the fifth or sixth year of its life, or during the years immediately following. The crisis which takes place at this period (a crisis hitherto very little studied) is as it were an initial puberty, less apparent than the real puberty which develops at a later stage. Like puberty, it is a crisis of development, and the psychological manifestations influence the whole being. Freudians insist upon the sexual aspect of the phenomena ; but they can be quite as advantageously studied from the outlook of the metaphysical anxiety which characterises them.[2] Most often this crisis seems to occur at the first contact of the child with *reality*, with objective life (the birth of curiosity) ; at the same time, it may be the first encounter between the objective and the subjective, between the practical and the

[1] Vide supra, Chapter IV, pp. 179–182.
[2] Cf. Bovet, Le sentiment religieux, " Revue de théologie et de philosophie," No. 32, 1919.

visionary, between the progressive tendency and the regressive tendency, between the "reality principle" and the "pleasure principle" (the latter being linked with the idea of the mother). The trouble is often expressed in dreams, or rather nightmares. Anguish is intensified according to the strength of the conflict, for anguish seems to be the specific symptom of the conflict between our tendencies. I have often had occasion to notice that, in the complexes aroused by the struggle, the symbols chosen to express the real have taken the form of *hard* objects such as iron and stone; or, again, the symbols may be associated with the memory of a "childish love." In Verhaeren's case, alongside the factory, we have the clock-faces at the watchmaker's, the man who related the story about the love of the lady-gnomes; we have the iron of the axe, and of the axles which clank—an image recurring later in connexion with trains. *Such infantile images are not in themselves regressive*; on the contrary, they are the first symbols of reality, of the progressive tendency, of the forward movement. It is only the *anguish* with which they are impregnated that discloses the regressive tendency. They have caused the anguish precisely because they jostled and alarmed the regressive and introspective tendency. When the poet tears himself away from his introversion and starts on his forward path, when he hurls himself into the real in order to live in it and hug it to his breast, it is quite natural that the same images should reawaken in him to express the real, the "forward march" once so dreaded and now beloved—which are even now, and in spite of himself, secretly held in awe. The anguish accompanying such images never leaves them. The real is accepted "with an open heart" (this is the new and wholesome side of the affair); but it has not been accepted without a subconscious protest, of which anguish is the symptom. Verhaeren can only gain and maintain his victory by daily combat; his temperament is such that he delights in a victory thus achieved with danger. He has no wish for "a regular happiness." He does not desire peace. He would blithely exclaim with Nietzsche (and, of course, in the same metaphorical sense): " I love peace as a means to fresh wars, and a short peace better than a long one ! "

> Mon cœur à moi ne vit dûment que s'il s'efforce.[1]
>
> [My heart cannot live duly unless through effort.]
>
> Je veux rester, je ne peux pas ; . . .
> Mieux vaut partir, sans aboutir,
> Que de s'asseoir, même vainqueur, le soir,
> Devant son œuvre coutumière,
> Avec, en son cœur morne, une vie
> Qui cesse de bondir au-delà de la vie.[2]
>
> [I would like to stay, I cannot ;
> 'Tis better to go, though you reach no goal,
> Than to sit down, even as a victor, at eventide
> To your accustomed task,
> While, in your mournful heart, life
> Ceases to leap beyond life.]

The constant desire to fight against oneself proceeds for the most part from the ascetic tendency ; it may also represent the confused consciousness of a vital need, for Verhaeren knows, or feels, that he must fight with his whole strength if he is not to succumb to the assault of his foes in the subconscious :

La force la plus belle est la force qui pleure
Et qui reste tenace et marche, d'un pas droit,
Dans sa propre douleur, qu'elle conçoit
Sublime et nécessaire, à chaque appel de l'heure.[3]

[The most beautiful strength is the strength which weeps
And which remains steadfast and goes forward, with unfaltering
   step,

[1] From La vie ardente, in Les flammes hautes.
[2] From Au bord du quai, in Les visages de la vie.
[3] From La joie, in Les visages de la vie.

LIFE IN ALL ITS ARDOUR

Wrapped in its own sorrow, which it conceives to be
Sublime and necessary, in response to every claim of the moment.]

Verhaeren seems never wholly to have overcome his
early complexes, never wholly to have triumphed over
his early conflict. (" Who has ever been cured of his
childhood ? ") We may even admit that he, as a fighter,
did not really yearn for victory. Rather he enjoyed the
struggle, resembling in this way *the gladiator who fed his own
beasts in order to fight them* :

> Nourrir, avec ferveur, les angoisses profondes
> Dont s'effare l'instinct mais dont vibre l'esprit.[1]
>
> [Fervently to feed the deep anguish
> Which affrights instinct but which makes the mind vibrate.]

Verhaeren has become extroverted, though not as
fully as his new intonation would lead us to believe ;
and there is nothing contradictory in supposing that in
his hymn to the real (just as previously in *Les flamandes*,
though to a less degree) he is involuntarily forcing the
tone, urged to this by a secret need to preach to himself,
for he feels that he is not fully converted. Thus the
old complexes—whose most powerful symbol is the
train—if they are no longer capable of preventing
the forward march, still have the power of making it
dangerous and fraught with anxiety. But the anxiety
and the danger, which may be mortal, serve to spur on
the combative energy, to intensify the will to run risks,
to stimulate defiance. Once again we return to the trains
in *La folie* and to those animals which

> N'arrêtent point l'essor
> De leurs ailes vers la lumière,
> Parce que ceux qui les montaient glissent à terre,
> Soudainement, parmi les morts.[2]

---

[1] From La joie, in Les visages de la vie.
[2] From La folie, in Les forces tumultueuses.

[Do not stop in the flight
Of their wings towards the light
Because those who were mounting them fall to the ground,
On a sudden, among the dead.]

We understand now what interior conflicts, what feverish anxiety, have been concentrated in these two lines, which are so tragically prophetic.

The new buoyancy bears along with itself the old emotions. We have already seen how Verhaeren's new faith, far from repressing his erstwhile devotion, absorbs it and makes it part of itself; we have seen how the mother reappears in the spouse. Autophilia, too, the introverted love which was so manifest in the symbols of the crisis, is still there. Verhaeren is advancing towards a pantheistic love of the world, but he loves himself as part of the world. This is a sublimated autophilia : no longer a mere retirement within himself; no longer " squatting " but erect, chest squared, inhaling and exhaling the universe. The extroversion and the introversion are now in a state of perfect equilibrium, as in the rhythmic breathing of a soul :

J'aime mes yeux, mes bras, mes mains, ma chair, mon torse
    Et mes cheveux amples et blonds
    Et je voudrais, par mes poumons,
Boire l'espace entier pour en gonfler ma force.

Oh ! ces marches à travers bois, plaines, fossés,
    Où l'être chante et pleure et crie
    Et se dépense avec furie
Et s'enivre de soi ainsi qu'un insensé.[1]

[I love my eyes, my arms, my hands, my flesh, my body,
    And my thick, fair hair,
    And through my lungs I would fain
Drink in space itself so as to increase my strength.

---

[1] From Un matin, in the sequence Les cris de ma vie, in Les forces tumultueuses.

LIFE IN ALL ITS ARDOUR

Oh, those walks through the woods, over the plains, along the dikes,
  When the whole being sings, and weeps, and cries,
  And spends itself with intensity,
And is drunken with itself as though it were mad!]

The Tumultuous Forces, as the very name suggests, are as it were the turmoil of waters when a river has at last broken through an obstacle. With Multiple Splendour the era of harmony is definitely entered upon.[1] This harmony in not the expression of a dull placidity. But dionysian art is being converted into apollinian art, the tempestuous visions are "finding repose in the form of statues":[2]

O ces frises de marbre autour des temples blancs,
Où s'incruste, dans la pierre dure asservie,
Le tumulte apaisé des gestes de la vie![3]

[Oh the marble friezes around white temples,
Wherein are petrified, in the hard, obedient stone,
The stilled tumult of the actions of life.]

And now the rhythms are approximating to classical regularity. The ancient myths of Hercules and of Perseus will arise in their undying youth, in all their well-knit vigour and nervous energy.

The struggle between the past and the future is finished —in so far as the struggle of a perennial fighter can ever come to an end. Verhaeren continues to sing of the past and to love it. But we need merely compare his new

---

[1] La multiple splendeur (1906); Les rythmes souverains (1910); Les blés mouvants (1912); Les flammes hautes (1914) [this work was not published until 1917]. During the same years we have Les heures d'après-midi (1905); Les heures du soir (1911); Toute la Flandre (1904–1911).— Les ailes rouge de la guerre (1916) must be placed in a category apart.

[2] Car aucune des visions qu'il avait eues
  Ne s'etait, à ses yeux, apaisée en statue.
    (From Michel-Ange, in Les rythmes souverains.)

[3] From Les vieux empires in La multiple splendeur.

evocations with those of *Les moines* to notice the difference. Then it was a question of the dead past; and even when this past seemed to persist, we felt it was doomed. But in *Les vieux empires* (*La multiple splendeur*) all the Egyptians and all the Chaldeans, all the Rameses and all the Cambyses, all the Athens and all the Romes, pass in unending files like a legend of the ages; but they are the living, the active past; one feels that this past is pregnant with the future; the poet does not lose himself in the past and linger there, wrapt in melancholy dreams; all the successive civilisations appear to him like the successive storeys of the latter-day Babel. No longer does he endeavour to go " up-stream," against the current of the time; he comes down the stream of history and tarries amid the alluvial drift whence living man draws his life:

> Ainsi, au cours des temps plein d'ombre ou de flambeaux,
> L'homme s'est fait son corps, son verbe et son cerveau.[1]

> [Thus, adown the ages full of shadow or of light,
> Man has fashioned his body, his speech, and his mind.]

This is the agelong work, slow of construction and never ending, the work of humanity as it grows. The poem closes with this refulgent verse:

> La flamme et la splendeur de la vie embrasée.

> [The flame and the splendour of glowing life.]

Verhaeren deals here with humanity's past just as he dealt with his own childhood in *Saint Georges*; he does not mean to be lost in the past but to draw it towards him and to nourish himself upon it. The present, the real, action—these are the goals of his enthusiasm: and through action he strives towards the future:

[1] From *Les vieux empires*, in *La multiple splendeur*.

LIFE IN ALL ITS ARDOUR 257

Je sais, je sais
Le charme exquis des souvenirs inapaisés,
Mais mon cœur est trop fier et trop vivace
Pour se stériliser
Dans le regret et le passé.
Souffles et vents illuminent l'espace,
Ma ville est trépidante aux bruits de l'univers
Et l'avenir frappe à ma porte—et je le sers.[1]

[I know, I know
The exquisite charm of restless memories;
But my heart is too proud and too mettlesome
To allow itself to become petrified
In regrets and in the past.
Breezes and winds illumine space,
My town is aquiver with the noises of the universe,
And the future is knocking at my door—and I serve it.]

The poet appears to be wholly released from the tyranny of introversion and from the irresistible attraction exercised over him by his "early affections." The poem entitled *Les attirances* in *Les rythmes souverains* presents us with the strange drama of a man who has been lured from his beloved's arms by the magnetic attraction of the modern city:

O la cité énorme, angoissante et tragique,
Comme elle entra fiévreuse et frémissante en lui !

[Oh the vast city, so full of anguish, so tragical,
How feverishly and shudderingly it permeated his being.]

We know what the *town* symbolises for Verhaeren: it is extroversion, enthusiasm for the real, for the present. The beloved who awaits the coming of her dear, in the distance, reminds us of her who hailed the ferryman, or of the child friend in *Les tendresses premières*:

Heures de paix, temps de naguère,
Charmes de celle, hélas ! qui l'attendait toujours
    Avec son âme et son amour,
A l'autre bout des mers et de la terre,

[1] From *Ma ville*, in *Les flammes hautes*.

Il négligea, brutalement, vos doux appels.
Son cœur grandi avait changé à un point tel
Qu'il ne s'angoissait plus que des forces profondes
Qui font d'un cœur humain le cœur même du monde.[1]

> [Peaceful hours, days of yore,
> Charms of her, alas, who ever awaited him,
>   With her soul and her love,
>   At the other end of the seas and of the earth,
> He callously neglected your gentle call.
> Owing to his mature experience he had altered so much
> That he was no longer tortured save by those profound forces
> Which make of a human heart the very heart of the world.]

Verhaeren feels that he is freed from the fascination of a regressive image by means of the more powerful attraction of reality. The poet is impelled towards men and things, not only by sympathy, but also by spontaneous admiration. The words "Admire one another" are placed as an epigraph at the beginning of *La multiple splendeur*; and Verhaeren carries out his own precept.

> Pour vivre clair, ferme et juste,
> Avec mon cœur, j'admire tout
> Ce qui vibre, travaille et bout
> Dans la tendresse humaine et sur la terre auguste.[2]
>
> [In order to live serenely and firmly and justly,
> With my heart, I admire everything
> Which vibrates and ferments and boils
> In human tenderness and on the august earth.]

Above all, the poet admires that which constitutes effort, the effort of the worker:

> Torses carrés et durs, gestes précis et forts,[3]
>
> [Bodies squared and hard, actions precise and strong,]

---

[1] From Les attirances, in Les rythmes souverains.
[2] From Autour de ma maison, in La multiple splendeur.
[3] From L'effort, in La multiple splendeur.

LIFE IN ALL ITS ARDOUR 259

the effort of the scholar, persevering and bold: here are the victors. He admires the effort of modern towns; the effort of Europe, the land of energy, straining towards reality ; the efforts of scattered humanity to unite—as the workmen from the south and from the north, tunnelling the mountains, meet at last.[1] The new faith which Verhaeren feels welling up within him, is striving towards a faith in human effort.

> Il n'importe que sous les toits
>   Dans les demeures,
> Quand le jour naît ou qu'il décroit,
>   Les prières au Christ en croix
>   Se meurent.
> Efforts multipliés en tous les lieux du monde,
> C'est vous qui recélez les croyances profondes :
>   Qui risque et qui travaille croit.[2]

> [What matter if beneath the roofs,
>   Within the dwellings,
> When day dawns or when it declines,
>   The prayers to Christ on the cross
>   Die.
> Efforts redoubled in every part of the world,
> It is you which sustain the profound faiths :
>   He who runs a risk and he who works, believes.]

The word *cross* is not too strong a symbol; for what Verhaeren seeks is a substitute for his sometime faith ; he finds it in this fresh enthusiasm :

> O prière debout ! O prière nouvelle !
> Futur, vous m'exaltez comme autrefois mon Dieu ! [3]

> [Oh the prayer one says standing! Oh new prayer !
> Future which exalts me as formerly did my God !]

The whole attitude is different ; the new religious sentiment is not regressive, it is addressed to the future

---

[1] See Le tunnel, in Les flammes hautes.
[2] From L'orgueil, in Les flammes hautes.
[3] From La prière, in Les rythmes souverains.

towards which every present effort is striving; but at bottom there exists the same ecstasy as in the past. The attitude of the prayer, the meaning of the faith, have changed because there was a vital need for the change : [1]

> Seigneur, toi seul connais ce qui s'est fait en moi ;
> Et comme il a fallu que l'urgence de vivre
> Eperonnât mon être et l'incitât à suivre
> Le montueux chemin qui m'éloignait de toi.[2]

> [Lord, thou alone knowest what has happened within me,
> And how the urgency of living had to
> Spur on my being and incite it to follow
> The uphill path which led me away from thee.]

The urgency of living, as we know, was the urgent need to escape from the crisis of despair, to find an extroverted and progressive faith, for the earlier faith was too infantile to satisfy the poet. The old faith has become impossible, for it is the cult of a child—which being interpreted means that it was for Verhaeren a regression towards childhood. The kings who came from the *east* to worship the *child* are symbolic of this naive faith :

> Mages des nuits d'argent dont les astres caressent
> Les fronts penchés vers la candeur et la bonté,
> Vos regards sont ravis et vos cœurs exaltés
> De croire au doux pouvoir nouveau de la faiblesse.
> Mais l'homme en qui l'audace a imprimé sa loi,
> Dont l'ample volonté est l'essor et la foi
> Et qui part conquérir pour soi-même le monde,
> Admettra-t-il jamais qu'en son âme profonde
> Le règne d'un enfant fasse ployer l'orgueil ? [3]

> [Kings of the silver night, whose stars caress
> The foreheads bent towards candour and goodness,
> Your eyes are rapt and your hearts exalted
> By the belief in the gentle power of weakness.
> But the man on whom courage has stamped her law,

---

[1] Traditional faith is not necessarily regressive ; but for Verhaeren it was so (roses, palms, etc., between little fingers).
[2] From L'ancienne foi, in Les flammes hautes.
[3] From Les mages, in La multiple splendeur.

LIFE IN ALL ITS ARDOUR

Whose abundant will is impetus and faith,
And who ventures forth alone to conquer the world—
Could such as he ever admit that in his inmost heart
The reign of a child should curb his pride?]

While seeking for a new faith, Verhaeren has met human effort :

J'entendais retentir tous les bonds de l'essor
Avec leurs sabots clairs sur le seuil de mon âme
Et je suivis leur course et leur galop de flamme
Vers les neuves cités dont s'exaltait l'effort.

La passion me vint et de l'homme et du monde. . . .
J'étais ivre de me sentir un être humain.[1]

[I heard resounding the leaps of impetus,
With their glistening hoofs, upon the threshold of my soul,
And I followed their course and their flaming gallop
Towards the new cities whence effort was springing.

Two passions seized me, that of man and that of the world. . . .
I was intoxicated at the thought that I was a human being.]

But, as he well knows, this passion and exaltation are no other than the old religious fervour transferred to other objects :

Car, bien que vous m'ayez abandonné, Seigneur,
Ma ferveur d'autrefois ne s'est point apaisée.

[For though thou hast forsaken me, Lord,
My bygone fervour is not assuaged.]

Again we encounter Magdalen, who has become Théroigne. In another poem this is made clearer still :

Si je n'ai plus en moi cette angoisse de Dieu
Qui fit mourir les saints et les martyrs dans Rome,
Mon cœur, qui n'a changé que de liens et de vœux,
Eprouvre en lui l'amour et l'angoisse de l'homme.[2]

---

[1] From L'ancienne foi, in Les flammes hautes.
[2] From Au passant d'un soir, in Les flammes hautes.

[If I no longer have within me the anguish of God
Which brought the saints and the martyrs to death in Rome,
My heart which has merely changed its bonds and its vows
Feels within itself the love and the anguish of man.]

The love and the anguish of man above all, but not exclusively. We have just had the line about "the passion of man and of the world," and a little earlier we read "in human tenderness and on the august earth." Though he outsoars mankind, Verhaeren never loses sight of the earth which sustains him; his faith does not merely consist of human fervour; it is a cosmic emotion, and by this very sign the religious character of the faith is marked. Verhaeren has made a definite profession of faith. It forms his answer to an enquiry circulated among writers of the day (1905):

"What is to be the future of poetry? I hesitate, and yet believe in poetry with all the strength of my faith. It seems to me that poetry will soon profess a lucid pantheism. More and more are healthy and honest minds coming to accept the unity of the world. The old distinctions between soul and body, between God and the universe, are being obliterated. Man is a fragment of the architecture of the world. He is conscious of the whole, of which he is a part; he understands it. He discovers things, he curtails the mystery enshrouding things, he understands their mechanism. As he penetrates their mysteries, both his admiration of nature and his admiration of himself become firmer. He feels that he is enfolded and dominated, and at the same time that he enfolds and dominates things. Confronted by the sea, he conquers it and builds harbours; the rivers, he dams up; the towns, he constructs; when he wishes to explore the skies, he fashions thousands of marvellous instruments; to know matter and to scrutinise his own being, he builds laboratories; during the last century he has increased his strength, his energy, and his will a hundredfold; he is creating a colossal work which he superposes on the work of time; by dint of prodigies he is himself becoming the personal god in whom his forefathers believed. Now I ask you, is it possible that lyrical inspiration should remain indifferent before such an unchaining of human power, and should delay celebrating so stupendous and magnificent a spectacle? The poet need only let himself be taken possession of by that which he sees, hears, imagines, guesses, in order that youthful, thrilling, new works should issue from his heart and his brain. His art will then be neither social, nor scientific, nor philosophical; it will be simply art as it was understood in those days elect when all that was most worthy of admiration was sung with fervour, when the most characteristic and the most heroic elements of each age found expression in song. We shall live in harmony with the present, and in closest contact with the future; caution will cease to curb the boldness of our pens; no longer will the poet be afraid of his own frenzy, or of the red and surging poetry wherein it will find expression.—These are my hopes."

Faith in man and in the world are one. Verhaeren has a dynamic outlook on the world; we feel his admiration for effort, for the struggles of the energetic will, for the endless labours of the millenarians; his outlook is permeated with the evolutionary spirit. He no longer sees the skies with their constellations set in perfect geometrical order, but as a "forest"[1] swarming with suns aglow, suns born from nebulas, whose heat flings worlds into space. Everything is making an effort, everything labours, as does the human crowd.

Le monde est fait avec des astres et des hommes [2]

[The universe is made of stars and of men]

to such an extent, that the tangled struggle of the stars might well serve as a symbol of the human conflict,

[1] A la gloire des cieux, in La multiple splendeur.
[2] From Le monde, in La multiple splendeur.

or vice versa. In one and in the other are manifested the great dynamic law of the universe marching forward and fighting as it goes :

> Et s'enivrer si fort de l'humaine bataille
> —Pâle et flottant reflet des monstrueux assauts
> Ou des groupements d'or des étoiles là-haut—
> Qu'on vit en tout ce qui agit, lutte ou tressaille
> Et qu'on accepte avidement, le cœur ouvert,
> L'âpre et terrible loi qui régit l'univers.[1]

> [To become so mightily intoxicated with the human battle
> —A pale and floating reflection of the giant assaults
> Or the golden groupings of the stars up there—
> That one lives in all that moves, that fights, that quivers ;
> That one eagerly accepts, with an open heart,
> The bitter and terrible law which governs the universe.]

Verhaeren divides his enthusiasm equally between the world and man, between " the multitudinous whirling gold of the skies " and the gold, no less multitudinous and whirling, which hallucinates the eyes of men dwelling in cities and spurs them forward to effort. In *Les villes tentaculaires*, Verhaeren devotes a poem to the Stock Exchange and to the feverish hunt for gold. He waxes enthusiastic as he writes. Such enthusiasm may seem strange on the part of a man so simple in his tastes, so kindly ; on the part of a sage whose needs were so easily satisfied, and to whom no action was so alien as the dollar hunt. But explanation is hardly needed as soon as we realise that the poet's cult of gold is, above all, symbolical : we know that, ever since he wrote *Les flamandes*, gold has been for him the symbol of an exalted life ; at first this life was sensual, but as soon as St. George signed the golden cross on his forehead, as soon as a new inspiration took possession of Verhaeren, gold was to become the symbol of the ecstasy of the soul, of Venus transformed into Théroigne. Gold still symbolises life in all its wealth and fruitfulness ; but the fruitfulness

[1] From La vie, in La multiple splendeur.

is now human or cosmic effort rather than the fruitfulness of the flesh and of golden harvests. Thus human gold merges into celestial gold in the same whirlpool of symbolic splendour. When the poet sings of the Bank, he reanimates, in his song, all the old complexes, and the gold is still interpenetrated with the whilom significance: we can hear the primitive instinct which he symbolised of yore vibrating through the lines as harmonics:

> Et tout là-bas, au coin d'un carrefour géant,
> Du haut de tes grands toits, *œillés de vitres rondes*,
> Tu règnes, de pôle en pôle, sur l'Océan,
> Toi, la Banque, âme mathématique du monde !
> *Les plus vieux des désirs retentissent en toi.*[1]

> [And high aloft, at the corner of the giant cross-roads,
> From the height of your great roofs pierced with round windows like eyes,
> You reign, from pole to pole, over the oceans,
> You, the Bank, the mathematical soul of the world !
> *The most ancient of desires reverberate within you.*]

Consider also the lines in *La bourse* (*Les villes tentaculaires*):

> La rue énorme et ses maisons quadrangulaires
> Bordent la foule et l'endiguent de leur granit
> *Œillé de fenêtres* et de porches où luit
> L'adieu, dans les carreaux, des soirs auréolaires.

> [The wide street and its massive blocks of houses
> Hem in the crowd, and dam it up with their granite
> Windows blinking like eyes, and their square porches
> Whence shine forth the farewells of haloed evenings.]

Soon, however, the image acquires a deeper significance; in addition to the earlier meaning it comprehends new meanings; it comes to embrace all the wealth of a prodigal universe:

> O formidable pluie éparse sur le monde !
> O l'antique légende ! O chair de Danaé !
> O cieux brûlés de feux et d'étoiles fécondes
> Qui vous penchez le soir sur l'univers pâmé !

[1] From L'or, in Les rythmes souverains.

O tourbillons de l'or où les yeux s'hallucinent,
Or, échange et conquête ; or, verbe universel ;
Sève montant au faîte et coulant aux racines
De forêt en forêt, comme un sang éternel.
Or, lien de peuple à peuple à travers les contrées,
Et tantôt pour la lutte et tantôt pour l'accord,
Mais lien toujours vers quelque entente inespérée
Puisque l'ordre lui-même est fait avec de l'or.

[Oh formidable rain scattered over the world!
Oh the ancient legend! Oh flesh of Danaë.
Oh skies consumed with fire and with fecund stars,
Skies bending over the swooning earth at night!
Oh vortex of gold hallucinating our eyes,
Gold, exchange and conquest ; gold, universal speech ;
Sap rising to the top and flowing down to the roots
From forest to forest like an endless stream of blood.
Gold, link between peoples throughout all lands,
Now causing strife and now bringing concord,
A link ever tending towards an unhoped for understanding,
For order itself is builded of gold.]

Verhaeren may have fancied that he was singing about gold as money, and he may have rationalised his song by thinking that gold is the lever of human energy. In reality, gold fascinated him much as the trains and the clock-faces had tortured him. But the fascination was in the realm of the symbolic ; were we to see in Verhaeren a mere panegyrist of the almighty dollar, we should be seriously misled ; the poet's whole life would rise up in witness against us.

Another thing which Verhaeren glorifies, apparently to excess, is the great modern town. True, he harboured an intense love for the town of to-day, but his love in this case resembled his love of gold : he loved it as an artist (which by no means implies that he loved it as a lover), without desiring it, and with a certain aloofness. Verhaeren lived in a retired corner of the Walloon country, at Caillou-qui-Bique. He came in close contact with the neighbouring peasantry. The peasants, knowing him to be a writer, called on him for help when they were faced with the onerous task of letter writing. The poet acquitted himself with goodnatured and smiling amusement.[1] One recalls his bent body; his rather clumsy gait, as of a man following the plough. Verhaeren loved the open air and the wind, he loved the long walks " through the woods, across the plains, along the dikes." While ranging over the countryside he composed his songs. When he wanted to be in close touch with Paris, he did not live in the capital but in the fresh oasis of Saint-Cloud. No one could, therefore, accuse him of a great love of the town, any more than of a love of gold as such. The town Verhaeren sings is a symbolical town. Albert Mockel understood this very well : " When Verhaeren writes of throbbing towns, he is thinking of himself ; one of these towns is *his* town, and one of them is his own soul portrayed in a living picture."[2] The town, which is his own town, is silhouetted in *Les flammes hautes* :

> J'ai construit dans mon âme une ville torride.
>
> Gares, halles, clochers, voûtes, dômes, beffrois,
> Et du verre et de l'or et des feux sur les toits.
>
> Passant tu n'y trouveras pas
> Autour des vieux foyers de quiétude
> Les fauteuils lourds, boîteux et las
> Où sommeillent et se chauffent en tas
> Les habitudes ;
> Ni sur les murs des ardentes maisons
> Les antiques images,
> Ni les bergers, ni les rois mages,
> Ni le bœuf, ni l'ânon,
> Ni la Vierge Marie,
> Ni le Christ calme et doux
> Que j'aime encor, mais plus ne prie
> A deux genoux.[3]

---

[1] Stefan Zweig, Erinnerungen an Emil Verhaeren (personal memories—privately printed).
[2] Op. cit., p. 131.   [3] From Ma ville, in Les flammes hautes.

[Within my soul I have built a torrid town.

Stations, market halls, steeples, arches, domes, belfries,
The roofs all aflame with fire and with gold.

Passer-by, you will not find here
Around the peaceful firesides of yore
The massive, tired, decrepit arm-chairs
Wherein are dosing and huddling for warmth
The habits of a lifetime ;
Nor will you find on the walls of the glowing houses
The ancient images,
Neither the shepherds nor the Kings of the East,
Nor the ox nor the ass,
Nor the Virgin Mary,
Nor the calm and gentle Christ
Whom I still love but to whom I no longer pray
On my bended knees.]

But there is no trace in the Town of the habits of the introvert who shuts himself up snugly within himself ; the old-time faith ; the maternal Virgin Mary ; the infantile images which illuminate the birth of the God-Child. Verhaeren's Town stands at the antipodes of these regressive things :

Rien ne s'y meut torpidement, à reculons.

[Nothing moves torpidly there, nothing moves backwards.]

More and more is the Town a symbol of extroverted fervour, of vibrant human effort, of all that constitutes the poet's new faith :

Oh ! l'exaltante et brûlante atmosphère
Que l'on respire en ma cité :
Le flux et le reflux des forces de la terre
S'y concentrent en volontés
Qui luttent. . . .
Sois fier d'être vivant quand tel a peur de vivre ;
Utilise l'orgueil qui te porte et t'enivre,
Et ta pitié, et ta fureur, et ta bonté.

[Oh, the exultant and burning atmosphere
Which one breathes in my city!
The flux and the reflux of the earth's forces
Are concentrated there in wills
That strive. . . .
Be proud of being alive when some fear to live;
Make use of the pride which bears you up and exalts you,
Make use of your pity, your frenzy, and your goodness.]

In these lines Verhaeren reveals the deep significance of his Town. What he admires therein is the visible image of ardour for the fight and of energy in combat. If, among all the energies, he has chosen to symbolise those of the factory, the stock-exchange, and the goods-yard, it is not because he loves these above all others; he certainly does not prefer them to the struggle within himself, the struggle he wages day by day, and through which he hopes to reach the heights of fervent beauty. "He desires fever," writes Jean de Smet, "but he desires it to be within him."[1] There are other reasons for the choice of such symbols. First of all, the factory has been for Verhaeren, from childhood to manhood, the concrete image of action, of the real; later, the factory became the symbol of the industrial town, just as the clank of the axles was converted into the noise of the trains. In addition, these aspects of the town are malleable, they respond to the instinct of the great visualiser and great visionary; they best express for him the idea of throbbing, straining energy. In the same way, Victor Hugo saw, in the splendid action of the Sower, the plastic concentration of the action of all creators.

"Life, so contradictory and so intoxicating," wrote Verhaeren. To be intoxicated also by contraries—such will henceforward be the law inspiring his enthusiasm. His life has become an equilibrium of contrasts; a balance of the two tendencies, extroversion and introversion, town and country:

[1] Op. cit., vol. ii. p. 252.

> La ville et tous ses bruits
> Et ses trains d'or trouant la nuit
> Ont effrayé pendant longtemps les blancs villages,
> Mais aujourd'hui l'accord est fait et les marchés
> Voient de beaux gars endimanchés
> Mener vers eux mille attelages.[1]

> [The town and its manifold noises,
> And its golden trains piercing the night,
> For long affrighted the white villages ;
> But to-day harmony has been achieved, and the market places
> Are thronged with handsome lads in their Sunday clothes
> Who have driven thither in their thousand carts.]

Verhaeren, in his own life, expresses this reconciliation ; he expresses it by living part of the year in the town and part of the year in the country, by dividing his time between Saint-Cloud and Caillou-qui-Bique.

A balance between power and gentleness. At the date of *Les apparus dans mes chemins*, St. George revealed love ; the Saints, gentleness :

Elles sont quatre à me parler : leur voix d'ailleurs
Toutes frêles, entre leurs lèvres lentes,
Sont calmantes et rechauffantes,
Comme leurs robes et leurs mantes.

L'une est le bleu pardon, l'autre la bonté blanche,
La troisième l'amour pensif, la dernière le don
D'être, même pour les méchants, le sacrifice.
Chacune a bu dans le chrétien calice
Tout l'infini.[2]

[There are four of them who speak to me : and their voices,
Issuing so frail from their slow-moving lips,
Are soothing and warming
Like their robes and their mantles.

---

[1] From *Tityre et Moelibée*, in *Les blés mouvants*.
[2] From *Les saintes*, in *Les apparus dans mes chemins*.

LIFE IN ALL ITS ARDOUR

One of them is blue forgiveness; another, white goodness;
A third is pensive love; and the last is the gift
Of being—even for the wicked—sacrifice.
Each has drunk from the Christian chalice
The whole of the infinite.]

But now, we have, in the figure of St. John, the highest and purest expression of this divine and ardent gentleness, a gentleness which has vanquished power:

La mauvaise fureur n'habitait plus en lui. . . .
Il se faisait très faible et se sentait très fort.
Il recelait en lui le secret réconfort
    De ceux qui dominent la vie
Non par la force droite et belle infiniment,
Mais par l'humble vouloir et par l'effacement
    Et la douceur inassouvie.[1]

[Evil fury dwelt no longer within him. . . .
He made himself very weak and yet felt himself very strong.
He harboured within himself the secret refreshment
    Of those who dominate life,
Not by a power which is infinitely beautiful and upright,
But by a humble will and by self-effacement
    And inexhaustible gentleness.]

"He made himself very weak and yet felt himself very strong": this is a line that may be fully applied to Verhaeren. There are now, as it were, two currents in his poetry; sometimes the currents run alongside one another, at others they mingle and yet do not merge so as to become indistinguishable. The older current is one of force and of violence; it is of this that we think when called upon to describe Verhaeren's work. The other current is one of gentleness and tenderness; it took rise at the date when *Les apparus dans mes chemins* was being written; ever since then this current has been gathering strength. But the gentleness is that of a strong individuality, a gentleness full of the most fascinating awkwardness. Gentleness is the basis of

[1] From Saint-Jean, in Les rythmes souverains.

the poem about St. John; whereas the neighbouring frescoes depicting the Barbarians, Martin Luther, and Michelangelo, are consecrated to power. All the books devoted to the beloved, belong to the first category: *Les heures claires, Les heures d'après-midi, Les heures du soir*. In these collections we hear a perfect melody which flows alongside (without ever losing itself therein) the sombre and rich orchestration of mighty works.

Thus balance is secured between the personal and the general, between love of the countryside and passion for all mankind. We find that such great achievements as *La multiple splendeur, Les rythmes souverains* and *Les flammes hautes*, are garlanded on one side by the collections of the Hours and on the other by All Flanders: the trilogy of private life and the tetralogy of the native land. These more intimate works were being fashioned concomitantly with the others, forming a burden of love which accompanied the lyrical flights of the mind.

No one has ever succeeded in wedding, more intimately or with so touching a simplicity, an enthusiastic love for humanity with devotion to the native land. One represents the future, the other the past. Verhaeren loves humanity as an effort ceaselessly straining towards betterment; he loves Flanders as he would love a mother. The balance which these two sentiments have established within him is perhaps the most faithful image of the equilibrium between extroversion and introversion. This balance, this equilibrium, acquired after so strenuous a fight, was tested to the utmost when Verhaeren had to look on while his beloved Flanders was crushed under the heel of war. The tragedy rent his heart, and entailed the danger of a fresh crisis. His faith in humanity was wellnigh shattered; not without good cause, for the most serene of natures might have been shaken by such calamities. He was the least prepared of men to sustain the shock; "this limpid, childlike soul who trusted so naively in the goodness of men," writes Jean de Smet.

Verhaeren was correcting the proofs of *Les flammes hautes*, that supreme act of faith, when the tornado was let loose. He thought for a moment that the whole structure of his inner life was again splitting from summit to base, and was crashing down amid the ruins of his country in flames. In actual fact, as if by a special vindictiveness of fate, the clock-tower of his native village crumbled once more in a welter of flames?[1] The tragic images of bygone days are kindled anew : clock-towers on fire and reflected in the mirror of the accursed meres. Such images throng the lines of *L'exode*, the finest poem, it seems to me, of the collection *Les ailes rouges de la guerre* :

Et tout à coup voici les tours,
Les grandes tours qui s'éclairent de bourgs en bourgs,
Et qui tendent jusqu'à la mer la tragédie
Haletante de l'incendie.

La plaine et la forêt s'illuminent au loin.
Mares, fleuves, étangs et lacs sont les témoins
De la terreur qui dans les eaux se réverbère ; . . .
Et dans les clochers noirs les derniers tocsins sonnent.

[And now, of a sudden, here are the towers,
The great towers which throw their beacon flares from town to town,
And which spread to the sea's far strand
The breathless tragedy of the conflagration.

Wide spreads the glow over forest and plain.
Meres, streams, ponds, and lakes stand there as witnesses
Of the terror reflected in these many waters ; . . .
In the black belfries the last tocsins sound.]

Is Verhaeren's faith once more to be wrecked ? The poet feels as though something within him has been wounded to death. In the preface to *La Belgique sanglante* he owns to a feeling of hate. Let us consider this hate : he is tortured by the idea that he is " no longer the same man," that he is " diminished " ; and we have the poignant

[1] On September 6, 1914 (Smet, op. cit., vol. ii. p. 131).

dedication to "the man I once was." Similar feelings are met with in his letters to Romain Rolland:[1] "I am filled with sadness and with hate. I have never felt hatred before; now I know what it is. I cannot rid myself of the feeling, and yet I fancy I am an upright man who formerly considered hate to be a degrading emotion."[2] These letters bear witness to the effort Verhaeren was making in order to overcome his hatred, for hatred was contrary to his nature and was undermining his faith in humanity, a faith which was the very foundation of his life. "How much greater and higher you are than I; you may well serve me as example," he writes to Rolland on December 3, 1914. "I own that while I am thus consumed with sadness and anger, I cannot be just. I am not standing by the side of a flame, I am in the very flame itself; I am suffering, I cry aloud. I can do no otherwise."[3] How far deeper would his personal grief have been, had he lived to see, three days before the armistice, the incendiary bombs falling on his little house at Caillou-qui-Bique and destroying it completely. Up to then it had been protected, thanks to Stefan Zweig's intercession.

This correspondence raises the curtain on a poignant drama of conscience; and Albert Mockel, who does not seem to know of the existence of the letters, has nevertheless recognised the similarity between the dramas within Verhaeren and Rolland respectively—dramas which worked out in very different ways in the two men. However, the two great writers never ceased to love one another. When Henri Mugnier asked Verhaeren to contribute to "Le Carmel," a magazine to which Rolland had promised his collaboration, he received the following answer from the Belgian poet: "Yes, you may count upon me. I shall be happy to write for a review where I shall have

[1] Quelques lettres de Verhaeren et Romain Rolland, published by Cahiers idéalistes français, Paris, No. 14, March, 1918.
[2] Letter dated October 24, 1914.
[3] Letter dated June 15, 1915.

such companions as Spitteler and Romain Rolland. For the moment I cannot follow the latter along the road he has entered; but I love him—I might say that I love him all the more since there is a certain danger in loving him. Remember me very cordially to him." [1]

The words "for the moment" are significant. Verhaeren no longer considers his attitude on the war as a definitive one; nor does he feel that the renunciation of his love for humanity is permanent. He has got a grip on himself once more. Verhaeren was simply the most passionate of lovers where his country was concerned; we should be guilty of grave injustice did we stigmatise such a man as a jingo. In 1916 I had the privilege (the reader will forgive me if I mention myself in this connexion) of conveying to Stefan Zweig the fervent admiration which Verhaeren still treasured for the Austrian writer. When we understand the intensity of Verhaeren's torture, we can readily condone his anger, and can all the more appreciate his attitude towards Rolland and Zweig.[2]

Faith in humanity and love for his fellows could not be extirpated from his great, tortured heart. His hate was itself nothing else than the obverse of his love; and his faith, shaken at the first onslaught, was too firmly founded and too vital not to be able to resist in the end; it arises again, less naively confident perhaps, but no less sure of itself. Having once been shaken, his faith becomes even firmer, as though buttressed with new powers:

L'urgence de revivre envahit nos cerveaux ;
Les vieilles vérités n'ont plus assez de force

[1] Letter dated January 26, 1916.
[2] In the opening issue of " Le Carmel " (April 1916) I published the first half of Zweig's Tower of Babel. Verhaeren wrote in enthusiastic appreciation, and expressed his desire to read the conclusion. To the third issue of the review (June 1916) Verhaeren contributed the poem entitled A celle qui a vingt ans.

Pour armer notre foi et dresser notre torse
En face de l'attente et de l'espoir nouveau.

Nous ne laissons rien choir de l'ancienne espérance ;
Mais nous la contrôlons afin de n'avoir point
Au lieu d'un frère un ennemi comme témoin
Du vieux combat dont l'homme attend sa délivrance. . . .

L'humanité a soif d'une équité profonde ;
L'angoisse du massacre est vivante en son sein,
Elle veut que d'après un plus tendre dessin
On sculpte d'autres traits au visage du monde.[1]

[The pressing need to relive is invading our brains ;
The old truths no longer have the power
Of arming our faith and raising up our body
Confronted by expectancy and by the new hope.

We shall forfeit nothing of the erstwhile confidence ;
But we shall control it so as no longer to have
Instead of a brother an enemy as the witness
Of the agelong combat from which man hopes to be freed. . . .

Man is athirst for a far-reaching equity ;
The anguish of the slaughter is alive in his breast ;
He wishes that there may be sculptured, in accordance with a
    more tender design,
Other features upon the countenance of the world.]

It is well that *Les flammes hautes*, whose printing was postponed owing to the outbreak of the war, should have been published (posthumously) after *Les ailes rouges de la guerre* ; for these aspiring flames will remain for all time Verhaeren's last testament. The shock is overpassed ; the poet takes up his pen once more to subscribe the words which were written prior to 1914 ; and in order to confirm the fact that he in no way goes back upon his words he adds this strophe to the collection :

[1] From *Les tombes*, in *Les ailes rouges de la guerre*.

L'orde guerre n'a point sapé ton vouloir droit
D'être homme de lutte et non homme d'effroi
Et de haïr jusqu'en tes os et tes entrailles
La fourmillante horreur des chocs et des batailles.[1]

[Foul war has not undermined your upright will
To be a man of struggle, but not a man of terror,
To be one who hates to his very bones and to his very bowels
The teaming horror of blows and of battles.]

This crowning work is dedicated "to those who love the future." Thus the concord between the past and the future, between the maternal fatherland and a virile humanity, a concord achieved by so bitter a struggle, has been able to resist in the long run the severest of tests.

There may seem to be a contradiction between the cry of hate and the affirmation of a belief in mankind; well, there is also a contradiction between gentleness and power, between the humanity of St. John who denounces all forms of pride, and the numerous hymns in which the poet celebrated the pride which saves. Verhaeren's lyricism is "contradictory and intoxicating" as life itself. Verhaeren lives wholly in the emotion of the moment; such an emotion will work him up to a frenzy, and it is for this very reason that he is able to write with so much power. We pointed out that these two currents of gentleness and power flowed along side by side without ever completely merging their waters. It is the same with all the contrasts existing in Verhaeren. In his frescoes, the opposing tones do not harmonise into a union giving birth to some more moderated shade; the juxtaposed masses balance one another by contrast. The contrast is evident, but we must not therefore be blind to the perfection of the balance. How did Verhaeren attain to so perfect an equilibrium, why did he keep to the last this intense need for contrast? That is what we shall learn by means of a further study of the symbols in his great works.

[1] From A l'homme d'aujourd'hui, in Les flammes hautes.

Verhaeren's inner victory, his conquest of so splendid a balance, is best expressed (it seems to me) by the myth of Perseus in *Les rythmes souverains*. Just as St. George issued from the Count of Mid-Lent, and the Amazon from St. George, so Perseus is the new incarnation of the warrior woman. We have here a typical example of the evolution of a symbol. The kinship between Perseus and St. George is apparent at the first reading of the two poems, but Verhaeren confirms the impression by actual words:

L'orgueil
Qui domine votre âme et en défend le seuil
Contre la plainte amère ;
Parfois même, pour en triompher mieux,
Et la ployer sous son talon victorieux,
Par l'héroisme pur, il l'exaspère ;
Et c'est alors qu'au plus profond de votre cœur,
Il prépare, dirige et résume, en vainqueur
La plus belle des batailles humaines.

Jadis, dans les légendes souveraines,
Au temps des Dieux, maîtres des cieux profonds,
C'était lui le Saint-Georges et le divin Persée
Qui transperçaient du bel éclair de leur pensée
La douleur hérissée en son corps de dragon.[1]

[Pride
Which dominates your heart and defends the threshold of your soul
Against bitter lamentation ;
Sometimes even, to triumph the better,
And to crush lamentation beneath a victorious heel,
Out of sheer heroism pride exacerbates the wound ;
Then it is that, in the recesses of your heart,
Pride prepares, directs, and recapitulates, as a conqueror,
The most splendid of human battles.

In times of yore, in the splendid myths,
In the days of the Gods, masters of the fathomless skies,
It was he, St. George, and the divine Perseus,
Who transpierced, with the effulgence of their thoughts,
The bristling body of the dragon, sorrow.]

[1] From *Les souffrances*, in *La multiple splendeur*.

LIFE IN ALL ITS ARDOUR

Perseus is, therefore, the symbol of ascetic pride which intensifies the evil before triumphing over it; Perseus is heroism incarnate. But, as is always the case with symbols, the abstract words "pride" or "heroism" present only one of the manifold aspects of the image. The symbol itself is always richer in meaning than any of the explanations one may give of it; and we cannot hope to discover the full significance of a symbol unless we analyse it in every detail.

Perseus, like St. George and the Amazon, fights the dragon of the old evil. Like the Amazon, he wishes to deliver "suffering humanity," which is symbolised in this poem by the figure of Andromeda chained to the rock and menaced by the dragon. In this symbol we encounter an objectivation which did not yet exist in *Saint Georges*. Then the struggle was an inner one merely, it was a fight for a subjective deliverance; the intimate significance of this symbol is enshrined in the secret recesses of both the Amazon and Perseus. We have in Perseus a duplex symbolism such as we often meet with in Verhaeren's works since the crisis. Objectively and consciously, Perseus represents the proud, the fearless hero who is to redeem mankind; subjectively and unconsciously, he represents the inner struggle of the poet which led to ultimate victory and harmony. Here Verhaeren haps upon the original and spontaneous meaning of the myth; this myth belongs to the same family as those of Orpheus and of buried treasure. In such ancient legends, psychoanalysts fancy they have discovered a common factor: the endeavour to liberate that part of the psychic energy which has become introverted and is pent up in the subconscious. Similar figures occur spontaneously in the dreams and fantasies of introverts; analysts have shown their general identity, and have explained them as manifestations of the "collective unconscious." Certainly, such an interpretation applies to Verhaeren's works. Further, it is obvious that at the date when *Les rythmes souverains* was composed (the very title is a hymn to victory) Verhaeren had become master of himself and had acquired inner harmony; the "descent into hell," the delving into the subconscious, which is embodied in the three plays, is now at an end; Verhaeren carries his soul into the broad daylight after having struck off the chains which bound it to the maternal imago and and to the affections of early childhood. He delivers Andromeda.

Jean de Smet [1] traces a kinship between Perseus and the Ferryman; and the woman who hails the ferryman in *La passeur d'eau*

> La tête effrayamment tendue
> Vers l'inconnu de l'étendue.[2]
>
> [Her head stretched out in affright
> Towards the unknown expanse.]

seems to him the first sketch of Andromeda (or of suffering humanity) calling for a saviour. The analogy is certainly less salient than that between St. George and the Amazon; but there does seem to be an outline draft of the same motif in the lines just quoted. It is normal that a spontaneous symbol should express in a single image both the objective and the subjective aspects of a feeling; that is to say, on the one hand, the creature which holds part of our soul in thrall, and, on the other hand, this portion of the captive soul. Speech effects the same synthesis when a mother calls her child "my love," or when we speak of something as "my terror." It is, therefore, perfectly normal that "she who hails," a figure reminiscent of early affections and summarised in the "little friend," should simultaneously express these early affections, this introverted and captive soul. So long as sentiments continue to manifest a regressive

---

[1] Op. cit., vol. ii. pp. 192, 193.
[2] From Le passeur d'eau, in Les villages illusoires.

LIFE IN ALL ITS ARDOUR 281

tendency, so long will the two aspects be as one. But at the date of *Les rythmes souverains* the deliverance had taken place, and as a consequence the separation of the two aspects has been effected. It is extremely interesting, in this connexion, to compare the two poems *Les attirances* and *Persée*. In the former, the female figure at the marge of the seas is nothing more than the object of early affections, and the hero forsakes her; in the latter, Andromeda is the very soul of Perseus, a soul long held captive at the marge of the seas, and the hero rescues her.

How does he rescue her? How, in other words, does he finally escape from his introversion? Why does Perseus succeed where the Amazon failed? Perseus' triumph is due to Pegasus, the wonder-horse which the hero conquers and tames. Now Pegasus has already made his entry by the side of the Amazon in *Les forces tumultueuses*. But Pegasus and the Amazon in those days required a separate poem each; in *Persée* the two motifs are fused. Here we have the key to the riddle. The enigma will be solved if we understand the cooperation of forces which the confluence of the images expresses. In *Les forces tumultueuses*, Perseus was the frank and explicit symbol of art, whereas the Amazon signified proud energy. More specifically, the Amazon was the sister of Théroigne and had to signify Verhaeren's tendency towards " social activity." Such activity, however, was not really part of himself, it could not fully satisfy him or bring about inner harmony. But now Verhaeren has realised that art is the only true realm for his activity, the object of his pride and of his combative energy. All his powers must be concentrated towards the mastery of art, art which has become the auxiliary for his deliverance: here is the explanation of the symbol of Perseus becoming the master of Pegasus.

As we have often seen before in the course of our analysis, the deductive interpretation is subsequently confirmed by the details of the poems and helps us to understand these details. Perseus does not conquer Pegasus without a struggle. At first he tries coercion:

> Le cheval outragé se cabra brusque et droit;
> Sa grande aile d'argent, en un effort tragique,
> L'affranchit de la boue épaisse et léthargique,
> Et ses reins révoltés rejetèrent leur poids.
> Persée eut beau crisper ses doigts dans la crinière
> Et resserrer les flancs dans l'étau des genoux,
> Aucune entente encor secrète et familière
> N'existait entre lui et le grand cheval roux.

[The indignant horse suddenly reared up straight;
His great silver wing, with a dramatic swing,
Freed him from the thick and sluggish mire,
And his rebellious back flung off its burden.
All in vain did Perseus cling to the mane
And squeeze the horse's ribs in the vice of his knees,
No secret and familiar understanding
As yet existed between him and the great red roan.]

Critics have resented Verhaeren's choice of words, and they accuse him of having maltreated art; they have spoken of his feverish creation of neologisms, and even of his "prancing" methods of expression (I cannot remember the author of the last-mentioned jibe)—and though they agree that some of these neologisms are veritable inspirations, they insist that for the most part such phraseology is incompatible with good taste and is repugnant to the French genius. Verhaeren is accused of having accosted poesy like a barbarian; but his "barbarism" has created such masterpieces that we cannot regret it. Undoubtedly, however, a perfect mastery of idiom is the outcome of greater reserve, and Verhaeren attained this mastery as the years went by In *Les rythmes souverains* he attained it in a "sovereign" manner. "He has given up the strange words of his vocabulary. He no longer offers us his thought, as in the days of *Les débâcles*, in some demented phrase which seems to arise out of chaos and to pitch back into chaos again after a sublime flight : he now directs his thought, he develops it, he orders it. . . . The cult of modern progress and the eloquent passion for humanity coincide with an art more akin to French art. Its fullest realisation may be found in *Les rythmes souverains.*"[1]

The forward march from the romantic to the classic corresponds in Verhaeren, as it did in Goethe, to the attainment of extroversion and of harmony. Vodoz has shown that Victor Hugo went through a similar evolution. Perseus comes to recognise that coercion is dangerous :

Aussi, le jour qu'il vit, sous la hêtrée épaisse,
Pégase, immense et las, au fond du bois dormir,
Rabaissa-t-il ses bras tendus pour le saisir
Et son geste brutal se changea en caresse. . . .

Ce fut par un matin couronné de rosée,
Que Pégase épousa le désir de Persée. . . .
Certes rebelle au mors, certes rebelle aux rênes,
Mais ne se cabrant plus avec effarement
Dès qu'une main touchait sa croupe souveraine. . . .
Avec le rythme aimé de quelques lentes phrases
Qu'il murmurait, disait ou chantait tour à tour
On eût dit que Persée envahissait Pégase.

[Thus, on the day when he saw, among the shady beeches,
Pegasus, huge and tired, sleeping in the forest depths,
He dropped his arms stretched forth to seize the horse
And his rough gesture was changed into a caress. . . .

It was on a morning garlanded with dew
That Pegasus espoused Perseus' wish. . . .
Still rebellious to the bit, still rebellious to the reins,
But no longer rearing in fright
As soon as a hand touched his regal flank. . . .
With the loved cadence of certain slow-spoken phrases,
Which he murmured, or said, or sang,
It seemed as if Perseus were invading Pegasus.]

[1] Mockel, op. cit., p. 182.

The poet's mastery of his art is in truth the mastery of himself, the liberation of the captive Andromeda.

There is yet another aspect of Perseus which we must not lose sight of. It is one which Verhaeren has himself emphasised : pride, a combative and ascetic pride, pride at triumphing over self, which in its turn was a factor in the triumph. But as a part of the same feeling, this triumph can never rest upon its laurels ; it continues to struggle ceaselessly, and with vigour ever renewed. In the sentiment are fused and harmonised, in a sublimated form, two tendencies which were in evidence at the time of the crisis, and which—despite all appearances to the contrary—seemed to grow from the same plant : the two tendencies are *autophilia* and *asceticism*. The former remains powerful, but it becomes increasingly purified until I feel I may speak of it as a platonic love of self. This love becomes holy and incites towards prayer :

> Et tout à coup je sens encor,
> Comme au temps de l'enfance, au fond de moi, frémir
> L'aile qui dort
> Des anciennes prières. . . .
> Les temps l'ont imprimée aux sursauts de mon cœur,
> Dès que je suis allègre et violent d'ardeur
> Et que je sens combien je m'aime.[1]

> [And all of a sudden I feel vibrating once more,
> As in the days of my childhood, in the depths of my being,
> The folded wing
> Of the prayers I used to say. . . .
> Time has engraved them on my leaping heart
> When I am joyful and strong with passion
> And when I feel how well I love myself.]

The link between this love and pride is manifest. In the poem entitled *L'orgueil* we read :

> O croyance en mon front, en mes yeux, en mes mains,
> Croyance en mon cerveau que la recherche enivre. . . .

[1] From La prière, in Les rythmes souverains.

LIFE IN ALL ITS ARDOUR

Je m'aime et je m'admire en tel geste vermeil
  Que fait un homme à moi pareil
  En son passage sur la terre.[1]

[Oh, belief in my brow, in my eyes, in my hands,
Belief in my brain which the pursuit of knowledge intoxicates. . . .

I love myself and I admire myself in the glorious gesture
  Which a man like me makes
  In his passage through life.]

In the same poem we find the link between pride and asceticism revealed in the following line:

Tout mon orgueil s'exerce à bellement souffrir.

[My pride is wholly devoted to bearing sorrow magnificently.]

But in two verses from another poem we have autophilia, asceticism, and pride expressed in a single concise formula:

Nous admirons nos mains, nos yeux et nos pensées,
Même notre douleur qui devient notre orgueil.[2]

[We admire our hands, our eyes, and our thoughts,
Even our suffering which becomes our pride.[1]]

We must notice that this pride is always balanced with an admiring love for man and for the world. In the two strophes which precede the above we are given the precepts that form the nucleus of *La multiple splendeur*:

Si nous nous admirons vraiment les uns les autres . . .

Nous apportons, *ivres du monde et de nous-mêmes*,
Des cœurs d'hommes nouveaux dans le vieil univers.

[If we really admire one another . . .

We bring, *drunken with the world and with ourselves*,
The hearts of new men into the ancient universe.]

[1] From L'orgueil, in Les flammes hautes.
[2] From La ferveur, in La multiple splendeur.

Precisely because Verhaeren believes in the world and in life, he can now believe in himself and in his art—a belief towards which he was vainly striving at the time when he wrote of the Monks and of his dead faith. This belief in self and in art is what will henceforward justify both pride and asceticism. We recall how of yore the ascetic tendency had lost all motive, all rationalisation; it seemed to us that this was in large part the cause of the crisis. Now Verhaeren has a definite goal; if he masters himself, if he renounces, he knows why.

I may quote in this connexion an admirable passage from Albert Mockel:

"Verhaeren was inclined towards asceticism, his indifference to material things bears eloquent witness of the fact. He who had sung the faëryland of the senses was, in his own life, at the antipodes of sensuality. I know of only one passion to which he succumbed and that was to the Havana tobacco leaf. It was a delight to see him choose a cigar; he seemed to be anticipating its aroma, tasting its delicacy in advance. But even this passion had been curbed. . . .

"He had decided to give up everything for his work, to devote himself entirely to his art; he kept resolutely to his plan of life. . . . The animation of the street, a crowd in a hall, all the manifestations of the living world, were a source of the keenest enjoyment to him; and yet he refused to enter places of public refreshment. He feared the habits so easily acquired and so difficult to break, he remembered the waste of time such habits entail. . . . Once for all he forbade himself these things and kept his resolution; if he had to meet anyone in Paris, he would arrange for the meeting to take place in the Louvre.

"The same determination was displayed in the care of his health, which had long been poor. By dint of attentive effort he became robust, and was in superb condition; but it had required a perseverance which

I can qualify only as admirable to obtain this result; he had to give up many of his pleasures, such as reading till the small hours, going to concerts, or to the theatre. He knew that good health, both of body and of mind, were essential to his work. He acquired it at the sacrifice of many little amenities which it invariably seems hard to give up." [1]

The ascetic tendency which made of Verhaeren " the poet of energy " was in truth profoundly rooted in his nature. So much is this the case that the *tree*, which has for long been the symbol of asceticism in the poet's work, henceforward comprises in itself the past struggle and the present victory. We may recall *L'arbre*, the triumphant tree, in *La multiple splendeur* :

Mais pour s'épanouir et régner dans sa force,
O les luttes qu'il lui fallut subir, l'hiver ! . . .
Tout lui fut mal qui tord, douleur qui vibre,
Sans qui jamais pourtant
Un seul instant
Ne s'alentît son énergie. . . .

[But in order to spread its branches and reign in its full vigour,
What struggles it had to undergo, in winter days ! . . .
It suffered from every twist, from every vibration
Without ever, notwithstanding,
For one moment
Allowing its energy to slacken.]

When this gnarled tree dominates the autumn, the poet, who feels himself to be in the autumn of life, identifies himself most intimately with the old fighter of tempests :

En octobre, quand l'or triomphe en son feuillage,
Mes pas larges encor, quoique lourds et lassés,
Souvent ont dirigé leur long pélérinage
Vers cet arbre d'automne et de vent traversé. . . .
Et j'appuyais sur lui ma poitrine brutale,
Avec un tel amour, une telle ferveur,
Que son rythme profond et sa force totale
Passaient en moi et pénétraient jusqu'à mon cœur.

[1] Op. cit., pp. 167-168.

[In October, when gold triumphs in the foliage,
My steps, which are still fairly vigorous, though somewhat
    heavy and tired,
Have often made their long pilgrimage
Towards this autumnal tree through which the wind would blow.
And I leaned my rough breast against it
With so much love, with so great a fervour,
That its profound rhythm and its entire strength
Passed into me and penetrated my very heart.]

Even more faithfully does the Willow Tree in the *Guirlande des dunes* express the crisis and the victorious fight:

> Un soir de foudre et de fracas,
>   Son tronc craqua,
> Soudainement, de haut en bas.[1]
>
> [One evening of lightning and noise
>   Its trunk was riven,
> Quite suddenly, from top to base.]

This disaster is well known to us: it is the clock-tower rent in twain. But the "gnarled and twisted tree" holds firm:

> Est-il tordu, troué, souffrant et vieux!
>   Sont-ils crevés et bossués, les yeux
>   Que font les nœuds dans son écorce! . . .
> J'ai admiré sa vie en lutte avec sa mort,
> Et, je l'entends, ce soir de pluie et de ténèbres,
> Crisper ses pieds au sol et bander ses vertèbres
>   Et défier l'orage—et résister encor.
>
> [How gnarled, and hollowed, and suffering, and old
>   is it!
> How torn and bruised are the eyes
> Which are formed by the knots in its bark!
> I have admired its life at grips with its death,
> And now I hear it, in this evening of rain and darkness,
> Convulsively clutching at the soil with its feet, every vertebra
>   taut,
> Defying the storm, resisting to the last.]

[1] From *Un saule*, in *La guirlande des dunes*.

LIFE IN ALL ITS ARDOUR

Verhaeren loves trees so passionately because they are the symbol of himself, even to the scars on their tortured bark. He can write:

> Ce saule-là, je l'aime comme un homme.
> [I love that willow as though it were a man.]

This line recalls how Beethoven "loved a tree better than a man." In *Les flammes hautes*, the Forest is buffeted by the same struggle. Already in the days when it was still in good health (as for Verhaeren in the days of *Les flamandes*):

> . . . montaient en floraisons
> Et les venins et les poisons :
> L'hostile jusquiame et le gouet malévole,
> Si bien qu'au ras de sol tout autant que là-haut
> L'embûche se dressait et donnait son assaut
> A l'ardeur méritoire et loyale des choses.[1]
>
> [. . . there were rising in inflorescence
> Both venoms and poisons—
> The hostile hyoscyamus and the malevolent arum—
> So that, on the ground-level just as much as higher up,
> The ambush had been made ready and was delivering its onslaught
> Upon the well-deserving and trusty ardour of things.]

At length came the inevitable crisis:

> L'insidieux poison des fleurs violettes
> Mêlait son maléfice au souffle des tempêtes. . . .
> Chênes, ormes, bouleaux, sapins, tilleuls, érables
> S'exaltaient tout à coup de leur front à leur pied
> En un branle profond, énorme et regulier. . . .
> Quand même, immensément, avec force, là-haut,
> Les vents faisaient chanter la forêt toute entière.[2]

---

[1] From La forêt, in Les flammes hautes.
[2] From the same poem.

> [The insidious poison of violet flowers
> Mingled its maleficence with the stormy winds. . . .
> Oaks, elms, birches, pines, limes, maples
> Swayed exultantly from crest to root
> With a huge and regular rhythm. . . .
> What time, with immense force, up aloft,
> The winds were making the whole forest sing.]

And now, as previously with the tree, Verhaeren identifies himself with the forest : " The forest is a world, and its life is mine." Need I remind the reader of that Leading Tree in the Avenue which leads the others like a prophet, but whose strength is due solely to its mad confidence and its obstinate energy ?

> Le premier arbre est grand d'avoir souffert. . . .
> L'arbre ployé criait, mais redressait quand même,
> Après l'instant d'angoisse et de terreur passé,
> Son branchage tordu et son front convulsé.[1]
>
> [The leading tree is great for it has suffered much. . . .
> The bent tree cried aloud but uplifted again,
> As soon as the moment of anguish and terror had passed,
> Its twisted branches and its writhing crest.]

All these trees are akin. Gnarled and twisted as of yore, they are ever fighting, ever ascetic ; but their asceticism has acquired an inexplicable air of triumph. There seems to be a continuous desire to conquer, to overcome self, as does the superb Hercules of *Les rythmes souverains*. In this poem, the hero not knowing what further exploit to undertake in order to outdo all his other exploits, tears up a forest, makes of it a pyre, and thus dies in beauty—dies fighting after " kindling a star upon the earth." This imperious tendency to combat, and the tendency to asceticism, are, as we have already seen, the tendency which prohibits " regular happiness," and excludes any harmony which is not dynamic, which is not a balance of fighting and contrasted forces. Verhaeren's " Life in all its Ardour " is a balance of this

---

[1] From Le premier arbre de l'allée, in Les flammes hautes.

LIFE IN ALL ITS ARDOUR

kind, and the splendid poem in which he sings it indicates clearly that this balance of contrasts issues from the old ascetic tendency and moves towards the "anguish" which "twists" his inner forces:

Et vous, haines, vertus, vices, rages, désirs,
Je vous accueillis tous, avec tous vos contrastes,
Afin que fût plus long, plus complexe et plus vaste,
Le merveilleux frisson qui m'a fait tressaillir.
Mon cœur à moi ne vit dûment que s'il s'efforce ;
L'humanité totale a besoin d'un tourment
Qui la travaille avec fureur comme un ferment,
Pour élargir sa vie et soulever sa force.[1]

[And you, hates, virtues, vices, rages, desires,
I welcomed you all, with all your contrasts,
To prolong, to render more complex and vaster,
The wonderful thrill which made me quiver.
My heart cannot live duly unless through effort ;
Humanity-at-large has need of an anguish
Which fiercely works it like a ferment
To expand its life and sustain its power.][2]

Here we have once more a splendid pride, an ascetic and combative tendency, the need for an inward clash between the contrasting forces of the human spirit. This mingling is the most notable characteristic of Verhaeren. Of a sudden we encounter a new expression of it, concisely phrased and with the familiar image of "twisting," in the closing strophe of *Les flammes hautes*:

Vous m'êtes tous tributaires devant le temps
Qui seul est juge et maintiendra mon œuvre vaste,
Où j'ai d'un poing *vainqueur tordu* tous vos *contrastes*
Pour qu'en tonne l'orage en mes vers exaltants.[3]

---

[1] From La vie ardente, in Les flammes hautes.
[2] These words "to expand its life" are equally applicable to the Tree of La multiple splendeur.
[3] From Ma gerbe, in Les flammes hautes.

[You are all tributary to me under the eyes of time,
Who is the sole judge, and will uphold my huge work,
In which, with a *victorious* hand, I have *twisted* all your *contrasts*
So that the storm of them may resound in my panegyric verses.]

Such are the last words of Verhaeren's work, *Ultima Verba*. In them he condenses what we have come to recognise as the most salient features of his personality of victory and strife. It would be impossible to achieve a better conclusion, one more faithful to the writer.

CONCLUSION

WHEN science has given a novelty to the world, it is unwise to proclaim from the housetops that the world will change in consequence. We need not pronounce judgment on our fathers; neither need we be too severe on the traditional methods of artistic and literary criticism, nor trumpet abroad that these methods are obsolete, and that instead of all such chatter we are now going to undertake a really scientific discussion. There is a modicum of good even in chatter! Doubtless it would become our critics better did they but realise that what they give to the world is merely an exchange of impressions, a kind of courteous colloquy upon beautiful things; they might then, perhaps, refrain from judgments which are as contradictory as they are fallible. Such colloquies are permissible—far more so than judgments, especially where matters of taste are concerned.

On the other hand it is desirable to seek out a concrete platform, where we can meet when we wish to talk about art—where we may hope to reach certain objective truths which are matters of science and not of opinion. We may be allowed to understand art as well as to feel art. Emile Hennequin's endeavour to lay the foundations of "scientific criticism" was laudable.[1] But as a matter of fact such a scientific point of view belongs far more to the psychologist than to the critic; if, after all, Hennequin's effort remained no more than a sketch,

[1] Hennequin, La critique scientifique, 1888.

this may have been due to the exiguity of his psychological attainments. We cannot be accused of playing with illusions if we affirm that since Hennequin wrote in 1888 much water has flowed under the psychological bridges. Psychology is still a youthful science, and has many surprises in store; but we are already enabled to say that it has taken the definitive step forward which has placed it in the rank of the sciences as an autonomous science and a real science. Psychology is no longer content to make use of the methods proper to the physical sciences; it has sought out, and to a large extent has already found, methods proper to itself. The narrow intellectualism which paralysed the associationist school has been abandoned; we have come to recognise that the psychic life is rooted in the affective life, and that the conscious cannot be studied apart from the unconscious. In accepting an affective and subconscious logic which is doubtless disconcerting to rational logic—in granting a validity to those reasons of the heart which the reason of the brain cannot understand—psychology has taken a perilous leap, but does not seem to have suffered from the venture.

We are now in a position to outline a psychology of art without implying that it can replace criticism, and yet confident that it can regenerate criticism, and may in due time furnish the critics with a more objective outlook. Aesthetic appreciation will probably remain a subjective thing. It is no less subjective than physical pain. But when physiological science tells us positively that such or such a pain corresponds to such or such a lesion, we are given an objective basis for physical suffering, and the physician can say: " You suffer because of . . ." This is the way in which we may hope to see psychology aiding criticism. If we come to recognise that certain constant features in the psychological genesis of a work which moves us, correspond to certain aesthetic emotions, then we can say : " This work moves us because of . . . ."[1] We psychologists are not yet in a position to give a precise diagnosis, but we already perceive how valuable such a method of criticism could be. Thus, our study of Verhaeren's works has shown that many of the poems universally regarded as masterpieces are precisely those which are most fraught with symbolical meaning. Such is the case with *Le moulin* in *Les soirs*; such is the case with *La dame en noir* and *Les nombres*, in *Les flambeaux noirs*; with *Saint Georges*, in *Les apparus dans mes chemins*; with *Le passeur d'eau* and *Le sonneur*, in *Les villages illusoires;* with *Les usines*, in *Les villes tentaculaires;* with *Le paradis*, in *Les rythmes souverains*. These are the poems which everyone thinks of when asked to mention Verhaeren's finest achievements. These are the poems which have found a place in Albert Heumann's collection.[2] In the course of our analysis we have seen that these poems are the outcome of a very strong and very precise condensation of images. That is why they have guided us into the most intimate recesses of Verhaeren's soul. Such condensations would seem to favour the genesis of great works. This is natural, for condensation is the sign of an emotion or of a conflict in the soul of the poet; such poems give expression to the profoundest of feelings, and for this reason they react powerfully upon the reader's emotions. A noteworthy fact is that the real object of the emotion or of the conflict may be subconscious, may be quite unknown both to the author and to the reader, and yet an intimate vibration is awakened which may not be understood

[1] Needless to say the problem of aesthetic emotion is far more complex than the problem of pain. Though the same lesion causes an analogous pain in everybody, we cannot affirm as much of the moving power of a work of art. The problem is a twofold one ; to account for a poetical emotion, for instance, we must consider, on the one hand, the psychology of the work itself ; and, on the other, the psychology of the reader. Consult, in this connexion, Roubakine, Psychologie bibliologique ; cf. also an article by Ferrière in " Archives de Psychologie," Geneva, No. xiv.

[2] Choix de poèmes, avec une préface d'Albert Heumann, fourth edition, 1916.

but will certainly be felt. We are led to the view that it is wise and proper to analyse the symbols employed by a poet, and especially those which he introduces into his masterpieces; seeing that the most moving of works are at the same time, and in general, the most explicative of works. We shall have to reconsider our judgments regarding works which have hitherto been placed in the second rank if, during the course of analysis, such works are shown to be pregnant with meaning. This is the case with Verhaeren's plays; and we have found that the lack of appreciation of the plays is due to a prejudice against lyrical drama. In the same way, many of the poems which have been valuable in elucidating the analysis should be reconsidered, and might then deserve to be placed in a collection where they have hitherto been denied admittance. To be convinced of this, we need but reread, from the artistic point of view, the poem about the Idol of Benares (*Là-bas*, in *Les débâcles*); or any of the *Chansons de fou*, in *Les campagnes hallucinées*; or *La joie*, in *Les visages de la vie*; or *L'amour*, in *Les forces tumultueuses*; or *Ardeurs naïves*, in *Les tendresses premières*; or *Saint Jean* and *Persée*, in *Les rythmes souverains*.

Psychology, in addition, furnishes us with yet another method of judging a work of art. What is the place of the symbol in poetry? It does not suffice to say that the use of a symbol is permissible; we must realise that it is essential. Nothing is more wrong-headed than to consider the symbol (or for that matter the simile or the metaphor, those simplified symbols) as an affected or roundabout method of expression which should be replaced by a direct method of expression. The symbol *is* the direct method of expression. Whenever the imagination is left to its own devices, and whenever we dream, the spontaneous method of the symbol is employed as a means of expression. In truth, the imagination is not left to its own devices. It has, indeed, escaped from rational control, but only to enter the service of sensibility. *Thus it is that the symbol comes to be the language of sensibility itself.*

The underlying principle of the symbolist school seems to conform in every way to the nature of things. This school has set itself the simple task of bringing to our notice the symbolical significance of expressions and actions, a significance which is usually concealed. In order to do so, the adepts of this school detach an action from its environment; such a method may be employed to explain the action, without any loss of precision or of realism. In this connexion Jean de Smet [1] has insisted upon the realist character of *Les villages illusoires*; here we enter the realm of "symbolical realism"—a happy phrase which we owe to Edouard Dujardin.[2] Doubtless the best symbolists are those who do not trouble over much about style, and who, therefore, preserve the full savour of the symbol. Is not Burne-Jones a painter faithful in his depiction of every detail? But no matter how real the action, it is separated from its surroundings, is transferred to other combinations dictated by the psychological law of the condensation of images. We have an example of this in *Les cordiers* (*Les villages illusoires*), a poem full of realistic and yet mystical action. We are given the "humming of the wheel," the "rakes" which are "staked out at regular intervals along the road" and upon which the "flaxen hemp stretches its coils." Up to this point we have nothing more than a Dutch painting. But in the very next line we escape from direct description: "continuously, for days and for weeks," a line wherein is condensed the woof of the hemp with the woof of time. The poet does not crudely translate his thoughts, though we must admit that Verhaeren does so occasionally and has been rightly censured for the lapse. For instance, in *Les pêcheurs* he writes of "the slimy bottom of the diseases," "the small fry of his wretchedness," and "the dead waters

[1] Smet, op. cit., vol. ii.   [2] Dujardin, op. cit.

of his remorse." Such expressions, says Jean de Smet, are unduly specific. This is not always true but it is very often the case, for, in general, the condensation of images (giving rise to the symbol) is the outcome of more than one factor ; and by allowing such crude translations into words, the symbol suffers amputation, it is reduced to two factors only, and the harmonics which should be heard vibrating are stifled. In a word the symbol is sacrificed, and we approach the realm of what is often called direct expression, but is really abstract expression. The sacrifice of the symbol is as legitimate as abstract expression itself, but we must remember that in making this sacrifice we stray from the symbol and from affective expression.

We have already seen [1] how, in general, the translation of our thoughts and feeling into abstract expression is prone to impoverish the symbol. If the "woof" of the Ropemakers, say those of mediocre artistic appreciation, is really time, surely it would have been better to speak simply of time and not to "use a metaphor." As a matter of fact, the poet does not use a metaphor ; the metaphor uses him. Furthermore, he instinctively feels that this metaphor represents time, and also destiny, and (as overtones) many other things which are not very clear to him, and which need not be. What is needful is that we should detach the action of the Ropemakers from its concrete surroundings ; this is far more important than that we should link it up too intimately with an abstract idea, for this would lessen its significance just as much as the concrete surroundings would have done. It is for this reason that the poet shows us the threads as "coming from the infinite" alternatively with the woof prolonging itself into "days and weeks" and the ropemaker "drawing the horizons to himself." The diversity of metaphors prevents the symbol from becoming stereotyped into an allegory ; and the harmonics, instead

[1] Apropos of Perseus in Chapter Six.

CONCLUSION

of being stifled, are induced to vibrate over and over again.

This is, I believe, the basic principle of the symbolist school. Psychology completely justifies it—justifies even the vagueness with which these poets have been so irrelevantly reproached. Of course there may be other forms of art, but this form is peculiarly true and is admirably consonant with the nature of the psyche.

From what has gone before we see that at this stage psychology permits us to formulate with precision certain critical judgments. But we need not let ourselves be encumbered by these critical preoccupations; the psychology of art is still in its infancy, and we must not risk deforming it and weighing it down with a burden it is not fit to carry.

Finally, the first rule of methodical investigation is to divide. We must apply to aesthetical psychology the methods which James and Flournoy applied to religious psychology: that is, we must clearly differentiate between an "existential judgment" and a "proposition of value" or "spiritual judgment." In the present instance the "judgment of value" is the prerogative of criticism. Psychology will do well to keep to the "judgment of fact," and to the "biological interpretation" of the phenomena of art.

A remarkable and important law is taking shape in this field of enquiry. We might name it *the law of the subjectivation of images*; this law appears to us to be the corollary of the law of condensation. We have constantly encountered it in the course of the present study, and we have seen that works which were apparently objective in conception tended towards the realisation, in symbolic form, of a subjective drama within the soul of the poet; such realisation may be involuntary and subconscious, but it is rendered all the more striking by this very fact. Thus *Les moines*, designed to present "the Christian world which is dead," expresses at the same time Verhaeren's loss of faith; in a later work, when the poet describes the hour of chaos and of confused preparation which the modern world is traversing, he likewise expresses the "tumult" and expectancy experienced by himself when he feels surging up within him the tide of a new faith. The depopulation of the countryside, the irresistible attraction exercised by the "tentacular towns," mark the end of the crisis of introversion; they point the way to an extroverted life and to human effort. Perseus' victory is symbolical of the conquest of inner harmony over the last assaults of the crisis. Even more typical are the plays which, as we saw, grouped themselves into a trilogy of the Oedipus complex. They express quite involuntarily, but with amazing intensity, the longing for the mother and the revolt against paternal authority, two sentiments buried in the depths of the subconscious and belonging to the days of earliest childhood.

Now all this is not peculiar to Verhaeren, nor is it pecular to poetry. Analysts have found analogous subjectivations in many kinds of artists; Maeder, among others, has brought this characteristic into relief in his discussion of Hodler's paintings.[1] That a work of art is always more or less subjective, that it always bears the stamp of the author's individuality, goes without saying; but what we are beginning to perceive is, *how* it has become a subjective expression, in virtue of what intimate mechanism this development has occurred. The phenomenon we have just described is doubtless an essential part of the mechanism. It is not merely a certain disposition of the senses or of the temperament, a certain way of looking at things, which determines the originality of a work of art and which impresses it with the author's sign manual. It is also, and perhaps above

[1] Op. cit.

all, a spontaneous faculty for subjectivating images. In so far as this is the case, it is true that " in every portrait an artist makes, he draws his own likeness."

In addition we must, in order thoroughly to understand the artist's vision, penetrate into what might be termed his personal symbolism. In Verhaeren we have the faces of the clocks in the towers, the towers themselves, the contrast between black and gold, the trains, the reflections in stagnant waters, the garden and the factory, the monks and the cloister—all are examples of personal symbolism. This symbolism is determined by certain emotions, by certain conflicts, which ever since infancy have been associated with such images. By retracing the images to their source, we are enabled to discover the meaning of the obsessive symbols, which are so largely responsible for the peculiar characteristics of any poet's work.

We must remember, however, that this symbolism is never stationary; on the contrary it is in a constant state of flux. Here we encounter yet another basic law. It is therefore impossible to write, once and for all, the code of laws which shall govern a poet's symbols : the images undergo a progressive metamorphosis of shape and of sense, even though certain features remain indelible and help us to recognise the original symbol. Examples of such an evolution are not lacking in Verhaeren's writings : we have the huge round eye of the watchmaker, and the eyes of his clocks, which become the eyes of the towers, and even moons; the clank of the axles heard by the child in the shuddering night is to become the roar of trains; his uncle's little factory is the germ of the great industrial town; the Count of Mid-Lent, the bringer of celestial toys, is metamorphosed into St. George, St. George changes into the Amazon, and the Amazon into Perseus; and with each metamorphosis the meaning of the image is modified, the curtain rises on a new act of the same drama. Gold, which at first symbolised sensual abundance, comes to signify the fecundity of human effort; the black cross becomes the cross of gold, for inner torment is replaced by the fruitfulness of loving sacrifice.

The metamorphosis of symbols informs us as to the intimate evolution of the artist. The conversion of the black cross into a golden cross is Verhaeren's own " conversion "; Perseus, when compared with the Amazon, represents pure art replacing social action; Perseus, when compared with St. George, expresses the return of the poet to classicism after a sojourn in the realm of romanticism.

The evolution towards more classical and more objective forms is manifest throughout the whole range of Verhaeren's works. The two aspects of the symbol, interior and exterior, were in evidence in *Les villages illusoires*; but subsequently the exterior aspect comes more and more to prevail. At the same time Verhaeren frees himself from the symbolism of the schools. This latter is pre-eminently subjective, and is peculiarly suited to give expression to the most secret sensibility. But his growing interest in the exterior world leads Verhaeren, as it led Goethe, back towards classicism. Of course we cannot affirm that the two tendencies invariably go hand in hand, but we can well understand that an interest in the objective world incites towards a greater objectivity in art. Neither would it be right to say, apriori, that classical art is superior to symbolist or to romanticist art. We may ask ourselves, with Albert Mockel, if we do well to rejoice, from the point of view of aesthetics, at this evolution of Verhaeren. For Verhaeren, as for Goethe, the return to classicism marked the beginning of extroversion, of the conquest of inner harmony; from this outlook we may certainly rejoice. But we must not therefore assume that the classical period of these poets was aesthetically superior, or that classical art in general stands at a higher level. What we have to realise is, that if symbolical poetry be preeminently subjective, and classical poetry preeminently objective, the balance of the two tendencies of introversion and extroversion (which is harmony incarnate) must lead a modern poet towards a synthesis of the two forms of art. *Classical symbolism* [1]—this is the goal Verhaeren set himself when writing the myths of his inspiration: *Pégase, L'amazone, L'amour,* in *Les forces tumultueuses*; *Le paradis, Hercule, Persée,* in *Les rythmes souverains*; and, finally, the drama *Hélène de Sparte.*

Our analysis of these symbols and of their metamorphoses has revealed to us the psychological characteristics and the mental evolution of our poet. The facts thus disclosed are confirmed by events in Verhaeren's life and by his professions of faith.

We have thus been enabled to discover some of the conflicts which took place in the Belgian poet's soul. In this connexion we have noted a phenomenon which psychologists (in the course of a therapeutical analysis, for instance) have glimpsed but never as yet sufficiently emphasised—a phenomenon which I shall characterise by the name of *polarisation of the conflicts.* From earliest childhood, most of the inner conflicts of man gather around the two nuclei formed by the idea of the mother and that of the father; thus each conflict may appear to be, at least to the subconscious, a renewal of the "mother-father" conflict. Some of these polarisations seem to be common to most individuals. Thus, in a boy, it is usual to find the tendency to introversion concentrating around the idea of the mother, whereas extroversion is associated with the idea of the father. Other polarisations are more individual, they depend rather upon associations of ideas and upon environment. Verhaeren's introversion finds a haven in the "garden," the art of the symbolist school; whereas his extroversion

[1] This term is peculiarly applicable to Carl Spitteler's work.

takes to itself the "factory," classical art. In general we could arrange the great conflicts of tendencies and of ideas in couples: just as we found the contrasts of images in Verhaeren could be grouped in such a way that the first word of each couple would be subconsciously associated with introversion, whilst the second would be associated with extroversion; the regressive tendency and the progressive tendency, the cult of the past and the cult of the future, autophilia and heterophilia, mysticism and love, asceticism and joy, the "garden" and the "factory," the "country" and the "town," Christian faith and pantheistic faith, death and life, symbolist art and classical art, individualism and the tendency to social activity, the "monks" and the "Flemish women," "black" and "gold." This is no arbitrary play of contrasts which could be continued ad infinitum just for fun; these contrasts are not, to quote Pascal's phrase, "false windows built in for the sake of symmetry." All the contrasting terms are held together, not by a logical bond, but by an intimate psychological tie.

Verhaeren's evolution may be described as follows: up to the end of the crisis, towards the poet's thirty-fifth year, he is a thorough introvert, strongly attached to his "early affections," and suffering from a longing for the mother; later he becomes an extrovert, he acquires an interest in the outside world, he has conquered and is master of all the second terms of the coupled contrasts. Then he encounters love, which he understands as the intimate gift of self, as action; he finds he is a socialist, he realises the beauty of modern life, he "accepts" the "factory" (a double symbol, representing for him paternal authority and the reality of life). This is what we have named Verhaeren's "conversion."

The tragical crisis which finds its final solution in this conversion belongs to the same order of crises as that of Faust; it is a crisis of extreme introversion from which the sufferer can discover an exit only by coming out of himself. The crisis would doubtless never have arisen, other things being equal, had Verhaeren never lost the faith of his adolescence, for he would then have found a perfect equilibrium for his introverted tendencies in some form of mysticism. We have, therefore, to look upon his loss of faith as a matter of prime importance in the causation of the crisis. But to what can we attribute the loss of faith ? This is a very difficult question, and I do not pretend to give a satisfactory answer. We may, however, say that the series of conflicts which we have brought to light during the present study were a contributory cause of Verhaeren's crisis. Just as some of the introverted mystics studied by Morel proved to be subjects of a strong Oedipus complex, so we have found the same complex in Verhaeren taking the form of a longing for the mother and a protest against paternal authority. But the mystics studied by Morel had a religious mother and a worldly father, so that, on the one hand, mysticism satisfied the introverted tendency towards which the longing for the mother led them, and, on the other hand, it formed an outlet for the secret protest against the father. Gustave Verhaeren was of a religious bent, he took young Emile with him on his monthly pilgrimage to the cloister at Bornhem ; the poet's father was more or less the model for Philip II, the "most Catholic king." Thus Verhaeren's inclination to mysticism, or, rather, his religious feeling, if it represents, from one point of view, the tendency to introversion, the longing for the mother, when contemplated from another angle, it represents the non-acceptance of paternal authority. Conflict had set up a focus of irritation in the mystical sentiment, and was secretly undermining it from the outset. We cannot assert that the poet was constitutionally predestined to his loss of faith, for he was of a profoundly religious and fervent disposition; but we cannot help feeling that the complex was to a certain extent a predisposing cause.[1] It is even possible that the drama of the loss of faith acquired preponderating importance in Verhaeren's soul, because the drama subconsciously represented for him the deepest of his conflicts, represented the full force of his inner anguish.

The fact remains that the fall of the religious sentiment dragged down with it the whole of the poet's erstwhile equilibrium. Already in *Les flamandes*, and still more in *Les moines*, this ruin is foreshadowed: the acute crisis of the subsequent years was the expression of its emergence above the threshold of consciousness. The evil was accentuated because religious faith had provided a rationalisation of the tendency to introversion; it had, so to speak, justified the tendency. Henceforth there was to be a ceaseless contradiction between tendency and reason.

In especial does Verhaeren's strong ascetic tendency function henceforward in the void. In *Les débâcles* it has been reduced to an insensate desire for self-inflicted injury. It thus forms one of the main factors of the evil, for it leads Verhaeren to yearn for even more suffering, to wish "to diminish" himself yet further, and "to forge distresses for himself at his own anvil."

This introverted world will no longer suffice to itself; all the energies dwell there in a state of chaos. In order to set up a new unity, a fresh hierarchy, the forces of extroversion had to be called to the poet's aid. But the extroverted forces (all the second terms of the contrasting couples) were so intimately related that it sufficed

[1] The *regicide* motif is for Verhaeren the symbol of protest against paternal authority (in especial is it the case in the drama of Philip II). The *dead king* symbolises for the poet his own loss of faith. The two symbols taken together afford us a glimpse of the bond between the loss of faith and the rejection of paternal authority. Cf. Les moines (supra pp. 97–8):

You alone survive, great, in the dead Christian world;
Alone, without bending your backs, you carry its burden
As if it were the dead body of a king enclosed in a golden coffin.

CONCLUSION

Verhaeren to accept one or two of them for all the others to follow. He welcomes love in the person of the noble woman who, he tells us, was responsible for his salvation. After having as a rebel thrown off every yoke, he comes to accept " paternal authority " in the form of a new duty, the duty to society. Around his love and his social activity, all the other terms of extroversion are gradually crystallised. By entering upon social work, Verhaeren was led to " accept the factory," he was led to a belief in the present, to faith in human labour. A new ideal, a new meaning to life, serves to justify the tendencies and to bring them under control. Harmony has been achieved.

We claim no merit for having brought our analysis to so satisfactory a conclusion, and for having found so faithful an expression of Verhaeren's personal life in the manifold symbols we encounter in his work. If any praise be due, it should be given to Verhaeren himself, whose writings are so spontaneous, so exceptionally sincere, that the task of analysis calls for no great exertion on the part of the analytical critic. If Verhaeren's symbols appear twisted and obscure at a first glance, they are not so because of a desire on the part of the poet to be affected or to astonish his readers. It is precisely when they are obscure that they are fundamentally spontaneous ; they are like dreams or nightmares which have been faithfully recorded, and they may be analysed with the same rigorous method as that employed in the analysis of dreams. Thus we find that the apparent inconsequence of one or other of the *Chansons de fou* [1] is a disguised presentation of the profoundest complexes in the poet's psyche. Later, when Verhaeren's symbols become simpler and more lucid, when they evolve towards classicism, we have another proof of his sincerity. As the

---

[1] There are six of these " Songs of Madmen " in *Les campagnes hallucinées.*

poet develops a wider interest in the world without, as he "objectivates" himself, he feels less impelled to sing of himself, and he tends towards an objective art which is to be a more faithful reflection of his new personality —a personality "which has fled the confines of self and has hastened to answer the call of the unanimous forces." Verhaeren consents even to run the risk of sacrificing originality to sincerity, for he gives up the visions, the special method of expression, and the rhythms which he had created, which were his signature, as it were, and of which he could be legitimately proud. Whereas other artists, less strong, cling desperately throughout life to the most mediocre of their eccentricities, since they see therein the guarantee of their artistic individuality, Verhaeren regally disdains a treasure of which the smallest jewel might make such seekers after originality weep with envy. Verhaeren loves running risks, he loves defiance; these are part of his heroism. He loves to exceed all his whilom exploits, as does his Hercules, even to the accomplishment of the impossible. Above all, he wishes to be sincere. When, therefore, the new soul he has created within himself demands of him a less spasmodic form of expression, an art less concentrated in self, more objective and even, if needs must, less personal—straightway he adopts such an art and makes it his own. His decision hardly seems to be a voluntary one. Verhaeren's sincerity is his instinctive conscience as an artist. A new state of soul creates a new art.

This perfect artistic sincerity, this wholehearted obedience to the dictates of an inward monitor, is what has rendered our analysis possible. The analysis, in its turn, confirms our conviction of Verhaeren's sincerity. In this way the work becomes a mirror of the soul—a symbolical mirror, it is true, but none the less faithful. All who knew Verhaeren, knew how simple and childlike he was; his whole life's work reflects his simplicity, his ingenuousness; and it is because it does so that it is so true.

APPENDIX

MADAME VERHAEREN has been kind enough to send me the following prose poem by her husband. It has not hitherto been published. The poem is dedicated to the memory of the aunt who was his real mother; his love for her was one of the most passionate of his " early affections." These lines will help us to appreciate all that the idea of the mother, the image of the Virgin and Child, and every analogous simile, represented for the poet. This dearly loved aunt certainly exercised a preponderant influence upon Verhaeren; one needs but to know of it in order to understand it.

CE SOIR

Ce soir, seul avec moi-même, je descends aux caveaux de mon cœur.

Là, reposent sous des croix, ceux dont j'ai consolé les agonies : toi, mon père ; toi, ma mère ; toi, ma douce et bonne tante qui mourus la première, voici bien des ans, en ce funèbre printemps sans fleurs, où tant de gens sont morts au village.

Toute mon enfance est restée comme pendue à ton cœur. Silencieuse, et comme absente de l'existence des autres, tu m'aimais avec une maternité refoulée, avec un rêve de femme seule, mélancoliquement à part, et seule.

As-tu jamais aimé autrement ?

Moi, je me confessais à toi, avant l'heure où l'on va chez les prêtres ; j'avais choisi une de tes poches pour y glisser les petits sous de mes épargnes ; les soirs de peur, je m'en venais frapper à la porte de ta chambre, et tu m'y accueillais avec des paroles calmantes. J'ai passé des heures et des heures, à te parler de mes petits camarades, à te raconter mes chagrins, larme à larme, à t'ennuyer de mes éxigences, et, je me souviens, qu'un jour, je t'ai battue !

Ce soir, seul avec moi-même, je descends aux caveaux de mon cœur.

Et tes yeux me reviennent dans la mémoire, comme de vieux joyaux ranimés soudain, doux yeux pâles, dont j'ai moi-même, pour toujours, abaissé les paupières, en ces heures mortuaires où des cierges, en plein jour, brûlaient autour de toi. Je te revois, en ta funèbre toilette : un petit bonnet blanc serrait l'ovale cireux de ton visage, tes mains étaient jointes, et sur tes doigts tombaient les grains d'un chapelet. Dans ce lit, si glacialement recouvert de grands draps blancs, je m'étais blotti bien des fois, sous de chaudes couvertures, et j'avais compté toutes les étoiles en papier peint dont son ciel se constellait.

THIS EVENING

THIS evening, alone with myself, I go down into the crypts of my heart.

There, resting under crosses, are all those whose death agony I eased: you, father; you, mother; you, my gentle and dear aunt who were the first to die, so many years ago, in that funereal spring when no flowers bloomed, when so many people died in our village.

My whole childhood seemed to hang on your heart. Silently, and as though absent from the existence of others, you loved me with a repressed maternity, with the dream of a solitary woman, sad, apart, and alone.

Have you ever loved otherwise?

I was wont to confess to you in the hour before I went to the priest; I had chosen one of your pockets in which to slip the pennies I saved; the nights when I awoke in a fright I would come knocking at your door, and you would welcome me with soothing words. Hour after hour I would tell you about my little comrades, I would confide to you my sorrows tear by tear, I would plague you with my unreasonableness, and, one day, I remember that I beat you!

This evening, alone with myself, I go down into the crypts of my heart.

And your eyes seem to me in memory like old jewels which have suddenly become bright again, eyes pale and gentle whose lids I myself closed for ever during those deathlike hours when the tapers, in broad daylight, glowed around you. I see you once again in your death robes: a small white bonnet framed the waxen oval of your face, your hands were clasped, and over your fingers fell the beads of your rosary. Into that very bed, so glacially covered with great white sheets, I had crept many a time and snuggled under the warm blankets, and I had counted all the stars on the coloured paper which looked like constellations on the tester.

Tu restas ainsi de longs jours, longue, avec tes pieds en pointe, et moi, qui, jamais, jusqu'à ces moments, n'avais regardé, de mes yeux, ni défunt, ni défunte, je ne te quittai qu'à l'instant de la mise en bière. Oh ! les clous à travers mon âme ! Et quand ton corps fut caché, pendant les dernières heures avant les cloches, pour toi sonnantes, ai-je embrassé le bois ! Oh ! l'ai-je embrassé le funèbre bois chrétien de ton cercueil !

Ce soir, seul avec moi-même, je descends aux caveaux de mon cœur.

S'il est vrai que les morts reviennent par les minuits propices, est-ce toi que je sens parfois, douce et bonne tante, quand la lune visiteuse s'incline, est-ce toi que je sens penchée à mon chevet ? Est-ce toi, cette Diane bienfaisante, telle que les légendes lointaines nous la montrent, non pas la mère, mais la tante, la vierge assise près des berceaux, patiente, tendre et sacrifiée, comme la sœur d'une sœur plus heureuse ! Est-ce ta caresse, cette impondérable et glissante lumière, qui me vient de si loin à travers l'air et la nuit de la terre ? Pauvre douce et bonne tante, dis, m'es-tu toujours celle qui pardonne et console ; suis-je toujours pour toi l'enfant ? M'aimes-tu encore, ô toi, la plus aimée parmi mes morts, la seule vraiment aimée, quoique déjà si morte pour tous les autres !

Ce soir, seul avec moi-même, je descends aux caveaux de mon cœur.

THIS EVENING

Many days you remained there, looking so long with your feet forming a point; and I, who had never before that day seen man or woman dead, I only left your side when they placed you in the coffin.

Oh the nails driven into my heart! And when your body was hidden during the last hours before the bells tolled, tolled for you, how I kissed the wood! Oh how I kissed and kissed the funereal, Christian wood of your coffin!

This evening, alone with myself, I go down into the crypts of my heart.

If it be true that the dead return when midnight favours their coming, is it you whom I feel sometimes, my gentle, my dear aunt, when the visiting moon declines, is it you whom I feel leaning over my bed? Are you the beneficent Diana whom the legends of old depict for us, not the mother but the aunt, the virgin sitting by the cradle, patient, tender, and self-sacrificing, as though she were the sister of a happier sister? Is it your caress, that imponderable light which comes gliding towards me from afar through the air and the night of the earth? Poor gentle and loving aunt, say, are you not she who always forgives and consoles; am I always a child in your eyes? Do you still love me, O you, the best loved among my dead, the only one I ever really loved, though you are so dead for all the rest of the world?

This evening, alone with myself, I go down into the crypts of my heart.

BIBLIOGRAPHY

ADLER, Ueber den nervösen Charakter, Bergmann, Wiesbaden, 2nd edition, 1919.

ARTUS-PERRELET, L., Le dessin au service de l'éducation, Delachaux et Niestlé, Neuchâtel and Paris.

BAUDOUIN, Charles, Etudes de psychanalyse, Delachaux et Niestlé, Neuchâtel and Paris, 1922.—English translation by Eden and Cedar Paul, Studies in Psychoanalysis, George Allen & Unwin, London, 1922.

BAUDOUIN, Charles, Suggestion et autosuggestion, Delachaux et Niestlé, 3rd edition 1922.—English translation by Eden and Cedar Paul, Suggestion and Autosuggestion, George Allen & Unwin, London, sixth impression (new edition), 1924.

BAUDOUIN, Charles, The Affective Basis of Intelligence, " Psyche and Eros," vol. i, No. 2, New York, 1920.

BAZALGETTE, Léon, Emile Verhaeren, Sansot, Paris, 1907.

BERGSON, Henri Louis, L'énergie spirituelle : essais et conférences, Paris, 1919.—English translation by H. Wildon Carr, Mind-Energy, Lectures and Essays, Macmillan, London, 1920.

BERGUER, Georges, Quelques traits de la vie de Jésus, Atar, Geneva, 1919.

BITHELL, Jethro, Contemporary Belgian Poetry, Walter Scott, London.

BOVET, Pierre, L'instinct combatif, Delachaux et Niestlé, Neuchâtel and Paris, 1917.—English translation by J. Y. T. Greig, The Fighting Instinct, George Allen & Unwin, 1923.

BOVET, Pierre, Le sentiment religieux, " Revue de théologie et de philosophie," Lausanne, No. 32, 1919.

BOVET, Pierre, Preface to Artus-Perrelet's Le dessin au service de l'éducation. See ARTUS.

BRINK, see JELLIFFE.

BUISSERET, Georges, L'évolution idéologique d'Emile Verhaeren, Mercure de France, Paris, 1910.

DOUTREPONT, Georges, Les débuts littéraires d'Emile Verhaeren à Louvain, Crès, Paris, 1919.

DUJARDIN, Edouard, De Stéphane Mallarmé au prophète Ezéchiel, Mercure de France, Paris, 1919.

FERRIÈRE, Adolphe, article in "Archives de Psychologie," Geneva, No. xiv.

FLOURNOY, Théodore, Une mystique moderne, "Archives de Psychologie," vol. xv, Geneva, 1915.

FOREL, Auguste, La psychanalyse et la guerre, "Le Carmel," Geneva, 1917.

FREUD, Sigmund, Drei Abhandlungen zur Sexualtheorie, Deuticke, Leipzig, 3rd edition, 1915.—English translation by A. A. Brill, Three Contributions to the Theory of Sex, 3rd revised edition, New York, 1918.

FREUD, Sigmund, Die Traumdeutung, 5th and enlarged edition, with contributions by Otto Rank, Leipzig and Vienna, 1919.—English translation by A. A. Brill, from 3rd German edition, The Interpretation of Dreams, George Allen & Unwin, London, 1913.

GOETHE, Johann Wolfgang von, Die Campagne in Frankreich, 1792.—English translation by R. Farie, Campaign in France in the year 1792, Chapman & Hall, London, 1849.

HENNEQUIN, Emile, La critique scientifique, Paris, 1888.

HESNARD, see RÉGIS.

HEUMANN, Albert, see VERHAEREN, Choix de poèmes.

HUGO, Victor Marie, Le Mariage de Roland. [This poem was written in 1846. Thirteen years later it was incorporated in the poet's La légende des siècles.]

"Imago," No. 3, Vienna, 1913.

JAMES, William, The Principles of Psychology, 2 vols., Macmillan, London, 1890.

JAMES, William, The Varieties of Religious Experience, Longmans, London, 1902.

JELLIFFE, Smith Ely, and BRINK, Louisa, Psychoanalysis and the Drama, Nervous and Mental Disease Publishing Co., Washington and New York.

JUNG, Carl Gustav, Wandlungen und Symbole der Libido, Deuticke, Leipzig and Vienna, 1920.—English translation by Beatrice M. Hinkle, The Psychology of the Unconscious, Moffat, Yard & Co., New York, 1916, Kegan Paul, London, 1921.

MAEDER, Alphonse, F. Hodler: eine Skizze seiner seelischen Entwicklung und Bedeutung für die schweizerisch-nationale Kultur, Zurich, 1916.

MOCKEL, Albert, Un poète de l'énergie, Emile Verhaeren, l'œuvre et l'homme, Paris, 1918.

MOREL, Ferdinand, Essai sur l'introversion mystique : Etude psychologique de pseudo-Denys l'Aréopagite et de quelques autres cas de mysticisme, Kundig, Geneva, 1918.

NIETZSCHE, Friedrich Wilhelm, Menschliches, Allzumenschliches, ein Buch für freie Geister, Chemnitz, 1878–9.—English translation, Human, All-Too-Human, being vols. 6 and 7 of Oscar Levy's complete edition, Foulis, Edinburgh and London, 1909–13.

OTT, Jean, Enquête sur Han Ryner, "Le Rythme," Paris, October, 1912.

PAULHAN, Les transformations sociales des sentiments, Flammarion, Paris, 1920.

PERRELET, see ARTUS-PERRELET.

PFISTER, Otto, Der psychologische und biologische Untergrund expressionistischer Bilder, Bircher, Berne, 1920.

PRESCOTT, Frederick Clarke, Poetry and Dreams, "Journal of Abnormal Psychology," vol. ii, No. 2, 1912.

RANK, Otto, Der Künstler, Ansätze zu einer Sexual-Psychologie, Heller, Vienna, 1907.

RANK, Otto, Traum und Dichtung ; Traum und Mythus. (Supplements to Freud's Die Traumdeutung. See FREUD.)

RÉGIS, Emmanuel, and HESNARD, A., La psychoanalyse des névroses et des psychoses, Alcan, Paris, 1914.

RIBOT, Théodule Armand, Essai sur l'imagination créatrice, Alcan, Paris, 1900.—English translation by Albert H. N. Baron, Essay on the Creative Imagination, Kegan Paul, London, 1906.

RIBOT, Théodule Armand, La logique des sentiments, Alcan, Paris, 1905.

RIGNANO, Eugenio, Psychologie du raisonnement, Alcan, Paris, 1920.

ROLLAND, Romain, Quelques lettres de Verhaeren et Romain Rolland, Cahiers idéalistes français, Paris, No. 14, March, 1918.

ROUBAKINE, Introduction à la psychologie bibliologique. La psychologie de la création des livres, de leur distribution et circulation, etc. 2 vols., Paris, 1922.

SMET, Joseph de, Emile Verhaeren, sa vie et ses œuvres, Part I, 1855–1894, Ryckmans, Malines, 1909; Part II, 1894–1916, Ryckmans, Malines, 1920.

SOURIAU, Paul, La rêverie esthétique. Essai sur la psychologie du poète, Alcan, Paris, 1906.

SOURIAU, Paul, La suggestion dans l'art, Alcan, Paris, 1893.

TRUC, Gonzague, La grâce, Alcan, Paris, 1918.

VERHAEREN, Emile.
[This bibliography of the poet's principal writings, including all those mentioned in the text, is arranged in chronological, not in alphabetical order. The translators are greatly indebted to the careful bibliography published by Amy Lowell in Appendix B of her Six French Poets, The Macmillan Company, New York, 1915.]
Les flamandes, 1883, reissued in Poèmes, see below.
Les moines, 1886, reissued in Poèmes, see below.
Les soirs, 1887, reissued in Poèmes, nouvelle série, see below.
Les débâcles, 1888, reissued in Poèmes, nouvelle série, see below.
Les flambeaux noirs, 1891, reissued in Poèmes, nouvelle série, see below.
Au bord de la route, 1891, reissued in Poèmes, see below.
Les apparus dans mes chemins, 1891, reissued in Poèmes, IIIme série, see below.

BIBLIOGRAPHY

Les campagnes hallucinées, 1893, reissued in 1904, see below.

Les villages illusoires, 1895, reissued in Poèmes, III ^{e} série, see below.

Poèmes : Les bords de la route ; Les flamandes ; Les moines—augmentés de plusieurs poèmes, Mercure de France, Paris, 1895.

Les villes tentaculaires, 1895, reissued in 1904, see below.

Poèmes, nouvelle série : Les soirs ; Les débâcles ; Les flambeaux noirs, Mercure de France, Paris, 1896.

Les heures claires, 1896, reissued, Mercure de France, Paris, 1909.

Les aubes, drame lyrique, Deman, Brussels, 1898.

Les visages de la vie, 1899, reissued, Mercure de France, Paris, 1908.

Poèmes, IIIme série : Les villages illusoires ; Les apparus dans mes chemins ; Les vignes de ma muraille, Mercure de France, Paris, 1899.

Le cloître, drame en prose et vers, Deman, Brussels, 1900.

Philippe II, tragédie, Mercure de France, Paris, 1901 ; reissued in Deux drames, Mercure de France, Paris, 1909.

Les forces tumultueuses, Mercure de France, Paris, 1902.

Les villes tentaculaires, precédées des Campagnes hallucinées, Mercure de France, Paris, 1904.

Toute la Flandre : Les tendresses premières, Deman, Brussels, 1904.

Les heures d'après midi, Deman, Brussels, 1905 ; reissued with Les heures claires, Mercure de France, Paris, 1909.

La multiple splendeur, Mercure de France, Paris, 1906.

Toute la Flandre : La guirlande des dunes, Deman, Brussels, 1907.

Les visages de la vie and Les douze mois, Mercure de France, Paris, 1908.

Toute la Flandre : Les héros, Deman, Brussels, 1908.

Toute la Flandre : La ville à pignons, Deman, Brussels, 1909.

Les rythmes souverains, Mercure de France, Paris, 1910.

Les heures du soir, Insel-Verlag, Leipzig, 1911.

Toute la Flandre : Les plaines, Deman, Brussels, 1911.

Hélène de Sparte, tragédie, Nouvelle Revue Française, Paris, 1912.

Les blés mouvants, Crès, Paris, 1912, reissued, Mercure de France, Paris, 1913.
La Belgique sanglante, Nouvelle Revue Française, Paris, 1915.
Choix de poèmes, avec une préface d'Albert Heumann, une bibliographie et un portrait, 4th edition, Paris, 1916.
Les ailes rouges de la guerre, Paris, 1916.
Les flammes hautes, Mercure de France, Paris, 1917.
Quelques lettres de Verhaeren et Romain Rolland, Cahiers idéalistes français, Paris, No. 14, March, 1918.

English Translations of Verhaeren

Poems by Emile Verhaeren, selected and rendered into English by Alma Strettell, with a portrait of the author by John Sargent, Lane, London, 1915.
The Plays of Emile Verhaeren, Constable, London, 1916. (The Dawn is translated by Arthur Symons, The Cloister by Osman Edwards, Philip II by F. S. Flint, Helen of Sparta by Jethro Bithell.)
Belgium's Agony (a translation by M. T. H. Sadler of La Belgique sanglante), Constable, London, 1916.
The Love Poems of Emile Verhaeren, translated by F. S. Flint, Constable, London, 1916.
Contemporary Belgian Poets, selected and translated by Jethro Bithell, Walter Scott, London, contains a number of metrical translations of Verhaeren.
Six French Poets, by Amy Lowell, Macmillan, New York, 1915, contains a few prose renderings.

Vodoz, J., Roland, un symbole, Preface by Georges Duhamel, Champion, Paris, 1920.

Wyzewa, Théodore de, Nos maîtres, études et portraits littéraires, Paris, 1895.

Zweig, Stefan, Emile Verhaeren, 2nd edition, Insel-Verlag, Leipzig, 1913.—English translation by Jethro Bithell, Emile Verhaeren, Constable, London, 1914.

Zweig, Stefan, Erinnerungen an Emil Verhaeren, privately printed.

INDEX

A celle qui a vingt ans, 275
A la gloire des cieux, 263
A la gloire du vent, 166
A l'homme d'aujourd'hui, 277
Action, 176
Action, L', 176, 177, 178
ADLER, 206, 208, 235, 315
Aegistheus, 228
AESCHYLUS, 203
Affective Basis of Intelligence, 18, 315
Ailes rouges de la guerre, 255, 273, 276, 320
All Flanders, 272, see also *Toute la Flandre*
Ame de la ville, 198
Amazon, 247, 248, 278, 279, 280, 281, 301, 302
Amazone, L', 247, 303
AMIEL, 21
Amour, L', 186, 244, 245, 296, 303
Amours rouges, 222
Ancienne foi, 260, 261
Andromeda, 200, 279, 280, 281, 284
Anthropologie, 25
Antwerp, 38, 42, see also Anvers
Anvers, 41, see also Antwerp
Apparus dans mes chemins, 160, 161, 162, 166, 172, 173, 176, 270, 271, 295, 318, 319
Appreciation of Poetry, 9
Aprement, 75
Arbre, L', 287
Arbres, Les, 130
Arche flottante, 2, 8
"Archives de Psychologie," 33, 295, 316
Ardeurs naïves, 45, 46, 50, 219, 296
Art flamand, 73
ARTEVELDE, 62, 63, 240
ARTUS-PERRELET, 41, 315
Aspects of Life, 185
At Sea, 185
Athens, 256
Attendue, L', 161
Attente, L', 185
Attirances, Les, 257, 258, 281

Au bord du quai, 252
Au carrefour de la mort, 80, 82, 83, 87 125
Au loin, 160
Au nord, 187
Au passant d'un soir, 261
Aubes, Les, 160, 176, 191, 239, 240, 319, see also *Dawn*
Autour de ma maison, 258
Aux moines, 97, 102, 103, 104
Aventurier, L', 225

Babel, 256
Bacchantes, 234
Baie, La, 115
Balthazar, Dom, see Dom Balthazar
Bank, 265
Banque, 265
Baptismales, 2
Barbarians, 272
BARD, 203
BARON, 317
BAUDELAIRE, 83, 84
BAUDOUIN, 2, 7, 8, 9, 10, 12, 17, 18, 315
BAZALGETTE, 38, 39, 88, 89, 212, 315
Beatrice, 48
Bêche, La, 151
BEETHOVEN, 101, 289
Belgique sanglante, 273, 319, 320, see also *Belgium's Agony*
Belgium's Agony, 320, see also *Belgique sanglante*
Bellringer, The, 190, see also *Sonneur*
Benares, 135, 139, 140, 141, 144, 296
BERGSON, 96, 243, 315
BERGUER, 33, 315
Bernardo, Fray, 212
Birth of Psyche, 2
BITHELL, 70, 108, 315, 320
Blacksmith, The, 190, see also *Forgeron*
Blés mouvants, 222, 255, 270, 319
Books, The, 191, see also *Livres*

Bords de la route, 75, 79, 80, 82, 83, 87, 125, 152, 153, 183, 244, 318, 319
Bornhem, 88, 89, 305
BOURGET, 104
BOVET, 41, 90, 101, 250, 315
Brabant, 168, 169
BREUER, 51, 239
BRILL, 316
BRINK, 316
Brussels, 38, 213
BUISSERET, 158, 160, 315
BURDEAU, 29
Burgraves, Les, 202
BURNE-JONES, 297

"Cahiers idéalistes français," 274, 318, 320
Caillou-qui-Bique, 266, 270, 274
Cambyses, 256
Campagne in Frankreich, 155, 316
Campagnes hallucinées, 52, 88, 150, 151, 160, 163, 186, 191, 192, 193, 194, 196, 197, 198, 199, 234, 296, 318, 319
Campaign in France in the Year 1792, 316
Canaan, 179
Carlos, Don, see Don Carlos
"Carmel, Le," 52, 274, 275, 316
Castor, 229, 230, 231, 232, 233, 236, 237
Ce soir, 220, 221, 310-312
Celle de l'île, 200
Celui du rien, 162
Chanaan, 178
Chansons de fou, 193, 196, 296, 307, see also Songs of Madmen
Chansons des rues et des bois, 71
CHATEAUBRIAND, 189
Chaumes, Les, 113, 114, see also Thatched Roofs
Chimay, 89
Choephori, 203
Choix de poèmes, avec un préface d'Albert Heumann, 295, 320
Christ, 165, 166, 182, 186, 198, 244, 259, 267, 268
Cinderella, 57
Clermont, Comtesse de, 211, 212
Clockmaker, The, 196, see also Horloger
Cloister, The, 320, see also Cloître
Cloître, Le, 201, 204, 206, 207, 208, 210, 218, 219, 223, 227, 230, 231, 239, 319, see also Cloister
Cloîtres, Les, 96, 97
Clytemnestra, 228
Clytemnestre, 228

COLERIDGE, 35
Comte de la Mi-Carême, 168, 169, see also Count of Mid-Lent
Comte de la Mi-Carême, 169
Conseil absurde, 123
Contemporary Belgian Poetry, 70, 315, 320
Conversions, Les, 99, 100
Cordiers, Les, 190, 297, see also Ropemakers
Count of Mid-Lent, 168, 169, 172, 181, 278, 301, see also Comte de la Mi-Carême
Couronne, La, 112, 132
Cris de ma vie, 249, 254
Critique scientifique, 293, 316
CROCE, 7
Crowd, The, 179, see also Foule
Crucifères, Les, 102
Cuisson du pain, 81

DA VINCI, 34
Dame en noir, 56, 74, 75, 117, 140, 150, 295, see also Lady in Black
Danaë, 265, 266
Dans ma plaine, 172
DANTE, 7, 25, 48, 240
Dawn, The, 320, see also Les aubes
De Stéphane Mallarmé au prophète Ezéchiel, 29, 316
Débâcles, Les, 56, 68, 106, 107, 109, 112, 117, 118, 119, 120, 121, 123, 124, 125, 126, 127, 128, 129, 130, 131, 132, 135, 136, 138, 139, 141, 143, 144, 147, 152, 158, 186, 192, 210, 227, 282, 296, 306, 318, 319
DEBOCK, Adèle, 38, 213
DEBOCK, Amelie, 38, 213
DEBOCK, (Emile Verhaeren's uncle), 39, 213
Début littéraire d'Emile Verhaeren à Louvain, 84, 316
Décembre, 181
Départ, Le, 199
Dessein au service de l'éducation, 41, 315
Dialogue, 127, 128, 143
Dialogue rustique, 222
Diana, 220, 312, 313
Dieux, Les, 137, 138
Divine Comedy, 240
Dom Balthazar, 89, 206, 208, 209, 210, 216, 219, 223, 227, 228, 230, 239
Don Carlos, 211, 212, 214, 215, 216, 217, 218, 219, 222, 224, 229, 231, 232, 233, 239

INDEX

Don Juan, 223
Donneur de mauvais conseils, 163, 195
DOUTREPONT, 84, 316
Douze mois, 319
Drei Abhandlung zur Sexualtheorie, 316
DUHAMEL, 320
DUJARDIN, 29, 31, 297, 316

E. U., 7
Early Affections, 35, 196, see also Tendresses premières
Eau, L', 188
Ecce Homo, 2, 8
Echo, 117
Eclats d'obus, 2
EDWARDS, 320
Effort, L', 258
Egiste, 228
Electra, 227, 232, 233, 234, 236, 237
Emile Verhaeren (Bazalgette), 31, 315
Emile Verhaeren (Mockel), 145, 156, 317
Emile Verhaeren (Smet), 189, 318
Emile Verhaeren (Zweig), 71, 108, 159, 320
En-avant, L', 249
En sourdine, 2
Enclos, L', 82
Energie spirituelle, 315
Enquête sur Han Ryner, 30, 317
Eperdument, 126
Erinnerungen an Emil Verhaeren, 267, 320
Escaut, 184, see also Scheldt
Escurial, 216
Essai sur l'imagination créatrice, 17, 36, 317
Essai sur l'introversion mystique, 33, 91, 317
Essay on the creative imagination, 317
Etudes de psychanalyse, 2, 315
Etrangère, L', 79
Eurydice, 240
Evolution idéologique d'Emile Verhaeren, 158, 315
Exode, L', 273

F. Hodler; eine Skizze seiner seelischen Entwicklung und Bedeutung für die schweizerischnationale Kultur, 317
FARIE, 316
Father Christmas, 168
Faust, 155, 304
Femmes, Les, 247
FERRIÈRE, 295, 316

Ferryman, The, 190, 280, see also Passeur d'eau
Ferveur, La, 285
Fièvres, Les, 163
Fighting Instinct, 315
Flamandes, Les, 70, 71, 72, 73, 74, 76, 77, 78, 79, 81, 82, 83, 85, 86, 87, 89, 90, 101, 106, 113, 120, 125, 129, 153, 167, 182, 186, 190, 192, 195, 197, 209, 222, 253, 264, 289, 306, 318, 319, see also Flemish Women
Flammes hautes, 63, 75, 101, 186, 252, 255, 257, 259, 260, 261, 267, 272, 273, 276, 277, 285, 289, 290, 291
Flambeaux noirs, 52, 56, 68, 74, 106, 107, 118, 120, 122, 133, 134, 135, 137, 138, 140, 141, 142, 143, 147, 148, 149, 150, 151, 158, 186, 190, 210, 227, 295, 318, 319
Flanders, 51, 56, 59, 61, 70, 71, 211, 212, 213, 224, 225, 227, 231, 237, 238, 272
Flandre, 51, 211, 224, 226, 227
Fléau, Le, 150
Flemish Women, 70, 304, see also Flamandes
Fleur fatale, 55, 133
Flight into the World, 159
FLINT, 320
FLOURNOY, 33, 40, 157, 220, 299, 316
Folie, La, 145, 249, 253
Force en nous, 2
Forces tumultueuses, 145, 159, 186, 187, 242, 244, 245, 247, 249, 253, 254, 281, 296, 303, 319, see also Tumultuous Forces
FOREL, 51, 52, 239, 316
Forest, The 289
Forêt, La, 289
Forgeron, Le, 190, see also Blacksmith
Forges, 89
Foule, La, 179, 180, 181, 182, 250, see also Crowd
FRANCK, 239
Fray Bernardo, see Bernardo
FREUD, 10, 17 20, 21, 23, 24, 25, 32, 36, 47, 51, 58, 111, 146, 205, 208, 235, 316
Furies, 232

George, Saint, see Saint George
Glaive, Le, 118, 123
GOETHE, 34, 155, 156, 158, 189, 283, 302, 316

Golgotha, 130
Grâce, La, 154, 318
Granges, Les, 81
GREIG, 315
Greniers, Les, 87
Gueux, Les, 86
Guirlande des dunes, 61, 66, 280, 319
GURNEY, 9

HAECKEL, 243
Hamlet, 121, 122
Helen, 227, 229, 230, 231, 232, 233, 234, 235, 236, 237, 238, 239, 240
Helen of Sparta, 231, 320
Hélène, 233, 234
Hélène de Sparte, 201, 204, 207, 209, 227, 228, 231, 239, 303, 319
HENNEQUIN, 293, 294, 316
Hercule, 303
Hercules, 21, 187, 255, 290, 308
Hérénien, 239, 240, 241
Herenthals, 38, 213
Hérésiarch, L', 98
Hernani, 208
Héros, Les, 62, 63, 319
HESNARD, 20, 33, 58, 219, 317
HEUMANN, 295, 316, 320
Heure mauvaise, 153
Heures claires, 160, 172, 174, 175, 272, 319, see also Serene Hours
Heures d'hiver, 117, 272
Heures d'après-midi, 173, 255, 272, 319
Heures du soir, 255, 319
Heures mornes, 130
HINKLE, 317
HODGSON, Ralph, 10
HODGSON, Shadworth, 35
HODLER, 33, 70, 300
Holy Office, 218
Hommage, 183
Horloger, L', 54, 58, 149, see also Clockmaker
Hours, 272, see also Heures
HUGO, 33, 71, 148, 155, 189, 199, 202, 269, 283, 316
Human, All Too Human, 126, 317
Humanité, 130

Idol, The, 296
Idole, L', 136, 137, 140
Ilion, 230
Illusory Villages, 187, 190, see also Villages illusoires
"Imago," 58, 316
Inconscience, 56, 119, 121

Inferno, 240
Infiniment, 117
Instinct combatif, 90, 101, 315
Interpretation of Dreams, 20, 316
Isis, 148
Ivresse, L', 183

Jacques d'Artevelde, 62, 63, 240
JAMES, 36, 157, 299, 316
JANET, 96
Jardin, 42, 44
Jean Christophe, 243
JELLIFFE, 316
Jesus, 120, 121, 246, 309
John, Saint, see Saint John
Joie, La, 186, 252, 253, 296
"Journal of abnormal Psychology," 26, 317
Juan, Don, see Don Juan
JUNG, 9, 40, 147, 156, 317

KANT, 25
Kato, 79, 86, 244
Kato, 78
Künstler, Der, 25, 317

Là-bas, 135, 136, 144, 296
Lady in Black, 56, 58, 143, see also Dame en noir
Laws of the Imagination and poetic Symbols, 8
Leading Tree in the Avenue, 290
Lear, 57
Légende des Siècles, 316
LEPAIGE, 38, 213
" Le Rythme," 30
LEVY, 317
Life in all its Ardour, 290, see also Vie ardente
Liminaire, 39, 184, 219, 221, 224, 225
LIONARDO, see Da Vinci
Livres, Les, 140, 149, 150, see also Books
Logique des sentiments, 17, 18, 19, 318
Lois, Les, 147
London, 133, 144
Londres, 144
Londres, 144
Louvain, 84
Louvre, 286
Love Poems of Emile Verhaeren, 320
LOWELL, 318, 320
Luther, 272

Ma gerbe, 291
Ma ville, 257, 267, see also Town
Madeleine, 244
MAEDER, 33, 70, 300, 317

INDEX

Magdalen, 244, 245, 246, 261
Mages, Les, 260
Maison du Peuple, 160
Malades, Les, 119, 128, 142
MALLARMÉ, 30, 31, 189
Mariage de Roland, 33, 189, 316
Maries, 113, 152
Marikerke, 48, 49
Marines, 83
Marinette, 21
Martin Luther, 272
MASSIN (Madame Emile Verhaeren), 160, 309
Matin, Un, 254
Méditation, 74, 77, 102
Meistersinger, 25
Ménélas, 228, 229, 233
Menelaus, 228, 229, 230, 231, 233, 237
Menschliches, Allzumenschliches, 317
MÉRINCOURT, see THÉROIGNE de MÉRINCOURT
Mes doigts, 141
Metamorphoses, 193
Meules qui brûlent, 191
Meurtre, Le, 138, 139
Michel-Ange, 255
Michelangelo, 272
MICHELET, 199
Mill, The, 195, see also *Moulin*
Mind Energy, 315
Miracle de vivre, 2
MOCKEL, 106, 145, 156, 160, 167, 208, 267, 274, 283, 286, 302, 317
Moine doux, 92, 94, 121
Moine épique, 95
Moine simple, 92, 93, 121
Moines, Les, 63, 70, 74, 88, 89, 90, 91, 92, 93, 94, 95, 96, 97, 98, 99, 100, 102, 103, 104, 106, 120, 126, 128, 129, 153, 190, 209, 210, 256, 300, 306, 318, 319, see also *Monks*
Moïse, 103, 104
MOLIÈRE, 237
Molossian Hounds, 117
Mon village, 59, 68
Monde, Le, 263
Monks, The, 70, 286, see also *Moines*
MOREL, 33, 40, 91, 96, 119, 147, 209, 305, 317
Mort, La, 116
Morte, La, 134, 135
Moulin, Le, 114, 295, see also *Mill*
Mourir, 116, 117
MUGNIER, 274
Multiple splendeur, 44, 67, 166, 186, 243, 255, 256, 258, 260, 263, 264, 272, 278, 285, 287, 319

Multiple Splendour, 255
Mystique moderne, 33, 316

Naiads, 234, 235
Narcissus, 91, 115, 117, 235
Nicholas, Saint, see Saint Nicholas
NIETZSCHE, 111, 112, 126, 129, 139, 158, 208, 243, 252, 317
Nombres, 148
Nombres, Les, 148, 149, 295, see also *Numbers*
Norns, 57
North Sea, 38
Nos maîtres, 30, 320
Novembre, 165
Numbers, 148
Numbers, 191, see also *Nombres*
Numidia, 42
Numidie, 41

Oedipus, 205, 206, 208, 209, 210, 218, 220, 221, 223, 225, 229, 231, 233, 235, 236, 237, 240, 300, 305
Oedipus at Colonus, 210
Oedipus Complex, 219
Oedipus Trilogy, 204
Olivier (pseudonym of Warlomont), 84
Oppidomagne, 240
Or, L', 265
Oreste, 228
Orestes, 228
Orgueil, L', 259, 284, 285
Orpheus, 239, 279
OTT, 30, 317
OVID, 193

Pan, 246
Pâques, Les, 65
Paradis, 42, 43, 295, 303
Parcae, 57, 190
Paris, 57, 267
Parsifal, 121, 122
Parsifal, 122
Pas, Les, 50
PASCAL, 304
Passeur d'eau, 45, 47, 55, 134, 189, 280, 295, see also *Ferryman*
Passion, 131, 133, 134
PAUL, 12, 315
PAULHAN, 205, 317
Péché, Le, 194, 195, 234
Pêcheurs, Les, 297
Pégase, 283
Pégase, 303
Pegasus, 187, 281, 282, 283
Pèlerinage, 193, 194
Penseur, Le, see Thinker

Penseurs, Les, 67
PERRELET, see ARTUS-PERRELET
Persée, 248, 278, 282, 283
Persée, 281, 296, 303
Perseus, 187, 200, 248, 255, 278, 279, 280, 281, 282, 283, 284, 298, 300, 301, 302
PFISTER, 33, 317
Philip II, 213, 214, 217, 218, 219, 224, 238, 240, 305
Philip II, 320
Philippe II, 201, 204, 209, 211, 218, 219, 222, 223, 225, 227, 231, 239, 306, 319
Plaine, La, 115
Plaines, Les, 72, 76, 113, 192, 225, 319
Plaines mornes, 192
PLATO, 111
Plays of Emile Verhaeren, 320
Plus précieux des cinq sens, 118
Pluto, 193
Poems by Emile Verhaeren, 320
Poète de l'énergie, see *Emile Verhaeren* (Mockel)
Poetic Mind, 7
Poetry and Dreams, 26, 317
Poetry of Dante, 7
Poets, Critics, and Class-Lists, 9
Pollux, 230, 236
Power within us, 2, 8
Premier arbre de l'allée, 290
PRESCOTT, 7, 26, 317
Prière, La, 259, 284
Principles of Psychology, 36, 316
Prometheus, 203
Proserpina, 193
Psychanalyse et la guerre, 52, 316
" Psyche and Eros," 315
Psychoanalyse des névroses et des psychoses, 20, 317
Psychoanalysis and Aesthetics, 2, 7, 8, 9
Psychoanalysis and the Drama, 316
Psychologie bibliologique, 295, 318
Psychologie du raisonnement, 18, 318
Psychologische und biologische Untergrund Expressionistischer Bilder, 33, 317
Psychology of the Unconscious, 156, 317

Quelques lettres de Verhaeren et de Rolland, 274, 318
Quelques traits de la vie de Jésus, 33, 315
Quelques-uns, 152

Rameses, 256
RANK, 25, 316, 317
Recherche, La, 67
Regency, 240
RÉGIS, 20, 33, 58, 219, 317
Rentrée des Moines, 102
Rêverie aesthétique, 26, 318
Rêves, Les, 243
Révolte, La, 55, 62, 64, 65, 99, 138, 197
" Revue de Théologie et de Philosophie," 315
" Revue Wagnérienne," 29
Rhin, 184
RIBOT, 16, 17, 18, 19, 20, 21, 23, 29, 35, 36, 317, 318
RIGNANO, 18, 318
Rispaire, Duke of, 223, see also Dom Balthazar
Roc, Le, 118, 120, 122, 133, 142
ROCHEFOUCAULD, 112
RODENBACH, 103
RODIN, 152
Rodolphe (Verhaeren's pseudonym), 84
Roland, un symbole, 33, 155, 320
ROLLAND, 274, 275, 318
Rome, 256, 261, 262
Ropemakers, The, 190, 298, see also *Cordiers*
ROUBAKINE, 295, 318
ROUSSEAU, 79, 96
Rues, Les, 114
RYNER, 30
" Rythme, Le," 317
Rythmes souverains, 41, 43, 187, 200, 248, 255, 257, 258, 259, 265, 271, 272, 278, 280, 281, 282, 283, 284, 290, 295, 296, 303, 319

Sadler, 320
Saint George, 156, 166, 167, 168, 169, 170, 171, 172, 181, 211, 242, 247, 248, 264, 270, 278, 279, 280, 301, 302
Saint Georges, 168, 170, 171, 278
Saint Georges, 161, 166, 172, 247, 256, 279, 295
Saint Jean, 271, 296
Saint John, 271, 272, 277
Saint Nicholas, 168
Saint-Amant, 37, 38, 46, 88
Saint-Cloud, 267, 270
Saint-Office, 217
Saintes, Les, 173, 176, 270
Saints, The, 270
Saints, les morts, les arbres, et le vent, Les, 164
S'amoindrir, 121, 123

INDEX 327

Santa Claus, 168
Sappho, 231, 233, 235
SARGENT, 320
Satan, 194
Saule, Un, 288, see also *Willow Tree*
Scheldt, 37, 38, 184
SCHOPENHAUER, 25, 29, 35, 236
" Semaine des Etudiants," 84
Sentiment religieux, 250, 315
Serene Hours, 173, see also *Heures claires*
Serve reine, 2
Seven against Thebes, 203
SHAKESPEARE, 25
Ship, The, 185
Si morne, 109
Sicile, 187
Sicily, 187
Sirènes, 187, 188
Sirens, 186, 187, 188, 189
Siva, 144
Six French Poets, 318, 320
SMET, 189, 192, 199, 243, 269, 272, 280, 297, 298, 318
Soir religieux, 102
Soir, Un, 141, 152
Soirs, Les, 55, 68, 106, 107, 113, 114, 116, 117, 119, 128, 130, 131, 133, 136, 137, 140, 142, 143, 144, 147, 158, 165, 192, 195, 196, 295, 318, 319
Song of Roland, 212
Songs of Madmen, 197, 307, see also *Chansons de fou*
Sonneur, Le, 60, 64, 65, 189, 197, 295, see also *Bellringer*
SOPHOCLES, 240
Souffrances, Les, 278
SOURIAU, 25, 318
Sous les porches, 142
Souvenir, 161
Sovran Rhythms, 185
Sower, 269
SPIESS, 118
SPITTELER, 220, 275, 303
STAËL, 189
Stock Exchange, 264
Stockholm, 52
STRETTELL, 320
Studies in Psychoanalysis, 2, 8, 17, 18, 315
Suggestion and Autosuggestion, 2, 8, 9, 146, 315
Suggestion dans l'art, 26, 318
Suggestion et Autosuggestion, 2, 315
Suppliants, 203
Symbole chez Verhaeren, 2
SYMONS, 320

Tabor, 181
Tamise, 134
Tendresses premières, 37, 38, 41, 42, 45, 48, 53, 54, 59, 65, 79, 93, 144, 149, 169, 174, 184, 209, 219, 224, 227, 257, 296, 319, see also *Early Affections*
Tête, La, 143, 145
Thabor, 181
Thames, 134
Thatched Roofs, 113, see also *Chaumes*
THÉROIGNE de MÉRINCOURT, 245, 248, 261, 264, 281
Thinker, The, 152
This Evening, 311-313
Three Contributions to the Theory of Sex, 235, 316
Thyades, 234
Tityre et Moelibée, 270
Tolstoï éducateur, 2
TOLSTOY, 152, 157, 158
Tolstoy the Teacher, 2
Tombes, Les, 276
Tours au bord de la mer, 61
Toute la Flandre, 37, 39, 44, 225, 227, 255, 319, see also *All Flanders*
Towards the Cloister, 113, see also *Vers le cloître*
Towards the Sea, 185, see also *Vers la mer*
Tower of Babel, 275
Town, 268, 269, see also *Ma ville*
Transformations sociales des sentiments, 205, 317
Traum und Dichtung, 25, 317
Traum und Mythus, 25, 317
Traumdeutung, 20, 316
Truandailles, 71
TRUC, 154, 157, 318
Tumultuous Forces, 185, 255, see also *Forces tumultueuses*
Tunnel, Le, 259

Ueber den nervösen Charakter, 206, 315
Ultima verba, 292
Usines, Les, 197, 295

Vache, La, 86
Vachère, La, 73
VANDERVELDE, 160
Varieties of religious Experience, 157, 316
Vent, Le, 164, see also *Wind*
Venus, 187, 244, 245, 246, 248, 264
Vénus, 244

Vergers, Les, 85
VERHAEREN, Adèle, 38
VERHAEREN, Emile, passim
VERHAEREN, Gustave, 38, 88, 213, 305
VERHAEREN, Marthe, see MASSIN
Vers la mer, 185, see also *Towards the Sea*
Vers le cloître, 112, 124, 125, 127, see also *Towards the Cloister*
Vers le futur, 198
Vers l'enfance, 120
VEUILLOT, 71
Vie, La, 264
Vie ardente, 63, 75, 101, 252, 291, see also *Life in all its Ardour*
Vieille, La, 163
Vieux chênes, 131
Vieux empires, 255, 256
Vignes de ma muraille, 115, 160, 165, 181, 183, 186, 187, 200, 319
VIGNY, 26, 103
Villages illusoires, 45, 46, 60, 65, 160, 161, 163, 164, 186, 189, 191, 225, 280, 295, 297, 302, 318, 319, see also *Illusory Villages*
Ville, La, 52
Ville à pignons, 319
Villes, Les, 52, 141, 144

Villes tentaculaires, 55, 62, 67, 115, 116, 139, 160, 186, 191, 197, 198, 264, 265, 295, 319
VINCI, see Da Vinci
Virgin Mary, 48, 92, 94, 113, 120, 121, 133, 170, 216, 217, 220, 267, 268, 309
Visages de la vie, 159, 160, 161, 176, 177, 178, 179, 180, 181, 182, 183, 185, 186, 188, 250, 252, 253, 296, 319
VODOZ, 33, 155, 189, 212, 283, 320
Voyageurs, Les, 140

WAGNER, 25, 122, 202, 203
WALLER, see WARLOMONT
"Wallonie, La," 118
Wandlungen und Symbole der Libido, 317
WARLOMONT, 84
"Weekly Westminster Gazette," 7
"Westminster Gazette," 7
Willow Tree, 288, see also *Saule*
Wind, The, 164, see also *Vent*
World as Will and Idea, 29
WYZEWA, 30, 32, 320

Zarathustra, 159
ZOLA, 83
ZWEIG, 71, 108, 159, 267, 274, 275, 320

For Product Safety Concerns and Information please contact our EU representative GPSR@taylorandfrancis.com
Taylor & Francis Verlag GmbH, Kaufingerstraße 24, 80331 München, Germany

www.ingramcontent.com/pod-product-compliance
Lightning Source LLC
Chambersburg PA
CBHW071154300426
44113CB00009B/1198